AUGUSTINE OF HIPPO AND HIS MONASTIC RULE

Augustine of Hippo and his Monastic Rule

George Lawless, OSA

CLARENDON PRESS · OXFORD

1987

Oxford University Press, Walton Street, Oxford OX2 6DP

Oxford New York Toronto
Delhi Bombay Calcutta Madras Karachi
Petaling Jaya Singapore Hong Kong Tokyo
Nairobi Dar es Salaam Cape Town
Melbourne Auckland

and associated companies in
Berlin Ibadan

Oxford is a trade mark of Oxford University Press

Published in the United States
by Oxford University Press, New York

British Library Cataloguing in Publication Data
Lawless, George
Augustine of Hippo and his monastic rule.
1. Augustine, Saint, Bishop of Hippo,
Regula   2. Augustinians—Rule
255'.406   BX2904.A2
ISBN 0–19–826741–X (pbk)

Library of Congress Cataloging in Publication Data
Lawless, George.
Augustine of Hippo and his monastic rule.
Bibliography: p.
1. Augustine, Saint, Bishop of Hippo. Regula.
2. Monasticism and religious orders—Rules—History.
3. Augustinians—Rules.   I. Title.
BX2904.Z5L39 1987   255'.406   87–5663
ISBN 0–19–826741–X (pbk)

Printed and bound in
Great Britain by Biddles Ltd,
Guildford and King's Lynn

In loving memory

Mrs Emilia Piasecki
Mr and Mrs Frederick King Weyerhaeuser

An elephant can swim in it
and a lamb can walk in safety

Gregory the Great in the letter addressed to Leander of
Seville and prefixed to his commentary on the book of
Job

[Barnwell Priory Observances commenting on the Rule
of Augustine]

Preface

WITH an average of four hundred publications annually (not a few of these are books), and every title generously signposted in the 'Bulletin Augustinien' of the *Revue des études augustiniennes*, the reader is justified in exclaiming: 'Why another study of Augustine?' What, then, are the original features of this book?

First of all, I have traced the beginnings and development of Augustine's monastic ideal during the years 386–96. Attention has been directed towards Augustine's selective transformation of many elements within the Classical heritage of late antiquity in order to accommodate his present purposes. The young Augustine was deeply affected by such ideas as wisdom and contemplation, the fostering of friendships and sharing of possessions, the political/ethical ideals of harmony and order, the good of the individual and its relation to the common good, and the Plotinian ἐπιστροφή or conversion. There were other heavy debts to Plotinus, such as the significance of beauty, unity, and multiplicity. In his personal life Augustine gradually effected many constructive changes by assimilating these values and by utilizing them still further in the service of the Church. This is another way of saying that Augustine's monastic ideal was heavily indebted to some of the richest intellectual refinements in the Graeco-Roman tradition.

Secondly, I have suggested that the leitmotif *auaritia*, *luxuria*, and *ambitio*, which had become a commonplace in Roman literature since the days of the Republic, was reflected in a subtle manner in the threefold renunciation of Rom. 13: 13, the Pauline text which appears to have loomed large at the moment of Augustine's conversion. Equally to the point, this same trinomial was subsumed in the single renunciation of Matt. 19: 21. Both biblical texts were cited by Augustine in the penultimate paragraph of Book Eight of the *Confessions* and are crucial to a correct understanding of his then voluntary surrender of sexuality, property, and power, an unmistakable adumbration of the future vows of religion: chastity, poverty, and obedience.

Thirdly, I have argued for the existence of a bona fide monastery at Thagaste during the years 388–91. The word itself is not so important; it need not be construed here in a technical sense. It hardly occurred to Augustine at the time of his conversion or afterwards, for that matter, to think of Christian perfection as a specialized calling for an élite group. Just as there were no compromises in the matter of his conversion, so too the uncompromising character of his personality lent itself both before and after his mother's death to his total commitment to Catholic Christianity. This is especially the case, as we shall note, by the time he returned from Italy to his homeland in the autumn of 388. I choose to date Augustine's monastic way of life from these early days at Thagaste.

Fourthly, there is available here for the first time within a single volume an English translation with facing Latin text of the *Ordo Monasterii*, the *Praeceptum*, and the *Obiurgatio* (= *Epistula* 211. 1–4). These documents constitute the basic dossier for the *Regula Sancti Augustini* and are indispensable for an understanding of the million maddening details that plague its history. Unlike all previous English translators of the *Rule*, I am mindful of its author's urging that it be read publicly once a week. For this reason, special care has been taken to preserve much of its parallel and antithetical structure along with many of its sonorous qualities.

Finally, again for the first time in English I present a comprehensive study of such disputed questions as the authorship of these documents, their respective dates of composition and their original public. My interest extends chiefly to the end of the Patristic period in the west, AD 636. While I am occasionally obliged to step beyond this boundary, the fortunes of the *Regula Sancti Augustini* in the Middle Ages require a book in itself.

Sixteen hundred years have passed since Augustine's 'conversion' in the garden of a rented house in Milan during the month of August 386, an experience which he depicted in his *Confessions*, the famous *tolle lege* scene. The word 'conversion' conveys multivalent meanings. Augustine's reading of Cicero's *Hortensius* during his nineteenth year was regarded by himself as his 'first conversion'. A 'second conversion' was effected in Milan by his reading of the Platonists (*libri Platonicorum*). Meanwhile, Ambrose, the bishop of Milan, encouraged him to read Isaiah, only now, unlike an earlier occasion in Rome after his disillusionment with Manichaeism, Augustine was to take the Scriptures seriously. Here is a 'third conversion' and so on.

I leave it to others to unravel the various historical and, more recently, psychological stages of Augustine's conversion. The former has been done many times; the latter is a risky enterprise. In both instances there is always danger of attempting too refined an analysis, a distillation of the evidence which, like mercury, refuses to be stilled for steady scrutiny.

Augustine's conversion was a complex process with much overlapping. Franco Bolgiani's incisive study of the *Confessions*, Book 8, properly described it as 'a unitary experience' in his *La conversione di s. Agostino e l'VIII libro delle 'Confessioni'* (Turin, 1956), 103–4. I wish to stress these continuities. It is my fundamental understanding, as explicated in Ch. II of this book, that Augustine's conversion to asceticism coincided with his conversion to Catholic Christianity. All that remained thereafter was his monastic option, prior to and distinct from his call to Orders. Or to put it another way, the development of Augustine's monastic vocation was linked with his progress towards full acceptance of Christianity. His moral conversion in the summer of 386 (Augustine had already convinced himself intellectually that Christianity was the one and only true religion) and his decision to live as a celibate servant of God went hand in hand.

While he possessed many affinities with St Basil the Great (this is a subject for fruitful research), one must not impose upon Augustine the earlier monasticism of Pachomius or Basil of Caesarea. Nor should one standardize Benedict's monasticism in such a way as to suggest that Augustine somehow fell short of its requirements. As with so much else, history must permit the Bishop of Hippo to remain his own self. As with their absorption of Greek thought, the Romans borrowed in a Roman way, so Augustine borrowed from his predecessors in his distinctive way by assimilating the monastic legacy in a manner truly flexible, open-ended, and dynamic.

'In patristic studies today, there are few literary problems so intricate as that of the documents which have been called "Rules of St. Augustine."' This judgement of Louis Bouyer's, in *The Spirituality of the New Testament and of the Fathers* (New York, 1963), 495 expresses an opinion that has prevailed for more than twenty years and helps to explain why Augustine's *Rule* has received scant attention from American, British, and Canadian scholars. In 1967, for example, Peter Brown's distinguished biography sidestepped the question of a monastic rule attributed to the Bishop of Hippo. Some years earlier the Church historian Gerald Bonner of Durham University was a notable exception when he assigned the title 'Augustine as a Monastic Legislator' to Appendix B of his excellent biography, *St. Augustine of Hippo: Life and Controversies* (London, 1963; 2nd edn. Norwich, 1986), 396–7.

Yet an extraordinary array of academic disciplines intersect to tell us much about Augustine's *Rule*: ancient history, textual criticism, liturgy, philology, palaeography, patristic and monastic theology, biblical and Classical studies. Those desirous of a historico-scientific commentary on the *Rule* will find it in Luc Verheijen's *Nouvelle Approche de la Règle de saint Augustin* (Abbaye de Bellefontaine, 1980), which covers more than half of the document's eight chapters. Since 1980 Verheijen's continuing research appears in the Louvain journal *Augustiniana*. Also deserving of special notice is Adolar Zumkeller's *Das Mönchtum des heiligen Augustinus* (2nd edn. Würzburg, 1968, Eng. tr. New York, 1986). I shall not trespass upon these areas of study except to recommend a useful commentary which was written for the non-specialist: Tarsicius J. van Bavel, *The Rule of Saint Augustine* (London, 1984). A word of caution, however, about this latter volume: the English version 'follows closely' a Dutch version which van Bavel describes as 'an interpretative translation' (p. 10). In a Platonic sense, then, we are presented with a translation that is twice removed from the original Latin text, with all the hazards that an imitation of an imitation implies.

The *Rule* of Saint Augustine is the oldest monastic rule with western origins, except possibly for the undatable document designated in the manuscript tradition as *Ordo Monasterii*, whose author remains to this day stubbornly anonymous (see Appendix II). Far from being a lifeless document from late antiquity, Augustine's *Rule* provides daily inspiration for more than one hundred and fifty contemporary Christian communities. Accordingly, this volume should help to fill, for the English-speaking world, a lacuna in Augustinian studies which has been allowed to exist for too long a time.

Georges Folliet, Director of Études Augustiniennes, Paris, felicitously assisted me by granting permission to reproduce Luc Verheijen's critical texts of the *Ordo Monasterii*, the *Praeceptum*, and the *Obiurgatio*. Pergamon Press, Oxford, has permitted me to recycle in Appendix II a portion of my article '*Ordo Monasterii*: A Double or Single Hand?', *Studia Patristica*, 17 (1982), 511–18. A segment of Ch. V has appeared in *Augustinianum*, 25 (1985), 65–78 under the title, 'Augustine's First Monastery: Thagaste or Hippo?' Vittorino Grossi, OSA has permitted me to refine this material still further in its larger historical context.

For biblical quotations I have, with the kind permission of the Oxford and Cambridge University Presses, occasionally used the New English Bible (2nd edn. 1970). Where Augustine's Bible (the Old Latin version, a forerunner of Jerome's Latin Vulgate) would not yield such a rendering, I have translated directly from the original. All reference-numbers follow the Vulgate. I wish to acknowledge permission from Doubleday & Company, Inc. to reproduce citations from John K. Ryan, *The Confessions of St. Augustine* (New York, 1960. Translation copyright © 1960 by Doubleday & Company, Inc.).

I am particularly grateful to Simon Tugwell, OP, Regent of Studies at Blackfriars, Oxford. His constructive criticisms and carefully nuanced comments considerably enriched my understanding of early Christian spirituality. Thanks are also due to M. Benedict Hackett, OSA for reading the entire text and to Adolar Zumkeller, OSA for reading two chapters of the final revision. Their suggestions were both helpful and incisive. No mistake here is theirs. Frequent reference to Luc Verheijen, OSA indicates the heavy debt which everyone owes to this scholar's lifelong prodigious research on the subject matter of this book.

I should be grievously at fault were I not to acknowledge my colleague, José Guirau, OSA and the many times he came to my aid as Librarian of the Patristic Institute, Augustinianum, Rome. Joseph Gildea, OSA graciously obliged me by reading the final revision in its entirety. To Marion Fitch I am much obliged for unfailing courtesy and skill in typing the complete manuscript. I am not less indebted to J. K. Cordy and Leofranc Holford-Strevens of the Oxford University Press for their helpful counsel and splendid editorial assistance. Special thanks to Neil J.

McGettigan, OSA. In his regard I borrow the salutation of an author who affectionately addressed all correspondence to her editor 'My bestest friend'.

G.P.L.

Feast of the Conversion of St Augustine
24 April 1986

Contents

Appendices

List of Tables

Forms of Citation

1. *Works by Augustine*

THE Latin titles utilized in this study are listed along with their date(s) of composition, except for Augustine's *Epistulae*, *Enarrationes in Psalmos*, and *Sermones*, which have their own peculiar chronology. In these latter three instances, I have regularly cited the date either in the text or the footnotes. The English title is always used in the text.

References to the *Praeceptum* and the *Obiurgatio* are indicated by the line(s) in the Latin text. Citations from my English rendering of these documents are indicated by the chapter and section of the *Rule* and by the appropriate section of the *Reprimand to Quarrelling Nuns*.

Acad.	*Contra Academicos*, 386
B. Vita	*De beata uita*, 386
Bon. Coniug.	*De bono coniugali*, 401
Ciu. Dei	De ciuitate dei, 413–27
Conf.	*Confessiones*, 397–400 [Cited in English from John K. Ryan, *The Confessions of St. Augustine* (New York, 1960)]
Cont.	*De continentia*, 395–426
Cresc.	*Contra Cresconium*, 405/6
Diu. QQ	*De diuersis quaestionibus octoginta tribus*, 388–94/5
Doc. Ch.	*De doctrina Christiana*, Books 1–3. 35, 396/9
En. Ps.	*Enarrationes in Psalmos*, Pss. 1–32 completed by 392
Ep.	*Epistulae*
Ep. Jo.	*In Epistulam Iohannis ad Parthos*, 407
Faust.	*Contra Faustum*, 397/8
Lib. Arb.	*De libero arbitrio*, Book 1, part of Book 2, 388–95
Mor.	*De moribus ecclesiae Catholicae et de moribus Manichaeorum*, 388
Op. Mon.	*De opere monachorum*, 400/1
Ord.	*De ordine*, 386

Quant.	*De quantitate animae*, 388
Retr.	*Retractationes*, 426/7
Sanc. Virg.	*De sancta uirginitate*, 401
Serm(m).	*Sermo(nes)*
Sol.	*Soliloquia*, 386/7
Symb.	*De fide et symbolo*, 393
Tr. Jo.	*Tractatus in Iohannis Euangelium*, (1–54) 406–21; (55–124) from 422

2. *Other works*

ACW	*Ancient Christian Writers* (Westminster, Md., 1946–)
AM	*Augustinus Magister* (3 vols., Paris, 1954)
AS	*Augustinian Studies* (Villanova, 1970–)
BA	Bibliothèque augustinienne, *Saint Augustin: Œuvres* (Paris, 1936–)
CCL	Corpus Christianorum, series Latina (Turnhout, 1953–)
CSEL	Corpus scriptorum ecclesiasticorum Latinorum (Vienna, 1866–)
FC	Fathers of the Church (New York, 1947–60; Washington, DC, 1961–)
JTS NS	*Journal of Theological Studies* (Oxford, 1900–), new series (1950–)
Lambot, SS	*Sancti Aurelii Augustini sermones selecti duodeuiginta* (Utrecht, 1950)
Misc. Agost.	*Miscellanea agostiniana* (2 vols., Rome, 1930–1)
PL	Patrologiae cursus completus, series Latina, ed. J.-P. Migne (Paris, 1844–64)
RA	*Recherches augustiniennes* (Paris, 1958–)
RB	*Revue bénédictine* (Maredsous, 1883–)
RB 1980	T. Fry (ed.), *RB 1980: The Rule of St. Benedict* (Collegeville, 1981)
REA	*Revue des études augustiniennes* (Paris, 1955–)
Règle	L. Verheijen, *La Règle de saint Augustin*, i. *Tradition manuscrite*, ii. *Recherches historiques* (Paris, 1967)
SCh	Sources chrétiennes, série latine (Paris, 1943–)
SP	*Studia Patristica* (Berlin, 1957–)

VC   *Vigiliae Christianae* (Amsterdam, 1947–   )
Vita   M. Pellegrino, *Possidio, Vita di Agostino*,
             Verba Seniorum 4 (Alba, 1955)

Chronology

Part One

AUGUSTINE'S MIND AND
MILIEU, 386–396

I

Ambitio, auaritia, luxuria

AUGUSTINE was rarely alone. As a schoolboy he associated with a group of hooligans (*euersores* or Wreckers). Although he deplored their destruction of property, he nevertheless enjoyed their company (*Conf.* 3. 3. 6). It was the companionship of others which strengthened his motivation to commit an act of wanton theft. In that well-known youthful escapade which he recounted in the *Confessions*, 2. 4. 9–2. 10. 18, Augustine did not steal pears out of need or desire, for he had superior pears in his own garden and threw the stolen fruit to the pigs.[1] Augustine enjoyed the mischief of thievery with his friends and twice said he would never have done it alone (2. 18. 16; 2. 9. 17). Still but a youth after having become a father at the age of seventeen, Augustine began to share his life with the mother of his son and remained faithful to his concubine for thirteen years (4. 2. 2). Soon after in deference to his mother (6. 13. 23), and in anticipation of a socially and legally acceptable marriage did another take her place (6. 15. 25).

In keeping then with his gregarious temperament, Augustine proposed at Milan in the year 386 to live his life in common with ten adults. All were friends, and from their number two individuals would be elected annually on a rotation basis, like the Roman magistrates. Principally, they were to provide for the domestic needs of the others, who would live a peaceful life away from the crowd (*remoti a turbis otiose uiuere*, 6. 14. 24). Total sharing of goods, a common fund, and a single household would characterize the group. Wives would be welcome, of course, as well as men with prospects of a future marriage like Augustine himself. This latter feature proved to be as unattractive as it was impracticable. Eventually the plan was scrapped.

---

[1] The pear theft, which takes up more than half of Book 2 of the *Confessions* 'becomes intelligible as a paradigm, not of the worst sin Augustine ever committed, but of the essentially negative character of sin'. See G. Bonner, 'Augustine's Doctrine of Man: Image of God and Sinner', *Augustinianum*, 24 (1984), 496.

So it is not at all surprising at the dramatic moment of his conversion in August 386 that Augustine was not alone in the garden, but with his beloved friend Alypius (8. 12. 30). Again, in the remarkable episode at Ostia, when Augustine was touched with mystic ecstasy, his mother was there with him to share that unusual experience (9. 10. 23–6). Nor were the friendships and the loves of his life without their measure of sorrow. Within a period of three years, Augustine mourned the untimely death of a friend and professional colleague, Verecundus (9. 3. 5), his mother (9. 11. 28), his dear friend Nebridius (9. 3. 6), and Adeodatus, his son (9. 6. 14). Many years previously he had wept over the death of a nameless friend whom he had led astray from the Christian faith (4. 4. 7). And indeed, Augustine was not alone at Cassiciacum. Several others, including some pupils and relatives, added lustre to those serene months at the villa of Verecundus before Augustine, the recent convert to the Christian faith, officially enrolled himself as a catechumen in Milan at the beginning of Lent 387. It is fair to say of Augustine:

His own temperament and the expectations cultivated in him by Manichaeism, Neoplatonism and the desire to live a community life made him ambitious for the best: he could never, as we say, settle for the second best. This made the whole process of his conversion, slow, difficult—but, of course, deep and far-reaching in its results.[2]

At the risk of appearing over-schematic, one may further suggest that four turning-points charted the direction of Augustine's life: (1) his reading of Cicero's *Hortensius* at the age of eighteen, (2) his baptism, (3) his ordination to the presbyterate, and (4) his ordination to the episcopate. A sense of continuity persisted throughout:

He had made up his mind, even before he accepted Christ, to live a life of philosophy in community . . . The pattern of Augustine's later life was set even before he was converted: there was afterwards no sudden, unexpected or incomprehensible change.[3]

During his first short-lived stay at Rome in 383, Augustine became acquainted with organized community life in the house of the

[2] J. O'Meara, 'Studies Preparatory to an Understanding of the Mysticism of St Augustine and his Doctrine on the Trinity', *AS* 1 (1970), 273.
[3] J. O'Meara, *The Young Augustine* (London, 1954; repr. 1980), 160.

Manichee Constantius.[4] At that time, however, he was on the verge of formally dissociating himself from the sect which had claimed his allegiance as an *auditor* or 'hearer' for nine years (5. 6. 10). Still, past associations with the followers of Mani were to stand him in good stead. Because his students in Rome refused to pay their fees (5. 12. 22), the prospects of a better teaching position lured him to Milan in 384, and Augustine secured a prestigious post as a result of his own merits through the influence of some erstwhile Manichaean friends and of Symmachus, prefect of the city of Rome (5. 13. 23).

All the while, Augustine's propensity for friendship fitted handsomely into the cultural milieu of the late fourth century. Common interest groups had long ago adopted a variety of forms: Plato's Academy, the Peripatetics, the Porch of the Stoics, the ascetic life of Pythagoras and his followers, Cynic asceticism, and a type of political club suggested by Cicero's *Laelius*. Within the Christian era, there had been Plotinus and then Porphyry with their respective disciples, and notably Augustine's own immediate contacts with the Manichees. In Greek thought generally, it was axiomatic to say that all things were common among friends.[5] Sharing of goods, a sense of withdrawal from the world, serious conversation, celibacy, and fasting frequently marked religioso-philosophical experiences of this sort.[6] As well as being an end in itself, *otium* or philosophic calm was intended to become a guarantor of felicitous relations among group members. Although scaled down appreciably, one finds here traces of Cicero's *otium cum dignitate*: 'the absence of domestic strife and the satisfaction of legitimate ambition.'[7] Cicero's political ideal of uniting the senatorial and equestrian orders of society had long since been doomed to failure, as it succumbed to the triple threat of *ambitio*, *auaritia*, and *luxuria*. In spite of the eventual failure of these idealistic ventures, the fact remains that 'the virtues of the Romans

---

[4] *Faust.* 5. 5. 7 (CSEL 25. 276–9).
[5] D. L. Mealand, 'Community of Goods and Utopian Allusions in Acts II–IV', *JTS* NS 28 (1977), 96–9.
[6] R. Kirschner, 'The Vocation of Holiness in Late Antiquity', *VC* 38 (1984), 105–24. See also P. Cox, *Biography in Late Antiquity: A Quest for the Holy Man* (Berkeley, 1983).
[7] F. E. Adcock, *Roman Political Ideas and Practice* (Ann Arbor, Mich., 1959), 65.

tended to be community virtues, strong in their setting of community life'.[8]

As a result, pagan paradigms with identifiable features such as the above significantly enriched the evolution of Augustine's monastic ideal. By the time he returned to Thagaste in 388 after an absence of five years from north Africa, Augustine had assimilated both consciously and subconsciously a variegated Graeco-Roman appreciation for communal living.

Pagan vices also, at least indirectly, provided another impetus to the future direction of Augustine's life. These vices with their deteriorating consequences had long ago been scrutinized and publicized by ancient authors. Contemporary students could recite by rote the proverbial 'causes' for the fall of the Roman Republic. Long before Marcus Aurelius, whether in the Golden or Silver Age of Latin literature, letter writers, essayists, historians, and satirists were often citing the evils of *ambitio*, *auaritia*, and *luxuria*. Like termites, this triad of diseases gnawed at social and political structures from within. The latter two vices, *auaritia* and *luxuria*, were deplored in the aphorism: 'self-indulgence lacks much, avarice everything'.[9] Augustine very likely recalled this adage or its equivalent from his former days in the classroom, when he trained students in the *suasoriae* and *controuersiae* of Roman declamation. Similar stock-in-trade leitmotifs were utilized by the sometimes sterile and turgid rhetoric of late antiquity to serve notice once again that history was about to repeat itself.

All these evils combined and worsened in such a way as to become a cancer that threatened the existence of Graeco-Roman civilization. *Respublica* and *imperium*, senators and generals, husbands and households had all been vulnerable to the metastases of these political and social ills. Cicero had long ago observed: 'Sick minds are characterized by hollow and deep desires for wealth, glory, irresponsible use of power, and depraved pleasures.'[10] Cicero had also written a treatise *On Glory* which is no longer extant. In a kind of unpredictable fulfilment of the Ciceronian aspirations for worldly glory, Christianity subsequently offered prospects of unending glory and an imperishable crown for the sake of a kingdom that was not of this world. A hundred years before Augustine's birth, many people were searching, first in the

---

[8] Ibid., 52.   [9] Publilius Syrus, *Sent.* 236 Meyer; cf. Seneca, *Contr.* 7. 3. 8.
[10] *De finibus bonorum et malorum* 1. 18. 59.

east and later in the west, for an 'alternative society'. As an alternative choice to the degeneracy of pagan society, Christianity extolled obedience and humility, which helped, respectively, to hold in check the abuses of power and of unbridled ambition. Another virtue, chastity, commended two centuries earlier by Tacitus as the most outstanding virtue of his mother-in-law,[11] helped to regulate an otherwise undisciplined sexuality. As recorded by Luke of the primitive Jerusalem community, sharing of possessions became a source of inspiration whereby Christians attempted to lay the axe to the roots of avarice.

Thus did Christianity with its attendant development of a monastic way of life set in bold relief many inherent weaknesses in the social fabric of the fourth and fifth centuries. At Cassiciacum Augustine will urge abstinence from 'all wantonness . . . excessive care and adornment of the body . . . ambition for posts of honour and power', and he will advise his circle of friends that 'love for money is an unfailing poison'.[12] These same standardized literary conventions will be invoked at Rome just one year later: ' . . . wherever he turns, *avarice* can confine him, *self-indulgence* dissipate him, *ambition* master him'.[13] Such texts could be multiplied.[14] Augustine's emerging Christian consciousness later at Cassiciacum and the following year in Rome was beginning to provide a new twist to these outworn rhetorical clichés. Similarly, the preaching of the Church Fathers was exploiting this indictment of ancient civilization, which had been so pithily presented by Roman writers. Hagiography, too, Possidius' *Life of Augustine*, for example, likewise accentuates many features of individual behaviour as a counter-cultural critique of paganism.

Because subtle motivations easily elude the historian's purview, it is naïve to suggest a stimulus–response theory to account for the appeal of western asceticism in the middle and late fourth century. So complex a phenomenon boldly resists such a *post hoc, propter hoc* interpretation.[15] Besides the political patronage of favourable

---

[11] *Agricola* 4.   [12] *Ord.* 2. 8. 25 (CCL 29. 121).
[13] *Lib. Arb.* 1. 11. 22 (CCL 29. 226).
[14] It comes as no surprise that *ambitio*, *auaritia*, and *luxuria* are cited (*Conf.* 2. 6. 13) in the catalogue of vices which Augustine enumerates in connection with the pear theft.
[15] R. MacMullen, *Paganism in the Roman Empire* (New Haven, 1981). See also G. Bonner, 'The Extinction of Paganism and the Church Historian', *Journal of Ecclesiastical History*, 35 (1984), 339–57.

emperors and other well-known historical factors, a psycho-social history might uncover some of the latent causes for the decline of paganism and the concurrent rise of monasticism. Persistent assaults of paganism, which held on tenaciously, paralleled continuing interest in asceticism, and we are reminded that Augustine was more of a pagan than one is ordinarily inclined to consider him.[16] Here is no instance of a simple linear displacement, either in the process of Augustine's conversion or in the sensate culture which his early life reflects. As catalogued by its diverse critics in both widely divergent eras and literary genres (specifically: the histories of Sallust, Livy, and Tacitus; the satires of Horace, Persius, and Juvenal; the philosophical essays of Cicero and Seneca), the excesses of Roman society in the long run became the turbulent ambience which agitated the emergence and growth of the ascetic and monastic milieu of a later time.

[16] J. J. O'Donnell, 'The Demise of Paganism', *Traditio*, 35 (1979), 45–88. The author says that Augustine during his bout with scepticism 'was more a [*sic*] typical pagan of his period than he has been given credit for being' (63). For another viewpoint see R. Guardini, *The Conversion of Augustine* (Westminster, Md., 1960), 135–44: 'Augustine did not "become" a Christian, since he had never been a pagan' (139).

II
Summer 386, Milan

1. The Prelude to Conversion

BY the time he resigned his professorship at Milan in August 386, Augustine was a churchgoer deeply impressed with the preaching of Ambrose. As a professor of rhetoric he had listened to the bishop several times (*Conf.* 6. 3. 4), at first paying attention to the preacher's delivery of the gospel, but eventually he became more and more attracted to the gospel of delivery (5. 14. 24). Nor were the Scriptures any longer unpalatable to him (3. 5. 9), as had been the case during his previous short-lived stay in Rome in 383. Alypius and Augustine were, in fact, reading St Paul when they were visited by a kinsman of theirs from north Africa. Pontician held an important job in the imperial service and he told his countrymen about Antony, the Egyptian anchorite. Although well-known in ascetic circles, Antony's life was wholly unfamiliar both to Alypius and Augustine (8. 6. 14), just as neither of them at that time had known about a monastery at Milan which was sponsored by Ambrose (8. 6. 15).

When they were free from their employment at Trier, Pontician and three of his friends paired off one afternoon to enjoy a leisurely walk. Two of the group came upon a house where God's 'servants' were living. There they also happened upon the *Life of Antony* by St Athanasius. One of the men was so moved by the example of Antony that he abandoned his secular career on the spot 'in order to serve God' (ibid.). After mutual consultation, both men took the decisive step of leaving all possessions behind in order to follow the Lord. Later on, Pontician and the fourth member of the party searched out their companions, who, in turn, told them of their resolve. Of the two men who were then and there determined to follow the Lord, we read: 'both are already Yours' (ibid.). When their fiancées heard what the two men had done, they dedicated their virginity to the Lord.

Augustine, meanwhile, depicts Pontician and his colleague thus:

'there is no change from their former state' (8. 6. 15). The following words describe both the holy men living at Trier and the two persons about to join them: 'brothers', 'servants' (twice, 14 and 15), 'to serve' (twice), and 'a comrade for so great a reward'. The will of the newcomers is portrayed as 'their purpose', 'resolution', and 'such determination' (ibid.). Whereas Pontician is a prayerful man and 'a faithful Christian' (8. 6. 14), the above terminology echoes the language of asceticism. A significant change had occurred in the hearts of Pontician's companions, whose lives had been reoriented towards God. This is no less true of Augustine:

Pontician told us this story and as he spoke, You O Lord, turned me back upon myself. You took me from behind my own back, where I had placed myself because I did not wish to look upon myself. You stood me face to face with myself . . . (8. 7. 16.)

Thus was I gnawed within myself, and I was overwhelmed with shame and horror, while Pontician spoke of such things. (8. 7. 18.)

As for me, *when I deliberated upon serving the Lord my God, as I had long planned to do*, it was myself who willed it and I myself who did not will it. It was I myself. I neither willed it completely, nor did I refrain from willing it. (8. 10. 22.)

In this last text the words in italics, *ego cum deliberabam, ut iam seruirem domino deo meo, sicut diu disposueram*, resemble the overture to a musical composition. That is to say, Augustine's moment of conversion in the garden, his formal enrolment as a catechumen, and his subsequent baptism sounded similar notes. Also in a wider sense, Augustine's later choice of a monastic calling is a variation or expression of the same theme. I dispute as too facile and possibly misleading the viewpoint which claims 'conversion was not to Christianity, but to Monachism—with its entire ascetic ideal'.[1] As attractive as such a thesis appears to be, historical evidence yields a more modest estimate: '(Augustine's conversion) took place in a very distinctive manner under the influence of the monastic ideal.'[2]

Much ink has been spilt assessing the significance of Antony for

[1] B. B. Warfield, *Studies in Tertullian and Augustine* (Oxford, 1930; Westport, Conn., 1970), 265.
[2] H. Leclercq, *L'Afrique chrétienne*, 2 (Paris, 1904), 69.

Augustine,[3] as it has been in other instances, for example, the influence of Cicero's *Hortensius* and the *libri Platonicorum* (the Neoplatonists, Plotinus and Porphyry) upon the development of Augustine's thought.[4] The *Vita Antonii*, meanwhile, will never erase the impact of Cicero to whom Augustine credited his initial taste for philosophy (3. 4. 7). Nor will the Bible completely efface the imprint of the Platonists. Augustine's intellectual stature would not permit this to happen; his blending of pagan wisdom with Christianity becomes an almost ingrained habit. On his deathbed the bishop of Hippo will utter both words of Plotinus and the Penitential Psalms.[5] Yet it is equally true to insist that the story of Antony, in Augustine's case, began almost immediately to radicalize the ancient philosophical tradition. In the long run, the pervasive influence of Platonist philosophy will be overtaken by the ascetic legacy, largely under the authority of the Scriptures.

Scripture's steady endowment of this legacy likewise reveals Augustine's assimilative and practical genius. Asceticism, for the new convert, was generally open both to external and internal forces. There was a continuum which flowed gradually, *gradatim*,[6] like the soul's Plotinian ascent or return to God. Apart from Augustine's apparently sudden volte-face regarding chastity, which is best explained as the working of grace, there were no leaps or bounds in his intellectual changeover from paganism to Christianity. Unlike Ambrose, Paulinus of Nola, or Jerome, Augustine had no abrupt interstices in his mind or milieu. So too after his conversion: the transition from asceticism to monasticism will again be gradual, almost imperceptible, assuredly irreversible.

---

[3] P. Monceaux, 'Saint-Augustin et saint Antoine: Contribution à l'histoire du monachisme', *Misc. Agost.* ii. 61–89. See also F. Bolgiani, *La conversione di s. Agostino e l'VIII libro delle 'Confessioni'* (Turin, 1956), 92–4.

[4] J. O'Meara, *Young Augustine*, 56–60 tends to downplay the significance of Augustine's reading of Cicero's *Hortensius* as a 'conversion which did not last' (58). Elsewhere he writes: 'The impression of the *Hortensius* likewise faded from Augustine's mind' (162). See the same author's 'Augustine and Neoplatonism', *RA* 1 (1958), 91–111 and more recently 'The Neoplatonism of Saint Augustine' in D. O'Meara (ed.), *Neoplatonism and Christian Thought* (Norfolk, Va., 1982), 34–41.

[5] *Vita*, 31. See H. T. Weiskotten, *Sancti Augustini vita scripta a Possidio episcopo* (Princeton, 1919), 140–3. Also A. H. Armstrong, *St Augustine and Christian Platonism* (Villanova, 1967), 33–4.

[6] Three instances of *gradatim* in the *Confessions* illustrate this movement from the external world of the body to the interior world of the soul (7. 17. 23); the ascent of the soul includes Monica (9. 10. 24) and the return of the soul to God (12. 28. 38).

Precisely because the many facets of so rich a personality were so intimately interrelated, it is permissible to say: 'What we usually denote as Augustine's conversion, should more properly be called his choice of a religious vocation.'[7] The same holds true for Alypius.[8] Both became 'committed Christians' or ascetics. Their monastic option lay in the future.

Soon (*moxque*, the word used by Possidius), after his conversion in the garden at Milan, Augustine abandoned every worldly hope 'with no further desire for a wife, children of the flesh, riches, or public office'.[9] These words of the bishop's first biographer and friend of forty years echo the convert's own account in that masterpiece of introspection, the *Soliloquies*, as these events were actually happening during the winter of 386–7. The Latin text contrasts its author's frame of mind, *nunc*, 'but now I spurn them all', with his previous persistent pursuits, *tunc*, 'riches, honours, and a wife'.[10] This self-portrait, given while he was waiting to be enrolled as a catechumen, is basically consistent with the bishop's later recollection of these happenings: 'I was hot for honours, riches, and marriage' (6. 6. 9). Riches and honours were the first allurements to loosen their grip on him.[11] Unlike Alypius, it was only later that Augustine's desire for marriage abated and he was able to decide in favour of celibacy (6. 12. 21–2).

The 'examples set by Your servants' (9. 2. 3) had enkindled Augustine's heart. But his 'plan' to resign his teaching post was known only to himself. This *consilium* became a 'vow and resolution' (9. 2. 3). Here the shift in meaning is worth noting. 'With a heart now completely in [God's] service' (9. 2. 4), Augustine finished the academic term. Fortunately, only a few class days remained. A professional colleague expressed regret at the time that he would no longer enjoy Augustine's company. But Verecundus would become 'a Christian and one of the faithful' (9. 3. 5). Augustine encouraged him 'to accept the faith in his own station, namely, married life' (9. 3. 6). Verecundus, however, had maintained that he would become a Christian only on terms which,

[7] L. Cilleruelo, *El monacato de S. Augustín y su Regla* (Valladolid, 1947), 24.
[8] F. Bolgiani, *Conversione*, 80: 'La conversione, la "vocazione" meglio, di Alipio segue da presso.'
[9] *Vita* 2 (Pellegrino, 44–6). See *Conf.* 8. 12. 30.
[10] *Sol.* I. II. 19 (PL 32. 880).
[11] R. P. Russell, 'Cicero's *Hortensius* and the Problem of Riches in Saint Augustine', *AS* 7 (1976), 59–68.

for himself, were impossible, that he would embrace both Christianity and celibacy together. This was an unrealistic ideal, since at the time he had a Christian wife. While this fact hints at the extent to which the ascetic ideal tended to depreciate married Christians, here also is another clue to Augustine's future designs.

As his chief propagandist, Athanasius had made it clear that Antony of Egypt was a monk in the sense of an anchorite. So does the Bishop of Hippo in his single use of the term *monachus* in the *Confessions* (8. 6. 14). At one time Augustine himself 'had been tormented at heart and had pondered flight into the desert' (10. 43. 70). But his temperament and all his experiences were marked by many social elements which were, in the long run, to supplement and enrich Pontician's vivid account of monasticism in the house at Trier, with its inhabitants and with Pontician's two friends who joined them. Augustine's resolution, like theirs, embraced both baptism and asceticism with his options pointing favourably in the direction of coenobitic life.

There is no doubt about Augustine's decision to serve God when he resigned his teaching position (9. 5. 13). Such was his intention before giving public notice to his students about engaging another teacher for the next academic term.[12]

But when a complete will to be at leisure and see that you are the Lord (Ps. 45: 11) arose and was made firm in me—you know all this, my God— I even began to be glad that this not untrue excuse was at hand.   (9. 2. 4).

Clearly Augustine's health was a secondary consideration;[13] the new goal he had set for himself was an ascetic one.

Finally, there is no reason to fault Augustine's memory or to suggest that he invested *seruus dei*, *deo seruiens*, and kindred words with an ascetic/monastic meaning which they did not possess some ten years previously as these events were taking place. Furthermore, as we shall note in Ch. V, the distinction between an ascetic and a lay monk was not always clear. We have no right to expect of Augustine's early vocabulary a precision or refinement which did not exist at the time. While *seruus dei* and *deo seruiens* textually admit of lay status, these words by no means exclude a monastic sense as Augustine will later conceive of it.

[12] *Vita* 2 (Pellegrino, 46): 'quod seruire deo ipse decreuisset'.
[13] There are many references to Augustine's poor health at this time: *B. Vita* 1. 4; *Acad.* 1. 1. 3; *Ord.* 1. 2. 5; *Sol.* 1. 9. 16; *Conf.* 9. 2. 4, 9. 5. 13.

2. Augustine and Romans 13: 13–14

In much the same manner as a pagan consulting the *Sortes Vergilianae*, and in response to the command: 'take and read; take and read' (8. 12. 29), Augustine's eyes alighted at random upon the Pauline verses:

Rom. 13: 13   *Non in comessationibus et ebrietatibus,*
non in cubilibus et impudicitiis,
non in contentione et aemulatione,

14   *sed induite dominum Iesum Christum*
et carnis prouidentiam ne feceritis in concupiscentiis.

It is a matter of interest that prior to his composition of the *Confessions*, Augustine's writings are 'astonishingly silent' and reveal 'an incredible indifference to Rom. 13: 13–14'.[14] In fact, a single reference to both verses appears in *Letter* 22. 1. 2 addressed to Bishop Aurelius of Carthage in 392.[15] Such silence is all the more surprising when we recall that Augustine had written two Commentaries on Romans shortly before his episcopal ordination.[16] Equally puzzling is the fact that Rom. 13: 13–14 is not featured in any significant way 'for at least some ten years after the appearance of the *Confessions*'.[17] To enter into the debate between the historicists and the fictionalists (as represented by O'Meara and Courcelle, respectively[18]), does not suit our immediate purpose.[19] One may wish to suggest that there is as much historical truth in the *Confessions* as there is in the Gospels. Our interest in Rom. 13: 13–14 derives not so much from the historicity of events portrayed in Book 8 of the *Confessions* as from the significance Augustine himself attached to these Pauline verses at so crucial a turning-point in his life.

[14] L. C. Ferrari, 'Paul at the Conversion of Augustine: *Conf* VIII, 12. 29–30', *AS* 11 (1980), 12, 17.   [15] *Ep.* 22. 1. 2 (CSEL 34. 56).

[16] See P. F. Landes, *Augustine on Romans*. Texts and Translations, 23 (Chico, 1982), 45 for Augustine's exegesis of the last phrase of the sequence Rom. 13: 13–14: 'et carnis prouidentiam ne feceritis.'

[17] Ferrari, 'Paul at the Conversion', 15.

[18] O'Meara, '*Arripui, aperui et legi*', *AM* 1 (1954), 59–65 defends the historicity of the narrative. For P. Courcelle's final reflections on the *tolle lege* scene, see his *Recherches sur les Confessions de saint Augustin* (Paris, 1968), 188–202. There is a succinct review of this debate among scholars in O'Meara, *Young Augustine*, 182–90.

[19] The issue arises again in connection with the Cassiciacum dialogues. See Ch. III n. 2.

'Not in revelling and drunkenness'

St Paul's injunction, in effect, proscribes a degree of independence which is inadmissible in the life of a Christian. His fundamental consideration was temperance or self-control, a preoccupation with Greek ethics generally. This admonition is prompted by concern for others and a respect for oneself which is rudimentary for all sound ethical behaviour. 'To be drunk as a lord' is a derogatory expression which implicitly condemns such unbecoming conduct. While intoxication is by no means the exclusive preserve of lords and princes, access to money and power presumably provides a measure of independence that enables wealthy persons to strike out in any number of directions; drunkenness is merely one. Excessive drinking was never, for Augustine, a serious problem (10. 31. 45). Yet one of his first pastoral duties as a priest at Hippo was to rebuke the flagrant insobriety of his congregation during their annual celebration of the local feast of St Leontius. Hence, *Letter* 22 with its singularly apposite use of Rom. 13: 13–14 possibly represents, at first sight, a more apt use of this text than its citation at the climax of Book 8 of the *Confessions*.

Another biblical text which had inspired Antony of Egypt to go into the desert, Matt. 19: 21, Jesus' invitation to 'the rich young man' to sell his possessions and to follow him, immediately precedes Augustine's reading of Rom. 13: 13–14. Some years afterwards, the bishop will cite Matt. 19: 21 no less than four times in a single epistle when he contrasts married and monastic life as different ways of serving the Lord.[20] With respect to common life, Matt. 19: 21 will eventually be upstaged by Augustine's decided preference for Acts 4: 32–5, which had idealized the early Christian community in Jerusalem.

Augustine's *Rule* mentions 'a single storeroom' for food and 'a single wardrobe' (5. 1). Both features are consonant with his own and his friends' earlier aborted attempt to live a common life at Milan. Later Augustine acknowledges that gifts ought to serve both the individual and the common good:

> Consequently, whenever anyone brings anything
> to sons or relations who reside in the monastery,
> an article of clothing,

[20] *Ep.* 157 (AD 414, CSEL 44. 449–88).

> or anything else that is considered necessary,
> the gift is not to be pocketed on the sly
> but given to the superior as common property,
> so that it can be given to whoever needs it.   (5. 3.)

Dependence upon one another is regarded as a source of spiritual strength, not a sign of indigence or weakness. Compassion, mutual consideration, and concern for both common and individual needs are so strongly evidenced in the *Rule* as to strike at the roots of any unwarranted independence, display of power, or egoism, which would be inherently destructive of common life.

'*Not in debauchery and licentiousness*'

Augustine's carnal desires held out until the final hour when the chorus of Continence sundered his deafness (8. 11. 25): 'Cannot you do what these youths and maidens do?' Previously he had envied Alypius' observance of chastity and assured his friend that married life likewise led to wisdom (6. 12. 21). Meanwhile, within Augustine two conflicting wills were raging, and he lamented the emotional and moral ambivalence of his dilemma (8. 10. 22). But the concluding sentence of Book 8 announced the triumph of grace:

For you had converted me to yourself, so that I would seek neither wife nor ambition in this world, for I would stand on that rule of faith where, so many years before, you had showed me to her (Monica). You turned her mourning into joy far richer than she had desired, far dearer and purer than that she had sought in grandchildren of my flesh.   (8. 12. 30.)

Unknown to Augustine, Paulinus of Nola and his wife Therasia, will soon vow continence. In the wake of their asceticism with its monastic overtones, Paulinus will be ordained a priest and eventually a bishop in southern Italy.[21] Neither Paulinus nor Jerome will ever meet Augustine, except (fortunately in both cases) through a prolonged exchange of letters. By this time perpetual chastity was fast becoming a symbol of sanctity. Other contemporaries of Augustine, Valerius Pinianus and his wife Melania the Younger, some years afterwards, will vow chastity

---

[21] J. T. Lienhard, *Paulinus of Nola and Early Western Monasticism* (Cologne–Bonn, 1977).

and later establish monasteries for men and women, respectively, at Thagaste and after a time move on to Bethlehem.[22]

The mother of Adeodatus returned to Africa in late 385 or early 386. She vowed never again to possess carnal knowledge of another man (6. 15. 25). Augustine's incapacity for continence contrasted sharply with the resolution of his former concubine. Because his fiancée was two years below the legal age for marriage (6. 13. 23), he soon took up with another woman merely to satisfy his sexual energies.

Two caveats are appropriate when evaluating Augustine's conduct during this time. First, baptism was a year away, nor was there any intimation that he would request this sacrament. On this score at least, Augustine was still far removed from the promptings of an informed Christian conscience. Secondly, modern criteria do not apply with equal merit to the social ambience of the late fourth century. Whatever charge of unmanliness, insensitivity, or injustice one may wish to level at Augustine for the abrupt dismissal of his anonymous concubine of some thirteen years, the relationship was terminated because Roman law prohibited marriage between persons of different social status. Any thought of regularizing their relationship, on the part of either Augustine or his concubine, was out of the question during those years of fidelity to each other. Legal and social customs precluded both persons from taking any such initiative. Ten years later Augustine's *Rule* (1. 7, 3. 4) would insist that there was to be no social stratification in the monastery as a vestige of the brother's former standing in the world.

In addition, as an ardent Manichee during most of these years, marriage would have severely compromised Augustine's allegiance to this religious sect. Possibly this allegiance to Manichaeism explains further why Adeodatus was an only child. Manichaeism took an unkindly view towards the birth of a baby, whereby particles of light, the soul, became enveloped in particles of darkness, the body.

Augustine never regarded the liaison with his anonymous concubine as a bona-fide marriage. Legal recognition of their

---

[22] J. Gavigan, *De vita monastica in Africa septentrionali inde a temporibus S. Augustini usque ad inuasiones Arabum* (Turin, 1962), 61, 83, 99, 113, 119. While this accurate and thorough coverage of north African monasticism embraces archaeological, epigraphical, and literary evidence, it is regrettably too little known and, for this reason, is too little cited.

cohabitation was lacking for two reasons: (1) there had been no intention to beget children, and (2) his concubine possessed a different social status. In the first instance, Adeodatus had been an unwanted child (4. 2. 2); once born, however, he forced himself upon his parents' love and Augustine loved him deeply (9. 6. 14). The second reason requires elaboration to which we shall return.

Roman society, meanwhile, was as tolerant of concubinage as is American society today. Even the Catholic Church appeared to be willing to look the other way. This, at least, is the legitimate interpretation of Canon 17 of the Council of Toledo which reads in part: 'Only let (the man) be content with one woman, whether wife or concubine.'[23] Nor were such persons to be cut off from communion with the Catholic Church. However, Canon 17 dates from the year 400, some fifteen years after the time in question; it also roughly coincides with the completion of the *Confessions*. Even allowing for the latest possible date when Augustine, as Bishop of Hippo, could have composed Book 10, which described the present state of his soul, he distinctly remarks there that concubinage is forbidden on moral grounds (10. 30. 41). Yet later in a pastoral treatise, the bishop implies that the fidelity of two people towards each other until death in a stable relationship is tantamount to a marriage.[24] By applying such a criterion to his own situation in early life, thirteen years of fidelity to one woman (4. 2. 2), in contrast to his pagan father's infidelity to Monica, surely endows his loving relationship with one of the basic ingredients of marriage. But this is to read history backwards. To assess the young Augustine in the light of later developments is improper, except to point out that varied pastoral experiences as a celibate priest and bishop had taught him much.

Moreover, steadfast Stoic and Neoplatonic convictions then embedded in western culture associated childbirth almost exclusively with civic duty. We shall have occasion to note again that the young Augustine was never keen on parenting.[25]

Nor was love linked with marriage in a more accurate rendering

---

[23] The Latin text reads: 'qui non habet uxorem et pro uxore concubinam habet, a communione non repellatur, tantum ut unius mulieris, aut uxoris, aut concubinae . . . sit coniunctione contentus.' See J. D. Mansi, *Sacrorum conciliorum noua et amplissima collectio*, 3 (Florence, 1759), 1001 for the full text.

[24] *Bon. Coniug.* 5. 5 (CSEL 41. 193–4).

[25] See n. 42–3 below.

of Pauline exegesis until the fifteenth century,[26] and even then acceptance of this link was afterwards pitifully slow. Sexuality only gradually emerged as a dignified dimension of conjugal love. Resistance to such an idea eventually breaks down within the twentieth century. Augustine's later rigorism with respect to the justification of sexual pleasure solely in the interests of child-bearing will inescapably reflect the established conventions of his time.

Furthermore, Augustine withholds the name of his concubine very likely out of respect for her privacy and in the interests of his own public ministry in the Church. The *Confessions* were read during his lifetime.[27] Besides, the book was never intended to be purely autobiographical; it was hastily composed and its author was selective in his choice of materials (3. 12. 21; 9. 8. 17). Nor does Augustine identify by name the dear friend of his youth (4. 4. 7–9), or a local African bishop who had urged Monica not to abandon hope (3. 12. 21), or his sister for that matter, and, surprisingly enough, although he frequently refers to his mother, Monica is mentioned by name only once in all his writings (9. 13. 37).

That Augustine loved the mother of his son is beyond dispute. He was faithful to her (4. 2. 2). His description of their parting is painful (6. 15. 25), and he is harsher with himself than with her.[28] Twice Augustine acknowledged Adeodatus to be the fruit of *his* sin (9. 6. 14).

In sum, chastity still eluded him. While battling against scepticism, the distinguished professor of rhetoric had very likely retained a residue of Manichaeism. His health was in imminent danger of collapse (9. 2. 4) and did, in fact, collapse.[29] His desire

[26] H. Crouzel, 'Marriage and Virginity: Has Christianity Devalued Marriage?' *The Way*, Supplement 10 (1970), 20.

[27] *Retr*. 2. 6 (CCL 57. 94).

[28] The following excerpt from a sermon preached at Cambridge University before an 'audience consisting predominantly of undergraduates' is unfair to Augustine: '[W]hen St Augustine was converted and thus suddenly abandoned the mistress with whom he had been living for years, telling her, in effect, to go to hell, he certainly became chaste in terms of the ecclesiastical definition. He no longer had any sex (and became in the process what amounted to an anti-sex maniac).' (H. A. Williams, *Poverty, Chastity and Obedience* (London, 1975), 8 and 69.) For a more informed appreciation of these matters, once again from Cambridge, see n. 43, also n. 45 below.

[29] P. Brown, *Augustine of Hippo* (London, 1967), 109 justifiably allows 'the physical manifestations of a nervous breakdown'.

for success in a secular career collided with his concern for the pursuit of wisdom in the company of others. A mistress, a son, his mother, even some relatives, meanwhile, were depending upon his employment. All these factors both precipitated and aggravated in varying degrees the crisis of that period.

Worldly ambition and personal sexual need directed Augustine's thoughts towards the marriage Monica had arranged for him (6. 13. 23). Augustine needed money and a wife who had some. It would not be out of order to inquire whose ambition was the more overreaching, the son's or the mother's. Like many mothers, Monica was pressing for a marriage which would enhance still further the social rank of her son. Elements of Milanese snobbery possibly blended with a mother's instinctive determination to secure the best. In his obvious obeisance to Monica, it is reasonable to ask whether Augustine was unduly deferential towards her. Or is Monica's behaviour all the more reprehensible for seeming to countenance or refusing to protest at the liaison with yet another woman? After all, she had previously barred her son from the house when he announced that he was a Manichee (3. 11. 19); even then she seemed not to have protested at his first liaison. We simply do not know.

Presumably, Monica's chief interest in the long run was to legitimate her son's status both civilly and ecclesiastically at whatever cost. Even though legal barriers were of a social nature and Roman law exhibited tolerance towards concubinage, Augustine's liaison with a woman outside marriage nevertheless presented an obstacle to baptism on moral grounds. Although the son gave no hint of the future, his mother's wishes were unmistakable. A short-lived liaison with a second woman was terminated as abruptly as the first. Monica's overriding concern had finally been laid to rest:

One thing there was, for which I desired to linger a little while in this life, that I might see you a Catholic Christian before I died. God has granted this to me in more than abundance, for I see you his servant, with even earthly happiness held in contempt. What am I doing here? (9. 10. 26.)

At long last Augustine was a committed Christian, *seruus dei*. His resolve to remain chaste was a fundamental expression of this service to God. Little by little Augustine assimilates and modifies the ascetic and monastic legacy which preceded him. And two treatises, *Continence* and *Holy Virginity*, will later enrich his transformation of that heritage.

'Not in quarrelling and jealousy'

This injunction likewise reflects the preoccupation of ancient Greek ethics with the virtue of temperance. Within a year of his ordination to the presbyterate Augustine will lament to Aurelius, Bishop of Carthage, the extent to which quarrels and jealousies were serious weaknesses among the clergy, more so than among the laity.[30] Possidius will note the same failing.[31] *Letter* 22, it will be remembered, offers the only full citation of Rom. 13: 13–14 before its appearance in the *tolle lege* scene. As we noted earlier, this particular Pauline passage is singularly appropriate in this instance, because Augustine uses it to rebuke both contentious clerics and bibulous laity. Augustine's pastorate subsequently brings him into contact with many monks and clerics. *Letters* 210 and 211 (this latter otherwise known in the manuscript tradition as the *Reprimand to Quarrelling Nuns*), furnish further evidence of the bishop's concern in this matter. Africans frequently manifested a litigious temperament. 'Either have no quarrels', he writes in his *Rule*, 'or put an end to them as quickly as possible' (6. 1). The same chapter of the *Rule* likewise cautions against 'insults', 'harmful words', 'words too harsh', and 'bickering'.

Such strictures, somewhat remotely perhaps, hint at the sense of order which Augustine inherited from the hierarchical categories of Neoplatonism. On the practical side, these levels of reality (not unlike Plato's harmony of the spheres in the myth of Er) had been incorporated for centuries into Roman political structures as expressions of the *concordia ordinum*. While the breach between the *optimates* and *populares* had long ago widened and corruption eroded the senatorial and equestrian ranks of society, Augustine's monasticism will later reflect much that was noble in the Graeco-Roman political/ethical tradition.

Injunctions against quarrelling and rancour were necessary for purifying the passions of the individual and for achieving that measure of virtue and tranquillity which epitomized the ethical orientation of later Greek asceticism. Access to the superior

---

[30] *Ep.* 22. 2. 7 (CSEL 34. 59).

[31] *Vita* 23 (Pellegrino, 124): 'Et dum forte, ut adsolet, de possessionibus ipsis inuidia clericis fieret, alloquebatur plebem Dei . . .'.

realms of contemplation is available only to those who subordinate lower goods to higher goods, thereby reflecting in the manner of their lives the beauty and proportion which are inherent in the hierarchy of the universe. These features of Augustine's early asceticism will be greatly transformed by his later understanding of 1 John 3: 15. Furthermore, the good of the city depends upon the moral values of its citizens, who exemplify the justice and order and harmony which exist among the higher and the lower elements in the universe. In the same way, Augustine will later insist that the *mores* of the monastery, indeed of every society, derive from the *amores* of its members to the extent that they repudiate self-interest for the sake of the common good. At the turn of the fifth century, he writes admiringly of 'well-regulated monasteries'.[32] But order and harmony also exist on a deeper level. By striking a distinctive Christian chord with the help of Luke 22: 25–6, Augustine says the superior of the monastery 'should regard himself (herself) to be fortunate as one who serves you in love, not as one who exercises authority over you' (7. 3.). Earlier he had written: 'Those responsible for food, clothing, or books are to serve their brothers (sisters) without grumbling' (5. 9). As an undergirding for common life then, 'compassion' is likely to instil obedience in its etymological sense of 'listening to' (*ob* + *audire*), listening to God and to one another.

One should pray, says Augustine, not so much to hear what one desires as to desire what one hears (10. 26. 37). Similarly, if desires are disciplined and if virtue is, in fact, 'the order of love',[33] and if priorities are properly ordered, presumably one's loves will be structured in like manner. Personal compassion and pastoral practice preclude any expectation of inexorable logic or extreme rationalization in Augustine's views of monastic life. The Doctor of Grace knew both the African temperament and human nature only too well. Besides, he consistently regarded himself as a convalescent in constant need of Christ's healing grace.[34] He was equally solicitous towards sick people and rich people inside the monastery and outside it. Poor people in the monastery should make every effort to understand concessions temporarily granted to wealthy individuals because of their different family background,

---

[32] *Op. Mon.* 29. 37 (CSEL 41. 587).   [33] *Ciu. Dei* 15. 22 (CCL 38. 488).
[34] Brown, *Augustine*, 177: 'The amazing Book Ten of the *Confessions* is not the affirmation of a cured man: it is the self-portrait of a convalescent.'

just as healthy persons should be grateful for their sound physical well-being.

For Augustine, perfect service becomes perfect freedom.[35] Ambition is made of sterner stuff, notably considerateness towards others. Chapter 6 of the *Rule* adds greater preceptive force to Paul's injunction about jealousy and quarrelling. There Augustine reminds us: daily forgiveness is available to everyone. Attentiveness to others of whatever social status generates obedience, as understood above. Compassion for oneself (here the bishop offers an unusual nuance), will, it is hoped, abet rivalry and discourage unbecoming behaviour:

> By being obedient, you manifest more compassion
> not only for yourselves, but also for him (her),
> because the higher position among you
> is all the more perilous. (7. 4.)

These are some of the qualities which endow Augustine's *Rule* with much of its characteristic tone.

In the *Rule* of St Benedict the second and third chapters enunciate, respectively, the role of the abbot and the function of the community in council. In this respect the composition of these *Rules* is quite different. While Benedict gives early attention to the governance of the community, Augustine gives early attention to the prayer-life of the community. Perhaps by this priority of treatment Augustine intends to say that the prayer-life of the community will determine the quality of human relations as these are prescribed in later chapters, chiefly, ch. 6.

Prayer will likewise facilitate greatly both the virtue of obedience and the concomitant role of the superior set forth in ch. 7. These penultimate chs. 6 and 7 are immediately followed by a prayer in ch. 8 which might likewise be interpreted as an apt demonstration of the practical connection between prayer itself and good order in community life.

'But put on the Lord Jesus Christ'

Although baptism was deferred until his thirty-third year, Augustine was signed with the sign of the cross and seasoned with the salt of exorcism immediately after birth (1. 11. 17). With his mother's milk he imbibed the name of Christ (3. 4. 8). At the age of

[35] *Quant.* 34. 78 (PL 32. 1078).

eighteen the sole unattractive feature of Cicero's *Hortensius* was
its failure to mention Christ (ibid.). Even though they frequently
invoked it, Christ's name held but a hollow significance for the
Manichees (3. 6. 10). During his first short-lived stay in Rome, he
could not conceive of the possibility of the incarnation (5. 10. 20).
At Milan Augustine was a Photinian for whom the divinity of
Christ was totally unintelligible (7. 19. 25). Nor could he conceive
of Christ as the mediator between God and man any more than he
could embrace the humility of Christ (7. 18. 24).

Yet the faith of your Christ, our Lord and Saviour, the faith that is in the
Catholic Church, was firmly fixed within my heart. In many ways I was as
yet unformed and I wavered from the rule of doctrine. But my mind did
not depart from it, nay, rather from day to day it drank in more of it.   (7.
5. 7.)

The absence of Christ's name from Augustine's reading of the
Neoplatonists eventually confirmed his status as a catechumen (5.
14. 25). The 'Church of Christ' had figured prominently in the
conversion of Marius Victorinus (8. 2. 4), and Augustine wished
ever so much to imitate this celebrated rhetorician and exegete
(8. 5. 10).

   Later at Cassiciacum the young convert contrasted his personal
love for the Church with Alypius' manifest reluctance to insert the
name of Christ in the Dialogues which were recorded there (9. 4. 7).
While readers of the *Confessions* must sometimes distinguish
between events as they occurred and their later reconstruction,
there is not the slightest whisper of doubt to suggest that
Augustine's response to the call of Christ was not at the same time
a return to the Catholic Church (9. 2. 4; 9. 13. 37). 'As to what I
did there (Cassiciacum) by way of literary work, which was already
in your service' (9. 4. 7), says Augustine, it reeked of the pride so
often found in the schools rather than the healing herbs of your
Church.[36] Even if one allows for the projection of a later cast of
mind upon these events, within a year, as we shall observe,
Augustine's first polemical treatise will sharply contrast the mores
of the Manichees with the asceticism of the Catholic Church.

   When the bishop reviewed his odyssey of soul at this turbulent
time of his life, he invoked, possibly from his subsequent reading

[36] R. J. O'Connell, *St. Augustine's Confessions: The Odyssey of Soul* (Cambridge,
Mass., 1969), 36.

of St Paul, two references to Christ (Eph. 5: 14 and Rom. 7: 25) as
the emancipator of his moral predicament (8. 5. 10–12). Or in all
fairness it could be that he was already familiar with these texts
from his days as a devout Manichee. This is not the place to
inquire about the extent of Augustine's knowledge of Paul during
the summer of 386, except to remark that the Manichees
entertained a high regard for the Apostle to the Gentiles. Again,
after reading the Platonists, Augustine had turned to St Paul (7.
21. 27); he had a copy of St Paul before him when Pontician had
visited him (8. 6. 14), and again after the outburst of tears in the
garden, he returned to the spot where he had left Alypius and 'the
volume of the apostle' (8. 12. 29). We are on safe grounds simply
to assert that 'from the time of his conversion, Jesus Christ was the
guiding light of his [Augustine's] soul'.[37]

Paul's triple injunction in Rom. 13: 13 is negative. Yet it is not
far-fetched to detect in this threefold renunciation elements of
asceticism which immediately take root and gradually grow in
varying ways in the lives of Augustine, Alypius, and Evodius.
Their desire to live together will culminate at Thagaste in
Augustine's boyhood home, an experiment in communal living
with extremely fortunate repercussions for the future of the
Church in north Africa. Not to revel obviously forestalls an
otherwise intolerable situation among individuals who are wholly
intent upon serving the Lord; renunciation of marriage frees each
of them totally for God's service; avoidance of jealousy and
quarrelling fosters loving service towards each other.

While Paul enjoins a triple injunction, Jesus' invitation to the
'rich young man' evokes a single renunciation as regards riches,
property, and possessions. Juxtaposition of Matt. 19: 21 with
Rom. 13: 13–14 in the *Confessions* (8. 12. 29) is a deliberate stroke
of Augustine's artistry. In and of itself, of course, ascetic
renunciation is valueless. 'Come, follow me' in Matt. 19: 21 echoes
the words with which Jesus called his disciples. 'Put on the Lord
Jesus Christ' of Rom. 13: 14 likewise insists upon this positive
aspect of asceticism. According to Jerome, this is precisely where
Crates of Thebes, a pupil of Diogenes, was deficient. Both he and
his wife Hipparchia had donated their wealth to the city of Thebes
in order to choose the Cynic life of mendicancy. As admirable as

---

[37] E. Portalié, *A Guide to the Thought of Saint Augustine* (Chicago, 1960), 152.

such asceticism could be, it could only possess bloodless appeal because of its failure to follow Christ.[38]

Leaving aside discussion of a 'liberal' and an 'ascetic' exegesis of Matt. 19: 21, there is no doubt that Antony of Egypt and Augustine both interpreted this biblical text in the latter sense. And more to our present purpose: this ascetic impulse embraced both the selling of property and the renunciation of marriage.

Rom. 13: 13–14 further represented, for Augustine, much more than 'a simple ethical exhortation of putting into practice the commandments of God'.[39] Just as Book 7 of the *Confessions* concludes with the way of humility and the incarnation of the Word, a truth which was a priori excluded from Neoplatonism, so also Rom. 13: 13–14 lends a memorable touch to the final moments of Augustine's long struggle. This Pauline text moves beyond its paraenetic purpose. Again it is not enough to enumerate its 'proclamation of the reality of salvation', its 'declaration of the world's redemption', and its 'affirmation of Christian life in Jesus Christ'.[40] At this particular time Augustine was already intent upon living an ascetic life (8. 10. 22); he was but a few steps away from becoming 'a committed Christian'.

Curiously enough, the single reference to Christ in Augustine's *Rule* occurs in its last chapter. Explicit reference to Christ is found ten years previously, again in the final chapter of *Answer to Sceptics*, Augustine's first entry in his *Retractations*. Christ Jesus is directly addressed once only in the *Confessions* at the beginning of Book 9 in the immediate aftermath of the *tolle lege* scene which terminates Book 8. Here Christ, the all-inclusive God-man, is both healer and helper. (The 'Lord Jesus' is directly invoked earlier in 1. 11. 17) At long last Augustine is set free from 'the gnawing cares of *favour-seeking*, of striving for *wealth*, of scratching *lust's* itchy sore' (9. 1. 1). These symptoms of bondage now become the obverse side of the coin; one might say they represent the image of Caesar. Christ has become Augustine's 'wealth' and is 'sweeter than every pleasure . . . higher than every honour' (ibid.). Such words as *honor*, *uoluptas*, *libidines*, and *diuitiae* recall familiar landmarks. Renunciation of power and possessions, and surrender

---

[38] Jerome, *Commentariorum in Matheum libri IV*, 3. 19. 28 (CCL 77. 172).

[39] M. Lods, 'La personne du Christ dans la "conversion" de saint Augustin', *RA* 11 (1976), 22.

[40] Ibid. See Goulven Madec's helpful critical comments in *REA* 23 (1977), 381–2.

of sexuality, suggest an effective antidote to the young Augustine's former worldly ways of ambition, riches, and sensuality. Rhetoric, as a profession, had become a dead letter; the spirit which gives life and freedom is the gospel.

'And make no provision for the flesh to gratify its desires.'

We have already noted in *Letter* 22 the single full citation of Rom. 13: 13–14 some five years before its appearance in the *Confessions* 8. 12. 29, and we must wait some ten years after its composition for another full citation of this text. Evidently Augustine broke the silence only once in order to comment tersely on the final phrase of v. 14: 'et carnis prouidentiam ne feceritis in concupiscentiis', to the exclusion of both v. 13 and the affirmative injunction of v. 14. Here his interest focused less on the word *concupiscentia* than on the phrase *prouidentia carnis*. Written during the last years of Augustine's presbyterate, *Propositions from the Epistle to the Romans* (ch. 77) stresses moderation when caring for bodily health in much the same manner as Augustine will later urge in his monastic *Rule* (5.5). While the phrase *in concupiscentiis* is devoid of sexual overtones in this instance, a recently discovered letter to Atticus, Patriarch of Constantinople, probably dated 420–1, reminds us of Augustine's continuing concern to nuance the meaning of *concupiscentia* in his writings.[41] All his life (the new letter gives lie to the rumour that the bishop was already dead), Augustine felt forced to face the criticism that he was at best a crypto-Manichee.

An early text, meanwhile, written during the late autumn or winter of 386/7, hesitates to depict marriage as 'the wise man's duty'.[42] Here we have a likely allusion to the expectations of Stoic ethics. Augustine explicitly says he then lacked certitude in regard to the duty of wise men to beget children. Such men, he maintained, were worthy of admiration rather than imitation. Augustine's following comment sits less easily with many of his critics: 'I know nothing which saps the citadel of a man's strength more than a woman's caresses and physical intimacies without

---

[41] *Epistula* 6* in J. Divjak, *Epistolae ex duobus codicibus nuper in lucem prolatae*, CSEL 88, *Sancti Aureli Augustini Opera* (Vienna, 1981), 32–8. See also G. Bonner, '*Libido* and *Concupiscentia* in St. Augustine', *SP* 6 (1962), 303–14.

[42] *Sol.* 1. 10. 17 (PL 32. 878).

which one can not have a wife.'[43] Porphyry's dictum 'omne corpus fugiendum est' is possibly reflected in the original Latin rather than any Christian tendency to disparage marriage.[44] But a few months away from being formally enrolled as a catechumen, the recent convert was still carrying the weight of his past learning. So much was happening at this juncture in Augustine's life that we shall content ourselves with the assessment of a competent historian whose name coincides with 'the world of late antiquity':

All one can risk saying is that, when, in later years, Augustine speaks of the Catholic Church as a field of warm and lasting friendships, among continent men and women, based on their service to others, the carefully mobilised phrases do not read quite like any other Latin author. A capacity for intimacy, above all, *fides*, for mutual trust and reliability in friendship, derived not merely from the post-conversion experience of the celibate bishop, but from late adolescence onwards, can be heard in these phrases—a tone as subtle, but as unmistakable as the ring of good crystal.[45]

Accordingly, the issue at the time was not so much a 'dysfunction' in sexual matters as it was the inherent weakness of Augustine's will.[46] Moreover, there is no need to wait for 'later years'. Before Augustine returned to his native Africa in early autumn 388, as we shall note in Ch. IV, he recorded his experiences, both immediate and vicarious, of coenobitism and eremitism in Rome and in the east.

[43] Ibid. See the excellent remarks on the abrupt dismissal of his concubine and 'Augustine's subsequent writing on the uncontrollable force of sexual desire in fallen man' in G. R. Evans, *Augustine on Evil* (Cambridge, 1982), 21.

[44] *Ciu. Dei* 10. 29 (CCL 47. 305).

[45] P. Brown, 'Augustine and Sexuality', *The Center for Hermeneutical Studies in Hellenistic and Modern Culture*, Colloquy 46 (Berkeley, 1983), 3 with perceptive responses from J. P. Burns, X. Harris, M. R. Miles, and R. O'Connell.

[46] Such was Augustine's recollection some ten years later in *Conf.* 8. 10. 22 cited above on p. 10.

III

Retreat at Cassiciacum

SEVERAL months in late 386 and early 387 were very likely the most tranquil in Augustine's life. Once again he was not alone. Monica managed the house; her other son Navigius was there. Also in residence were teenage pupils, Licentius and Trygetius; Augustine spent considerable time tutoring both of them. His cousins Lastidianus and Rusticus compensated for their lack of formal education with their excellent common sense. There were nine persons in all, including Alypius and Adeodatus.

Autumnal air was a tonic for Augustine's breathing and chest ailment. Set in the foothills of the Italian Alps some forty miles north-east of Milan, the villa of Verecundus provided a welcome respite from the ardours of teaching. When Augustine resigned from his teaching post in Milan for reasons of health and to serve the Lord,[1] the vintage vacation, 23 August–15 October, was, in effect, prolonged.

It is not our purpose here to take sides in the scholarly debate between the historicists and the fictionalists as to the degree of historical accuracy or poetic licence which is reflected in the final redaction of the recorded conversations at Cassiciacum.[2] The Dialogues certainly resound with recurring metaphysical issues of the ancient world. For example, *Answer to Sceptics* argues for the validity of human knowledge and discusses the dialectic between authority (faith) and reason. *A Life of Happiness* engages a theme which will remain, for Augustine, the underlying desire of all other desires. *On Order* examines the value of the liberal arts as propaedeutic to contemplation and forcefully affirms the existence of God's providence, notwithstanding the magnitude of evil in the world. Subsequently, Augustine coins the word 'soliloquy' and gives the title *Soliloquies* to his fourth extant book, which unveils his unique effort to recount his personal 'God-talk', that is, a

---

[1] *Conf.* 9. 5. 13 (CCL 27. 140).
[2] J. O'Meara, *St. Augustine: Against the Academics. ACW* 12 (Westminster, 1951), 32: '. . . the element of fiction is far from being negligible'.

dialogue between himself and his reason. Like the *Confessions*, the first chapter of the *Soliloquies* is a prayer of praise and faith.

Structurally, these early writings remind one of Plato's and Cicero's successful achievements in the same literary genre. While the contents of these Dialogues are imbued with elements of ancient philosophy, one also finds in them distinctively Christian perspectives, such as the authority of Christ,[3] the doctrines of the Trinity and the Incarnation,[4] a discussion about the divinity of Christ (which proves to be embarrassing for Trygetius),[5] and the fervent prayer of a Christian Platonist.[6]

Augustine still could not escape Aristotle's dilemma that one must philosophize in order not to philosophize.[7] When he was twenty years old, Augustine had read both Aristotle's *Categories* and Cicero's *Hortensius*.[8] While the *Hortensius* was for Augustine an exhortation to wisdom, the *Categories* was useful when he later elaborated his theory of Trinitarian relations. He never lost his philosophic bent of mind: ultimate concerns such as happiness, the possibility of certitude, knowledge, wisdom, authority, faith, evil, and God eventually became the chief concerns that would engage both pen and pulpit of this monk, priest, and bishop for forty-two years.

During these months at Cassiciacum, a flexible daily schedule permitted discussions at mid-morning and late afternoon, indoors and outdoors depending upon the weather. One particular night the discussions were prolonged into the following day. Navigius and Alypius had stayed the night in Milan; the others had gone to bed. Licentius, meanwhile, tapped the floor with a stick to frighten away some field-mice. Night's silence was so audible that the would-be sleepers could detect the uneven flow of water making its way to the nearby bathhouse in a conduit choked by autumn leaves. A lively nocturnal conversation between Licentius, Trygetius, and Augustine ensued on the subject of order and providence.[9]

On 13 November 386, Augustine's thirty-second birthday, the same bathhouse furnished a congenial setting for part of the

---

[3] *Acad.* 3. 20. 43 (CCL 29. 61). See n. 33 below for the text.
[4] *Ord.* 2. 5. 16 (CCL 29. 116).
[5] Ibid. 1. 10. 29 (CCL 29. 103).
[6] *Sol.* ch. 1 (PL 32. 869–72).
[7] A. Solignac, *Les Confessions*, BA 13 (Paris, 1962), 667–8 n. 13.
[8] *Conf.* 4. 16. 28, 8. 7. 17 (CCL 27. 54. 124).
[9] *Ord.* 1. 3. 6–1. 8. 21 (CCL 29. 91–9).

dialogue which is reproduced in *A Life of Happiness*. This first completed extant treatise was dedicated to Mallius Theodorus, whom Augustine regarded at that time as a Neoplatonic saint. But meanwhile the conversion of Marius Victorinus to Christianity had made much more of a mark upon Augustine: what had been for him the 'harbour' of philosophy with its muddied waters and lofty mountain-peak was beginning to cast more shadows than light. His happiness eventually became grounded in the pivotal mystery of the incarnation with its invitation to faith and hope and love.[10]

Each day began with a prayer;[11] it was customary to end the day with a prayer.[12] Augustine often wept for the healing of his sins.[13] About twelve years later he will recall his delight in the Psalms during these peaceful months.[14] The cure of a toothache he credited to his companions' prayers, telling them of his agony by writing on a wax tablet.[15] Monica rebuked Licentius for singing a psalm while attending to the needs of nature in the outhouse. As he was humming the eighth verse of Ps. 79, the teenager's ear evidently took a fancy to the cadence of the chant, Licentius amusingly reduced Monica's rebuke to the absurd level by saying: 'As if, should some enemy imprison me here, God would not hear my voice!'[16]

Before the evening meal, Licentius, Trygetius, and their mentor regularly read half a book of Virgil.[17] Discussions were suspended for seven days when Augustine's pupils read Books 2, 3, and 4 of the *Aeneid*.[18] Both students were already familiar with the *Hortensius* of Cicero.[19] Apparently Augustine had hoped that this book would leave its mark upon them in somewhat the same manner as it had affected himself. He wisely urged his pupils to go off by themselves and engage in conversations unrelated to their studies.[20] The teacher–student relationship widened to embrace everyone present. Alypius, for example, requested a résumé of a conversation he had missed on the theme of wisdom, and he was advised that philosophical discourse—or any conversation for that matter—resembles the harbour of the mind, while words are like

[10] Ibid. 2. 8. 25 (CCL 29. 121).
[11] Ibid. 1. 8. 25 (CCL 29. 101).
[12] *Ep*. 3. 4 (CSEL 34. 8).
[13] *Ord*. 1. 8. 22, 1. 10. 29 (CCL 29. 99, 104).
[14] *Conf*. 9. 4. 8–11 (CCL 27. 137–40).
[15] Ibid. 9. 4. 12 (CCL 27. 140).
[16] *Ord*. 1. 8. 22 (CCL 29. 99–100).
[17] Ibid. 1. 8. 26 (CCL 29. 102).
[18] *Acad*. 2. 4. 10 (CCL 29. 23).
[19] Ibid. 1. 1. 4 (CCL 29. 5).
[20] *Ord*. 1. 3. 6 (CCL 29. 91).

the sails of a boat. To recapture words after they have left port sometimes becomes a 'shipwreck of misrepresentation'.[21]

Nearly an entire day was spent reading Book 1 of the *Aeneid* and working on the farm.[22] Such an agreeable combination of work and study proved to be both restorative and relaxing: 'We got up, therefore, earlier than usual and, because it was urgent, did some work with the farm-hands.'[23] The harvest season was making its annual demands, household chores too, and writing letters.[24] There is no evidence to suggest that Augustine excused himself from the work routine. While the following observation stands its ground, it does not take into account these several months in northern Italy: '. . . [W]hen faced with the disorder of the Christian monastery of Carthage in the year 401, [Augustine] was facing a pattern of life of which he himself had had, largely speaking, no knowledge which might be described as experiential.'[25] At that time the issue had to do with monks in the environs of Carthage who refused to engage in manual labour. Augustine on that occasion will lament that pastoral ministry had made this type of work impossible in his own case. As he then enumerated the four staples of monastic life: manual labour, reading, study of the Scriptures, and prayer,[26] Augustine may well have recalled these tranquil days at Cassiciacum. Some seven years at Thagaste and Hippo prior to his episcopal ordination will afford Augustine additional credentials for reproaching such unruly monks. This may be another reason why Aurelius, bishop of Carthage, will request him to do so.

At the conclusion of the dialogue *On Order* Alypius thanks Augustine for furnishing its interlocutors with 'the rules of life and the paths of knowledge'.[27] Augustine had earlier suggested that a person approaches God through life's experiences and also in formal study.[28] This latter approach, *eruditio*, embraces the liberal

[21] *Acad.* 1. 5. 15 (CCL 29. 12).   [22] Ibid.
[23] Ibid. 2. 4. 10 (CCL 29. 23).   [24] Ibid. 2. 11. 25 (CCL 29. 31).
[25] R. J. Halliburton, 'The Inclination to Retirement—the Retreat of Cassiciacum and the "Monastery" of Tagaste', *SP* 5 (1962), 340. G. Bonner, *St Augustine of Hippo: Life and Controversies* (London, 1963; 2nd edn. Norwich 1986), 93 aptly remarks apropos of any reluctance to work on Augustine's part: 'Men do not get up early to work in the fields simply to lend verisimilitude to an idyllic rural existence. One does not easily imagine Horace doing so on his Sabine farm.'
[26] *Op. Mon.* 29. 37 (CSEL 41. 587).
[27] *Ord.* 2. 20. 53 (CCL 29. 136).
[28] Ibid. 2. 8. 25 (CCL 29. 121): 'una pars uitae altera eruditionis est'.

arts, a trademark of ancient Roman education which mirrored much of its conservative character. Long ago the pragmatism of Cicero, for example, had given a distinctively Roman flavour to the already inherently ethical orientation of ancient Greek philosophy. In the treatise *On Order* Pythagoras and to a lesser extent Varro offer rules for living the best possible life. Augustine reflects this heritage by saying that glimpses of beauty in one's search for God are available to the individual who 'lives well, prays well, studies well'.[29]

These rules, *praecepta*, pertaining to moral and intellectual activity are part and parcel of any worthwhile programme of study: *ordo eruditionis*.[30] In 'embryonic form',[31] some twenty-four of these precepts in the treatise *On Order*, 2. 8. 25–2. 19. 51, anticipate the precepts for common life later prescribed by Augustine in his monastic *Rule*.

Pedagogically, therefore, the composition of both the dialogue *On Order* and Augustine's *Rule* are strikingly similar. Pythagorean and monastic precepts are directed towards the same goal: contemplation. In a learned article Père Luc Verheijen correctly concludes: 'The Rule of Saint Augustine, when put into practice, possesses a range of experience very much more contemplative than one would generally acknowledge at first sight.'[32]

Reason and authority (faith) furnish lenses for filtering the data of human experience. Augustine had already declared at the conclusion of *Answer to Sceptics*: 'As for myself, I am firmly resolved never to deviate in the least from the authority of Christ, for I find none stronger.'[33] Once again the former teacher of rhetoric is becoming a disciple; *disciplina* (a word freighted with meaning, sometimes with sorry consequences[34]), will gradually overtake *eruditio*. Augustine, for example, will never rival the erudition of his contemporary Jerome. He will lament to Jerome his lack of time for study.[35] Meanwhile, mimetic aspects of ancient educational theory eventually merge with the compelling exhortation to 'put on the Lord Jesus Christ' (Rom. 13: 14) and the gospel invitation to 'come, follow me' (Matt. 19: 21). Little by little the

[29] Ibid. 2. 19. 51 (CCL 29. 135).
[30] See n. 28 above.
[31] L. Verheijen, *Nouvelle Approche de la Règle de saint Augustin* (Abbaye de Bellefontaine, 1980), 239.
[32] Ibid. 241.
[33] See n. 3 above.
[34] Brown, *Augustine*, 233–43.
[35] *Ep*. 73. 2. 5 (CSEL 34. 269).

nexus between doctrine and life tightens, for Christianity is, after all, a life that is lived—in a word, discipleship.

That a monastic impulse lay dormant in Augustine's soul during these tranquil days at Cassiciacum is by no means an extravagant claim. One must wait some twenty years for the bishop's formal description of a monk.[36] Meanwhile, this monastic impulse in the young Augustine manifested itself in his indefatigable desire for God and the intensely personal character of his experiences to such a pitch that his proselytizing temperament attracted others to share their lives with him. A social dimension regularly pervaded Augustine's activities.

Ten years before writing the *Confessions* its author had already opened the window of his soul, as we just noted, by coining the word *Soliloquies*, the singularly apt title of his final composition at Cassiciacum. Such a self-portrait shortly before his baptism in April 387 discloses the outlook of a monk of whatever epoch, whatever religious tradition. The whole of ch. 1 for example, is a prayer with its lapidary Latin leaping into the ear of the listener:

Iam *te solum* amo,
te solum sequor,
te solum quaero,
tibi soli seruire paratus sum,
quia *tu solus* iuste dominaris;
tui iuris esse cupio.[37]

Such hunger for God and single-mindedness of purpose as expressed in this penultimate section of so fervent a prayer fits the description of any monk, anywhere. And the prayer ends with some of Augustine's innermost convictions:

[36] Brown (*Augustine*, 135) says of Thagaste between the years 388–91: 'At this time, Augustine was a contemplative.' I consider Augustine to be a contemplative in both a philosophic and religious sense, that is, a Christian sense, at Cassiciacum. This is surely borne out by a critical reading of *A Life of Happiness, On Order*, and the *Soliloquies*. Nor am I willing to exclude *Answer to Sceptics* in this regard; the evidence is simply more pronounced and abundant in the aforementioned writings. For Augustine's descriptive definition of a monk, see my English translation of *En. Ps. 132*, § 6 (CCL 40. 1931) in Ch. IX, p. 158.
[37] *Sol.* 1. 1. 5 (PL 32. 872):

Now I love Thee alone,
Thee alone do I follow,
Thee alone do I seek,
Thee alone am I ready to serve,
for Thou alone hast just dominion;
under Thy sway I long to be.

> This only do I ask of Thy extreme kindness,
> that *Thou convert me wholly to Thee*,
> and Thou allow nothing to prevent *me*
> *from wending my way to Thee*.[38]

Surely the Latin original *ut me penitus ad te conuertas* and *mihi . . . tendenti ad te* is propaedeutic to an understanding of Augustine's later annexation of *ad deum* to the Lucan phrase of Acts 4: 32: *anima una et cor unum*. It likewise anticipates the memorable phrase *fecisti nos ad te* in the opening paragraph of the *Confessions*.

In Augustine's desire to know God and the soul,[39] interiority regularly possessed an intensely personal character. Nor was its social dimension ever to be neglected. A legitimate parallel may be drawn, furthermore, between the experiences of both Augustine and Plotinus on the basis of the final words attributed to the latter in Porphyry's arrangement of the *Enneads*: 'the flight of the alone to the Alone'.[40] While the Greek phrase μόνος πρὸς μόνον in itself was commonplace in the Platonic tradition (Plato had long ago employed the expression μόνος μόνῳ with erotic overtones in the *Symposium*, 217 в), the idea of flight was novel.[41] Linked as it was with Plotinus' doctrine of oneness, Plotinus clearly did not mean *fuga mundi* in the 'monastic' sense as found in Arsenius' apothegms 1 and 2 and other sayings of the Desert Fathers. On this point Augustine is closer to Plotinus than to Antony and the monks of the Egyptian desert.[42] Augustine is likewise influenced deeply by Neoplatonist notions of oneness, for example, the *Soliloquies*, 1. 2. 7; 1. 13. 22, select texts from Book II of the treatise *On Order*, and *True Religion*, 59 ff. The citations could be multiplied indefinitely.

Recent studies have rid us of traditional misconceptions which consistently regarded the philosopher in the ancient world as an individual who stood aloof from society in order to transcend it.[43]

---

[38] Ibid. 1. 1. 6.   [39] Ibid. 1. 2. 7, 1. 15. 27 (PL 32. 872, 883).

[40] *Enneads* 6. 9. 11; P. Henry and H.-R. Schwyzer, *Plotini Opera*, 3 (Oxford, 1982), 290.

[41] E. R. Dodds, 'Numenius and Ammonius', *Entretiens Hardt*, 5 (Geneva, 1960), 17.

[42] R. J. Halliburton, 'The Concept of the "*Fuga Saeculi*" in St Augustine', *The Downside Review*, 85 (1967), 249–61.

[43] P. Brown, 'The Philosopher and Society in Late Antiquity', *The Center for Hermeneutical Studies in Hellenistic and Modern Culture*, Colloquy 34 (Berkeley, 1980), 1–41.

In fact, Porphyry's *Life of Plotinus*, 9 tells us: 'Though he spent twenty-six whole years in Rome and acted as arbitrator in very many people's disputes, he never made an enemy of any of the officials.' Augustine's later life as a bishop will be strikingly similar in this and other spheres of activity. A detailed comparative study of Porphyry's *Vita Plotini* with Possidius' *Vita Augustini* would yield surprising information, albeit with many nuances. Still there was, to be sure, a certain congruity of vocation between the philosopher and the Christian ascetic. Plotinus' practice was actually rather social, even if he did not develop any theory of sociability or friendship. In the years to come, moreover, the role of the Christian bishop will be superimposed upon Augustine's ascetic/monastic ideal, without ever effecting their total eclipse.[44] While there are emphatic differences between the two men, Augustine's approach to monasticism can be viewed in some respects as filling out Plotinus' doctrine of 'the flight of the alone to the Alone', rather than contradicting it.[45]

Augustine's *Soliloquies* reveal the temperament of a person who does not begrudge but rather delights in communicating his experiences to others.[46] Whether one invites comparison with the Plotinian return/ascent of the soul to God and its way of inwardness, or with the Plotinian attraction towards the one over against dissipation towards the many, as Augustine frequently does in his writings, we have already observed the extent to which the doctrine of a personal God as revealed in the Incarnation totally altered his thinking. A monastic impulse or inclination was, therefore, already latent in his personality and one could explore at length and develop the thesis *anima Augustiniana naturaliter monastica*.

A rich Graeco-Roman heritage, then, is reflected in the group gathered at Cassiciacum during this idyllic interlude between Augustine's conversion in the garden at Milan and his baptism by Ambrose at the Easter Vigil in 387. Work (both physical and intellectual), contemplation (both philosophical and Christian), prayer and serious dialogue on a variety of themes—these were

---

[44] H. Chadwick, 'The Role of the Christian Bishop in Ancient Society', *The Center for Hermeneutical Studies in Hellenistic and Modern Culture*, Colloquy 35 (Berkeley, 1980), 1–47.

[45] A. Meredith, 'Asceticism—Christian and Greek', *JTS* NS 27 (1976), 313–32.

[46] *Sol.* 1. 13. 22 (PL 32. 881).

the happy notes which sounded in this lovely place of retreat. Cassiciacum was Augustine's Manresa with an important difference, however: it offered a communal experience as well as a deeply personal one.

IV

Second Sojourn at Rome

AUGUSTINE came to Rome for the first time in 383. Personal ambition and disenchantment with unmanageable students at Carthage had prompted him to leave Africa. In less than a year, the failure of Roman students to pay their tuition-fees and the lure of a professorship occasioned his move to Milan. After formal repudiation of Manichaeism about the time he left Rome, there ensued successively a period of scepticism followed by Neoplatonic enthusiasm, the beneficent influence of Ambrose's preaching, enlightenment by the Scriptures, and, finally, Augustine's conversion and baptism. Some time afterwards, Evodius, a former government official, joined Augustine's party in or near Milan, where they had remained for a while. About ten years later the bishop will cherish fond memories of pleasant liturgical experiences in the environs of this northern Italian city.[1] At Milan and Cassiciacum there had been no hint of the future.

Now the group was pressing on to Ostia on the Tiber. There is no evidence that they stayed in Rome. Apparently they intended to reach north Africa directly, then home. While resting from their journey and waiting for a ship to sail, Augustine and Monica were graced with the famous so-called 'vision of Ostia' which has become 'a battlefield for rival exegetes'.[2] There is no end to illuminating scholarship on the subject, the most recent of which serves our immediate purpose, since it suggests (somewhat surprisingly, perhaps because of its context), that '. . . there is here a new note in monasticism'.[3] After nine days' illness, Monica died at the age of fifty-six years. Book 9 of the *Confessions* is Monica's story, and no author would dare attempt to match its telling.

Unsettled political fortunes caused further delay of about one year before Augustine and his party could return to Africa. Maximus had invaded Italy and routed the young emperor

---

[1] *Conf.* 9. 7. 15–16 (CCL 27. 141–2).
[2] Bonner, *Life and Controversies*, 96.
[3] A. Louth, *The Origins of the Christian Mystical Tradition* (Oxford, 1981), 136.

Valentinian in 387. Like so many previous emperors, Britain's former military governor had come to power with the help of soldiers, and he now effectively blockaded the Mediterranean. In view of this crisis, Augustine and his friends returned to Rome. As in Augustine's case during his early days at Carthage, unsuspecting Christians were being attracted to bogus Manichaean rationalism and its vaunted asceticism. In Rome, therefore, Augustine began writing the first of many anti-Manichaean treatises, *The Ways of the Catholic Church and the Manichaeans*. Two other treatises, *Magnitude of the Soul* and *Freedom of the Will*, soon follow, both of which are dialogues with Evodius. This latter work will remain unfinished until shortly before its author's episcopal ordination.

Immortality of the Soul had been Augustine's last book before baptism, and it is unique for being the only one of his voluminous writings without a single citation from the Bible. Its composition was so convoluted as to be 'unintelligible' to its author at the end of his life.[4] He now has another go at the subject, shifting gears meantime from immortality to the make-up of the soul and its functions: *Magnitude of the Soul*.

The soul's activities are depicted in Plotinian terms as a seven-stage process: animation, sensation, art, virtue, tranquillity, ingress, and contemplation.[5] On Augustine's own admission, this sevenfold schema is arbitrary and breaks down further into a tripartite ascent: body—soul—God, stressing sequentially the significance of the soul to the body, to itself, and to God. Seven similar levels of ascent resemble a ladder of beauty and lend still another perspective on the soul's movement towards God. The importance of this model is equally germane to Augustine's aesthetic and ascetical theory.[6] In the concluding chapter of his monastic *Rule* Augustine will, in fact, urge the servants of God who live in the monastery 'to observe these precepts with love as lovers of spiritual beauty'.[7] Here at Rome, he describes eastern monks as 'completely happy in their contemplation of (God's) beauty'.[8] This anti-Manichaean treatise thus adumbrates a salient feature of the *Rule* written at Hippo some ten years later.

---

[4] *Retr.* I. 5. I (CCL 57. 16).
[5] *Quant.* 33. 70–34. 77 (PL 32. 1073–7).
[6] R. O'Connell, *Art and the Christian Intelligence in St Augustine* (Cambridge, Mass., 1978), 10–27.
[7] *Rule* 8. 1.   [8] *Mor.* I. 31. 66 (PL 32. 1338).

Curiously enough, Augustine depicts eremitic and coenobitic life without using the words 'hermit', 'coenobite', 'monk', or 'monastery'. Persons pursuing 'so exalted a peak of sanctity'[9] are called 'holy men', 'brothers', 'people who serve God', words which in their context clearly designate a structured ascetic life. The structure itself is referred to as a regimen or an established way of life: *ordo*, *institutum*, *mores*.[10] Augustine further specifies a dwelling, *diuersorium*, in Milan.[11] He will later recall Pontician's account of a 'house community', *casa*, at Trier.[12] Neither of these dwellings possessed the grandeur of Marcella's home on the Aventine,[13] but each points the way to steps Augustine himself will take soon after the return to his native Thagaste in less than a year.

Augustine is impressed with the organizational skills of Pachomius.[14] Shared possessions, chastity, and holiness are the hallmarks of common life. Here for the first time we meet, in the common ownership of goods, an indirect reference to Acts 4: 32, a text that will play so conspicuous a role in determining the shape of Augustine's monasticism.[15] Health is also an important criterion in matters of diet, fasting, clothing, or any genuine necessity.[16] There is no hoarding of surplus materials.[17] Other aspects of coenobitic life, such as prayer, reading of the Scriptures, and serious dialogue,[18] will resurface in Augustine's family home one year later at Thagaste. With the exception of manual labour and silence during working hours, all these elements of monasticism will appear in Augustine's *Rule*. Finally, common life in both *The Ways of the Catholic Church and the Manichaeans* and Augustine's *Rule* is oriented towards God:[19] its chief components are a mind and heart committed to this holy purpose.[20]

[9] Ibid.   [10] Ibid. 1. 31. 68 (PL 32. 1339).
[11] Ibid. 1. 33. 70 (PL 32. 1339); see n. 30 below.
[12] Conf. 8. 6. 15 (CCL 27. 122).
[13] For splendid memoirs of Marcella and Paula respectively see Jerome, *Epp.* 127, 108 (CSEL 56. 145–56, 55. 306–51).
[14] J. K. Coyle, *Augustine's 'De Moribus Ecclesiae Catholicae'* (Fribourg, 1978), 215, 230.
[15] *Mor.* 1. 31. 67 (PL 32. 1338): 'Nemo quidquam possidet proprium . . .'.
[16] Ibid. 1. 33. 71–3 (PL 32. 1340–1).   [17] Ibid. 1. 31. 67 (PL 32. 1339).
[18] Ibid. (PL 32. 1338): 'simul aetatem agunt, uiuentes in orationibus, in lectionibus, in disputationibus'.
[19] Ibid.: 'concordissima uita et intentissima in deum'.
[20] *Praeceptum* 5: 'sit uobis anima una et cor unum in deum'; 58: 'unianimiter et concorditer uiuite'.

In a telling passage, Augustine expresses his admiration for the virtuous lives of bishops, priests, and deacons. Their tranquillity of mind, however, is constantly threatened by pastoral obligations. Ministers of religion actually forfeit 'peace of soul' in order to live alongside the people they serve, whereas solitaries and coenobites, both women and men, are already living that life of contemplation which ministers aspire to. Although Augustine here exalts the active life of the minister as the best, *optimus uitae modus*,[21] he personally preferred, consistently through all the years, a life of contemplation.

Twice Augustine takes for granted as common knowledge that many Christian men and women practise perfect continence 'particularly in the East and in Egypt'.[22] This observation is obviously intended as a criticism of counterfeit Manichaean chastity. Shiploads of surplus supplies sent by monks to alleviate poverty and hunger are likewise portrayed as 'a well-known fact'.[23] Even allowing for possible exaggeration (owing to the polemical character of this treatise as well as its author's proselytizing temperament directed against his former co-religionists), other sources inform us that the West was becoming more familiar with eastern monasticism by this time. For example, when exiled from his episcopal see for the second time in 339, Athanasius had spent seven years at Rome. He had also travelled to Milan and Aquileia. Peter of Alexandria, his blood-brother and successor, stayed at Rome, after Athanasius' death, from 373 to 378. Marcella, Jerome's aristocratic patron and friend, had studied the *Life of Antony* and knew Peter of Alexandria personally.[24] Evagrius of Antioch had translated the *Life of Antony* into Latin *c*.370 and another, anonymous, translation had appeared before that date.[25] Pontician's account of Antony's conversion was hardly an isolated instance of edification, for he registered surprise at Alypius' and Augustine's unfamiliarity with the ascetic movement. Jerome

---

[21] *Mor.* 1. 32. 69 (PL 32. 1339). See Coyle, *Augustine's 'De Moribus Ecclesiae'*, 410–11 for a comparison of this passage with Augustine's viewpoints in *Epp.* 10. 2, 21. 1.

[22] Ibid. 1. 31. 65 (PL 32. 1337).

[23] Ibid. 1. 31. 67 (PL 32. 1339).

[24] J. N. D. Kelly, *Jerome: His Life, Writings, and Controversies* (London, 1975), 92.

[25] L. W. Barnard, 'The Date of S. Athanasius' *Vita Antonii*', *VC* 28 (1974), 169–75 and the response of B. R. Brennan, 'Dating Athanasius' *Vita Antonii*', *VC* 30 (1976), 52–4.

came to Rome in 382, and his influence upon monasticism persisted long after he left the Italian peninsula in 385.[26]

These were the years when many talented and dedicated women such as Paula, Eustochium, Melania the Elder, and her grand-daughter of the same name embraced a type of household asceticism which derived largely from eastern models.[27] Nor should western approaches to monasticism be discounted: for example, the efforts of Eusebius of Vercelli and Ambrose of Milan to semi-monasticize their clerics.[28] But no one in the West could at that time match the organizational skills of Pachomius or Basil of Caesarea. Benedict will be born some fifty years after Augustine's death, and Gaul will inherit the more immediate legacy of Cassian and Martin of Tours.

While Augustine had learned of Antony only shortly before his conversion, he dispelled his ignorance of monasticism soon after his baptism in Milan.[29] Within the year he mentions 'several houses in Rome'[30] where the monastic ideal included manual labour, which he refers to as 'an eastern custom'.[31] To claim that Augustine had read Jerome's famous *Letter* 22 to Eustochium strains the existing evidence.[32] Augustine's slender knowledge of Greek further prevented him from reading either Basil the Great or a Greek version of Pachomius, whose original text was written in Coptic.[33] Besides, Jerome translated Pachomius' *Rule* in 404 and the years 397–400 are usually assigned to the Latin adaptation of Basil's *Rules* by Rufinus of Aquileia.[34] It is beyond our purpose

[26] Kelly, *Jerome*, 335: 'Nor should we underrate his (Jerome's) contribution to the establishment of monasticism as a major expression of Christian life and culture in Europe.'

[27] Ibid. 91–103.

[28] For an excellent survey of early western monasticism see R. Lorenz, 'Die Anfänge des abendländischen Mönchtums im 4. Jahrhundert', *Zeitschrift für Kirchengeschichte*, 77 (1966), 1–61.

[29] *Conf.* 8. 6. 14–15 (CCL 27. 121–3).

[30] *Mor.* 1. 33. 70 (PL 32. 1339–40): 'Vidi ego diuersorium sanctorum Mediolani, non paucorum hominum . . . Romae etiam plura (diuersoria) cognoui . . .'.

[31] Ibid. (PL 32. 1340) 'Orientis more'.

[32] See L. Verheijen, *Saint Augustine's Monasticism in the Light of Acts 4, 32–35* (Villanova, 1979), 40–2 for a comparison of *Mor.* 1. 31. 67 with Jerome's *Ep.* 22. 35. Coyle is over-confident (*Augustine's 'De Moribus Ecclesiae'*, 214) when he writes: 'In any case, there can be no doubt that Augustine had read Jerome's *Epistula* 22.'

[33] P. Rousseau, *Ascetics, Authority, and the Church in the Age of Jerome and Cassian* (Oxford, 1978), 15–16.

[34] Kelly, *Jerome*, 228, 280–1.

here to tease out the Pachomian and Basilian elements in this early
account of monasticism by Augustine, except to remark that the
monastic impulse was felt in Rome at this time every bit as much as
it had been earlier in Milan. Conversations on the subject were
legion. So far as we know, Augustine writes on the basis of 'oral
reports'[35] and first-hand observation. His informative account of
monasticism in this early treatise derived from talks with Alypius,
Evodius, and others, as well as from direct contact with monasteries.
Then as now, Rome was the scene of much mobility. Travel was a
paramount feature of the general unrest which marked these
waning years of the Western Empire. Before he crossed the
Mediterranean never again to return to Italy, Augustine had
acquired a fairly sound grasp of both eremitic and coenobitic life.

If the monastic ideal as exemplified by Antony was the central
theme of Augustine's conversion, then the period of some ten
months to a year in Rome after Monica's death appreciably
enriched the recent convert's knowledge of this phenomenon.
Before Alypius, Evodius, and Augustine left Milan for Ostia they
'had come to form a tight, almost monastic group'.[36] Possidius, as
we shall note below, portrays Augustine as a lay monk after
he reached Africa.[37] Here is Augustine's recollection of these
events:

Qui habitare facis unanimes in domo, consociasti nobis et Euodium
iuuenem ex nostro municipio. Qui cum agens in rebus militaret, prior
nobis ad te conuersus est et baptizatus et relicta militia saeculari accinctus
in tua. Simul eramus simul habitaturi placito sancto. Quaerebamus
quisnam locus nos utilius haberet seruientes tibi: pariter remeabamus in
Africam. Et cum apud Ostia Tiberina essemus, mater defuncta est.

You 'who make men of one mind *to dwell* in a house' (Ps. 67: 7), *joined
with us* Evodius, a young man of our town who had served as a special
agent. He had been *converted* to You before we were, and he had been
baptized. Having *given up* his secular service, he *girded* himself for Yours.
We kept together with the intention of *dwelling together* in our *holy
resolution. We made our investigations* as to what *place* would be *best
suited for Your service,* and *together we were returning* to Africa. When we
were at Ostia my mother died.   (9. 8. 17.)

The seventh verse of Ps. 67 cited in the above passage figures
prominently in both Augustine's *Rule* (1. 2) and his *Reprimand to*

---

[35] Verheijen, *Augustine's Monasticism*, 43.
[36] Brown, *Augustine*, 126.   [37] See Ch. V nn. 18, 86.

Quarrelling Nuns (§ 2). These two loci, in fact, represent the only instances in the entire Augustinian corpus where Ps. 67: 7 is associated with Acts 4: 32a.[38] In our present context the two occurrences, *habitare* and *habitaturi* indicate a shared life under the same roof: *facis unanimes in domo.* It is God who has linked Evodius with the others, *consociasti nobis.* Augustine distinguishes between conversion, *conuersus est,* and baptism, *baptizatus.* Evodius is now girded for the Lord's service, *accinctus in tua*; his secular employment is done with, *relicta militia.* It is, therefore, a matter of Evodius' vocation. The anaphora, *simul . . . simul* emphasizes their unanimity and simultaneity of intention. Two plural instances of the imperfect tense, *eramus* and *quaerebamus* further accentuate this corporate and continuing character of the search. Their holy resolution, *placitum sanctum* and goal, namely, the place best suited for Your service, *seruientes tibi,* go beyond the expectations required of baptism. *Pariter,* a synonym for *simul,* combines with still another imperfect tense, *remeabamus,* expressing their reason for the journey home.

To suggest that the author of the *Confessions* imposed a much later cast of mind upon these events which happened at least ten years previously is not, in this particular case, convincing. The *Gestalt* of Augustine's mind, and his odyssey of soul both before and after Monica's death, seriously impugn the point of view that the coenobitic framework found in *The Ways of the Catholic Church and the Manichaeans* was 'in itself admirable only as a living organization of charity'.[39] Rather, it seems more likely and in agreement with much of the available information that Augustine actually entered into a form of monastic life with his companions at Thagaste. This lifestyle for which he eventually composed the *Rule* constituted a new chapter in the history of early western monasticism.

---

[38] Verheijen, *Augustine's Monasticism*, 66–9.
[39] Halliburton, 'Inclination' 339 citing J. Burnaby with approval.

V

North Africa

1. The Monastery at Thagaste

WHETHER or not Thagaste was the site of Augustine's first monastery is a much-disputed question. With his customary thoroughness and precision, André Mandouze has admirably reviewed the stance which many scholars have taken on this matter.[1] We shall content ourselves with a cursory presentation of three sharply contrasting points of view. Notwithstanding this range of contradictory opinion, I shall set forth reasons which compel me to characterize the life at Thagaste between the years 388–91 as providing a genuinely monastic experience.

First of all, there is the position which states: 'That St. Augustine was any more involved in the monastic life of the church of which he had become a member when finally settled at Thagaste would be hard to prove.'[2] This comment enunciated by R. J. Halliburton is fairly representative of a viewpoint that has recurred during the past twenty years. A recent echo of this opinion concludes on philological grounds, from the meaning of the term *seruus dei*, that we are 'not justified . . . to speak [*sic*] of a monastery at Thagaste'.[3] According to this first interpretation, the Thagaste community was religious chiefly in the sense that it espoused the ideals of philosophic contemplation then prevalent in the world of late antiquity. The people there may aptly be described as ascetics.

A second opinion, wholly at variance with the first, grants Thagaste legitimate recognition as a monastery. Perhaps its boldest formulation was expressed thus: 'Augustine founded in 388 his first small monastery in the house of his parents in Thagaste.'[4] A similar stance has been taken more recently:

[1] A. Mandouze, *Saint Augustin: L'aventure de la raison et de la grâce* (Paris, 1968), 200–9. [2] Halliburton, 'Inclination', 339.
[3] L. J. van der Lof, 'The Threefold Meaning of *Serui Dei* in the Writings of Saint Augustine', *AS* 12 (1981), 55.
[4] F. van der Meer, *Augustine the Bishop* (New York, 1961), 208.

'. . . Augustine returned to Africa in 388. He was determined not to accept Orders, but the monastery which he established with his friends at Thagaste proved to be too valuable to an ailing African Catholicism.'[5]

Still others adopt a middle position, conceding to Thagaste a somewhat limited claim as a monastery. A representative viewpoint from this third line of reasoning reads as follows:

Thus, the inspiration behind Thagaste must be sought in three sources: in indigenous African asceticism, in Egyptian monasticism, and in the Roman philosophical ideal of a life of leisure dedicated to cultural and philosophical pursuits.[6]

In other words, Thagaste is a 'halfway house' between Cassiciacum during the autumn and winter months of 388–7 and Hippo in the year 391. Yet the same author advises against 'too restrictive' a use of the term *monasterium*.[7] This tripartite division of opinion will engage our inspection, at the end of which I shall come down on the side of those who suggest that Augustine's foundation at Thagaste was, indeed, his first monastery.

Those who deny even a quasi-monastic status to the similarly minded group which settled at Thagaste suggest that 'from the company kept and the interests pursued, it would appear that it is in its essentials a continuation of the retreat of Cassiciacum.'[8] But Peter Brown correctly insists:

Thagaste could never be another Cassiciacum. Even during his stay in Rome, Augustine's writings show a new determination. From that time onwards, he intended to live a secluded life no longer, as in Milan, on the fringe of a society of intellectual laymen, but directly in the shadow of the organized life of the Catholic Church.[9]

Brown goes on to say:

Augustine was, yet again, changing his mode of life . . . The centre of gravity in Augustine's thought had begun to shift . . . The two years which Augustine had spent at Thagaste are marked by even more significant, though more mysterious, changes.[10]

[5] W. H. C. Frend, *The Early Church* (London, 1982), 202, and more recently: 'the monastic-type settlement' (666) and 'the monastery at Thagaste' (667) in id., *The Rise of Christianity* (London, 1984).

[6] C. Stancliffe, *St Martin and his Hagiographer: History and Miracle in Sulpicius Severus* (Oxford, 1983), 29.

[7] Ibid. 28–9.   [8] See n. 2 above.
[9] Brown, *Augustine*, 132.   [10] Ibid. 134–5.

Apart from a miscalculation with regard to the length of Augustine's stay in his parents' house, Brown's assessment is accurate.[11] An exchange of twelve letters with Nebridius, seven letters to as many other individuals, and three books written during this interlude reveal both a doctrinal and ecclesial flavour. On the basis of these writings, Brown justifiably disallows a detached attitude towards coenobitic life at Thagaste:

In the year before he was made a priest in Hippo, Augustine may already have tried to fill out his life—to organize his community, to found personal relations within it upon a permanent code of behaviour, to be responsible for the spiritual well-being of many other people, and to exercise some real measure of authority over them. As a result, the group of like-minded enthusiasts that had gathered round him in his retirement, came, by slow and subtle stages, to resemble a 'monastery', with Augustine as 'spiritual father'.[12]

With less diffidence Brown continues: 'Such a life (monastic) had already begun to influence Augustine in his first year in Thagaste.'[13]

There is evidence, as we shall see, to support this latter statement. Actual foundation of a 'monastery' in a technical sense is another matter. For the moment, I wish simply to propose that the Thagaste community need not have been designated as a 'monastery' by Augustine or anyone else in order to qualify as one. Moreover, the tentative language employed by the above scholars in their estimate of Thagaste: 'would be hard to prove', 'it would appear', 'may have already been tried', serves notice of the difficulties which beset the researcher of this disputed question.

Augustine returned to Africa in August or September 388.[14] He stayed only briefly in Carthage at the house of Innocentius; obvious haste did not permit a delay long enough to visit his dear friend Nebridius. Alypius and he were at that time 'servants of God' pressing on hurriedly to their boyhood home. In a reference to the miraculous healing of Innocentius, Augustine carefully distinguished between their status as 'servants of God' and the fact that neither Alypius nor he was a 'cleric' at the time.[15] There

[11] *Vita* 2: 'ferme triennio'. See Weiskotten, *Augustini uita*, 44, 148 on the use of 'ferme'.

[12] Brown, *Augustine*, 135–6.

[13] Ibid. 136.

[14] O. Perler, *Les Voyages de saint Augustin* (Paris, 1969), 147–8, 432.

[15] *Ciu. Dei* 22. 8 (CCL 48. 816): 'Venientes enim de transmarinis me et fratrem meum Alypium, nondum quidem clericos, sed iam Deo seruientes . . .'.

obviously existed in the bishop's mind some thirty-five years later an identity worth remembering. Monasticism was, of course, a lay movement in the early Church with a slower start in north Africa than in Italy. Distinction between ascetic and monk at that time was not so clearly differentiated as to be readily recognizable. For example, in a letter written at Thagaste, Augustine could recommend to the wife of Antoninus the *lectio diuina*, that is, reading of the Scriptures.[16] So commendable a practice was by no means the exclusive preserve of the monk. It was a Christian practice, and before that a Jewish one.

Augustine 'alienated' (possibly a legal term)[17] his family property and possessions as soon as he arrived at Thagaste. Now aged 34, he had returned to his birthplace with the fixed purpose of serving God in the company of others. Possidius' choice of words, *placuit ei*,[18] echoes Augustine's own *placitum sanctum*.[19]

Life at Thagaste was characterized by surrender of property and possessions (certainly in Augustine's case), fasting, fraternity, dialogue, prayer, spiritual reading (principally the Scriptures), and work of an intellectual bent. *Reply to the Manichaeans on Genesis* constituted Augustine's first published attempt at biblical exegesis. *The Teacher*, a dialogue with Adeodatus, explored theories of language and knowledge. *True Religion*, while exhibiting a 'very different language and style',[20] was a mature composition which has long been recognized as a significant turning-point in Augustine's life.[21] It could only have emerged from the ambience of a monastery, not the Academy.[22] With its fusion of learning and piety in the service of the church, Thagaste surpassed Cassiciacum.

Another feature of Thagaste was the instructive value of 'conversations'.[23] Some of these were no doubt represented by the range of topics in the *Eighty-three Different Questions* collected and published by Augustine shortly after his episcopal ordination.

[16] *Ep.* 20. 3 (CSEL 34. 48–9).

[17] *Vita* 3: 'in quibus (agris) . . . et a se iam alienatis.' See also Perler, *Voyages*, 149, n. 2.

[18] *Vita* 3.   [19] *Conf.* 9. 8. 17 (CCL 27. 143).

[20] L. R. Palmer, *The Latin Language* (London, 1954), 202.

[21] M. Wundt, 'Ein Wendepunkt in Augustins Entwicklung', *Zeitschrift für die neutestamentliche Wissenschaft*, 21 (1922), 53–64. The author's conclusion, however, that *True Religion* is more Neoplatonic than Christian does not hold.

[22] L. Cilleruelo, 'Evolución del monacato agustiniano', *Estudio agustiniano*, 15 (1980), 194.

[23] *Vita* 3: '. . . et praesentes et absentes sermonibus ac libris docebat.'

He tells us: 'these questions were dictated, without any order having been preserved by me, in response to the brothers who were asking me things when they saw me unoccupied'.[24] Questions 1–50 very likely coincided with the years 388–91; these chiefly reflected philosophical issues pertaining to God and the soul, some current Manichaean concerns, and several points of interest on the Trinity and the Incarnation.[25] The philosophical, theological, and biblical focus of these questions was largely determined by the educational background and intellectual interests of the inquirers.

An objection to calling Thagaste a monastic community in the strict sense emerges from the fact that the extant literature nowhere designates Augustine's family home as a monastery.[26] One year previously in Rome, Augustine had used the phrase *diuersorium sanctorum* to describe the dwelling of monks in Milan. Augustine had actually seen the place.[27] The terms *coenobium* and *monasterium* are both wanting in this lengthy and informative sequence, which portrays Pachomian monks, yet no one would deny these men their monastic identity. In fact, owing to its late start in Latin translations from the Greek, the word *monasterium* only gradually gained currency in the West.[28] *Letter* 48, too, written *c.*398 and addressed to Abbot Eudoxius and his monks on the island of Capraria, makes no mention of *monasterium*, yet its contents are as applicable to what we know about life at Thagaste as they are to its addressees.[29] Augustine's later *Commentary on Ps. 99*, § 12 employs *monasterium* in a sense which is wholly congruent with everything we know about Thagaste, and this fact suggests an indirect inference that the community there may

[24] *Retr.* 1. 26. 1 (CCL 57. 74), tr. D. Mosher.
[25] D. L. Mosher, *Saint Augustine: Eighty-three Different Questions*, FC 70 (Washington, 1982), 2–16.
[26] See n. 2 above; also van der Lof, 'Threefold Meaning', 54.
[27] *Mor.* 1. 33. 70 (PL 32. 1339). See also ch. 4, n. 30. For 'diuersorium' see Cassian, *Conlationes* 18. 5 (CSEL 13. 511): 'unde consequens fuit ut ex communione consortii coenobiotae cellaeque ac diuersoria eorum [sc. monachorum] coenobia uocarentur'; 18. 10 (CSEL 13. 517): '. . . monasterium nomen est diuersorii, nihil amplius quam locum, id est habitaculum significans monachorum . . .'.
[28] L. Th. Lorié, *Spiritual Terminology in the Latin Translations of the* Vita Antonii *with Reference to Fourth and Fifth Century Monastic Literature* (Nijmegen, 1955), 43–51.
[29] CSEL 34. 137–40. See L. Verheijen, *Saint Augustine: Monk, Priest, Bishop* (Villanova, 1978), 25: '. . . the life of Augustine and his friends at Thagaste already resembled that of the monks of Capraria, as described in *Letter* 48'.

suitably be depicted as monastic.[30] Furthermore, Augustine
entertains a decided preference for the Latin forms *seruus*, *seruus
dei*, *deo seruiens*, *famulus dei*, *sanctus*, *fratres*, *societas fratrum*
over the Latin derivative from the Greek, *monachus*, possibly
because he was chary of loan-words from Greek in his early
writings.[31] The Donatists, moreover, objected to 'monk' since the
word was not found in the Scriptures and this, too, helps explain
Augustine's later hesitation regarding its usage.[32] While all such
words must be contextualized and while further study of Augustine's
usage is desirable, a sufficient sampling is already available to
support the main argument of this chapter.

In addition to the evidence in the texts already cited, Augustine's
four rudiments of monastic life (manual labour, reading, prayer,
and study of the Scriptures)[33] likewise conform with our information about Thagaste, except for work of an intellectual nature, which
appears to have taken the place of manual labour. When we read
Augustine on Augustine, there is to my knowledge no passage
which militates against calling Thagaste a monastery in a bona-fide
sense. This is not to say that Augustine's monasticism awaited no
further development. Contrariwise, everything we read in Augustine's writings on monastic life corroborates our knowledge about
the years 388–91.

At the risk of providing an anti-climax to this chapter, it is fair to
suggest that the word 'monastery' of itself is not so important. In
this connection I invoke Augustine's own criterion, *non uerba sed
res*[34] or *non ciuitas sed ciues*.[35]

In a rare reminiscence of this period, the bishop equates
surrender of his 'father's few plots of land with [his] conversion to
the free service of God'.[36] While it is unscientific to read history
backwards, it seems fair to point out Augustine's consistency in
this matter and his subsequent behaviour as a bishop. For
example, he will urge Alypius not to admit a candidate to the

---

[30] Ibid. See CCL 39. 1401 for the text.

[31] Lorié, *Spiritual Terminology*, 24–43 for *monachus* and *frater*; see his index for
sanctus, *seruus*, and related words.

[32] *En. Ps.* 132. §6 (CCL 40. 1930–1).

[33] *Op. Mon.* 29. 37 (CSEL 41. 587).

[34] *Ord.* 2. 2. 4 (CCL 29. 108), *Cresc* 1. 13. 16 (CSEL 52. 339).

[35] *De excidio urbis Romae sermo* 6. 6 (CCL 46. 258): 'in parietibus et non in
ciuibus . . .'.

[36] *Ep.* 126. 7 (CSEL 44. 12–13). See also *Ep.* 157. 4. 39 (CSEL 44. 485).

'society of brothers' until the individual has disposed of his property and possessions.[37] He will insist that all his clergy either sell their possessions and give the money to the poor or make them over to a local church for the same purpose.[38] In his own case, he had distributed what little he had (*tenuis paupertatula mea*) to the poor.[39] Possidius' account, just noted,[40] confirms the bishop's recollection of this matter.

A further objection to calling Thagaste a monastery in the strict sense hinges on the word *otium*. Accordingly, the leisure depicted there is thought to be strongly representative of religious and philosophical currents in the Late Empire,[41] albeit Christian.[42] The sequence from *True Religion* 35. 65 leaves no doubt as to its profoundly contemplative and decidedly Christian character. Augustine argues for stillness; man's quest for unity with God must possess simplicity of heart. 'Be still (*agite otium*),' writes Augustine, 'not the stillness of inactivity (*otium desidiae*), but of thought (*otium cogitationis*).' He approvingly cites Ps. 45: 11: 'Be still and know that I am God.' One freely acknowledges elsewhere in this passage Neoplatonic resonances regarding the philosophical categories of time and space. *Otium*, however, in this context is a far cry from the leisure of the philosophers. Augustine defines it as: 'love for those realities which can only be loved with toil'. Then invoking Matt. 11: 30, he says that the yoke of Christ lightens man's toil. An allusion to John 1: 12 further enables individuals to become masters of this world, if they acknowledge their sonship in God. Meanwhile, the world with its embrace engenders fear, and nothing is more toilsome for people than to be at rest (*ut nihil sit laboriosius quam non laborare*). To claim that this passage, written at Thagaste, fits a definition of monastic leisure which is singularly conducive for contemplation is, indeed, a modest assertion. We possess here the seeds of the future bishop's mature thoughts on contemplation.[43]

---

[37] *Ep.* 83. 3 (CSEL 34. 389).
[38] *Sermm.* 355. 2, 356. 5 (Lambot, *SS* 125–6, 136).
[39] *Serm.* 355. 2 (Lambot, *SS* 125).   [40] See n. 17 above.
[41] G. Folliet, 'Aux origines de l'ascétisme et du cénobitisme africain', *Saint Martin et son temps,* Studia Anselmiana, 46 (1961), 25–44. Also the same author's ' "Deificari in otio" Augustin, *Ep* 10, 2', *RA* 2 (1962), 225–36.
[42] See the perceptive remarks by G. Madec, 'Augustin disciple et adversaire de Porphyre', *REA* 10 (1964), 368–9.
[43] *Thesaurus Linguae Latinae*, 9. 2. 1178. 79–1179. 16.

Here it is worth noting that Augustine actually feeds *otium* as a 'good thing' into western monasticism. For Cassian it is still a 'bad thing', as it is for Benedict. Nor does Cassian appear to make any significant use of Ps. 45: 11 and, incidentally, Basil seems to use this particular verse only to make a quite different point (*Shorter Rules* 218). The nearest analogue to Augustine is Basil's early retreat described mockingly by Gregory Nazianzen (*Letter* 4) as a mousehole (μυωξία, a neologism coined by Gregory), or 'in high-sounding terminology' a think-tank (φροντιστήριον), a monastery (μοναστήριον), a fairly recent word in the year 361 and finally, a school (σχολή). It is Augustine who makes monasticism 'contemplative', at least in the West. Even the Cappadocians did not do this, apart from their early experiment which came to nothing. But in Augustine's case, as we shall presently observe, the 'bishop's house' or the 'monastery of clerics' took a different turn from that of his original foundation at Hippo in 391, which remained a non-clerical community.

For Augustine, monastic life always possessed a social dimension. Who then were the *alii ciues et amici sui* referred to by Possidius with whom Augustine spent his days at Thagaste?[44] Besides Alypius who seems always to have been at his side, Evodius and Severus were destined to become bishops of Uzalis and Milevis, respectively, just as Alypius will become bishop of Thagaste. Honoratus will be ordained a priest in another locale. Adeodatus, Augustine's talented interlocutor in *The Teacher*, died in Thagaste at the age of seventeen. Nor does the presence of Augustine's son weaken the argument that the family home was a monastery. Antoninus, Augustine's ill-fated second choice as bishop of Fussala, will live in the monastery at Hippo from the time when he was a boy.[45] Others remain anonymous, because it is unclear whether they joined the community at Thagaste or later at Hippo.[46]

Incidentally, to emphasize friendship as though it were the *condicio sine qua non* for monastic life distorts the historical

[44] Gavigan, *Vita monastica*, 34 and Zumkeller, *Das Mönchtum des heiligen Augustinus*, 2nd edn. (Würzburg, 1968), 67.

[45] *Ep.* 209. 3 (CSEL 57. 349). One of the recently discovered letters of Augustine, *Ep.* 20*. 2 (CSEL 88. 95), says of Antoninus: 'puer creuit'. The son and daughter of Januarius, both of whom were legal minors, lived in respective monasteries for men and women, *Serm.* 355. 3 (Lambot, *SS* 126–7).

[46] Gavigan, *Vita monastica*, 34.

evidence. Possidius' account of Thagaste precludes possible
exaggeration of friendship, as greatly esteemed as this value was
by Augustine himself.

It could be that Augustine's praise of monasticism (which he
situated immediately following an encomium to Mother Church),
was composed at Thagaste.[47] But there could never be any
question of Augustine's failure to link monasticism with its
ecclesial setting, as he did in these concluding chapters of the first
book, *The Ways of the Catholic Church and the Manichaeans*.[48]
The same holds true for all his writings at Thagaste. His polemic
with the Manichees on the proper exegesis of Genesis, his
epistemology and psychology (which are irretrievably interconnected
in their approach to Christ, the interior teacher), and lastly, the
purport of genuine religion as opposed to a decadent paganism all
offer hints for the future direction of Augustine's monasticism and
his burgeoning ministry in the service of the Church. His *Sitz im
Leben* was fortified from the beginning by prayer and contemplation.
These prominent features of his *Sitz im Denken* were at the root of
all his actions as well as patristic thought generally; spirituality and
teaching were inseparable.

Augustine wrote to Nebridius and insisted that he would not
leave Thagaste. Neither Carthage nor the countryside would
please him at this particular time.[49] Cassiciacum's days had ended.
There is possibly a subtle and oblique hint to the effect that
contemplation could bring Nebridius closer to Augustine than any
sedan-chair supplied by their mutual friend Licinian for the
overland route between Carthage and Thagaste. Augustine then
forthrightly urged contemplation for Nebridius to face life's final
journey towards death.[50] (Nebridius, in fact, died shortly thereafter.)
'When I have some time,' Augustine writes begrudgingly, 'more
importunate matters demand my attention and they necessarily
use up all my leisure.'[51] A complaint to Romanianus about the
scarcity of writing materials, with a request for his patron to return
them, indicates a strain upon Augustine's apostolate of the pen.[52]
A second visit to Caelestinus, who is likewise requested to return
some of Augustine's anti-Manichaean books, is not possible; there

[47] Coyle, *Augustine's 'De Moribus Ecclesiae'*, 70–6.
[48] *Mor.* 1. 30. 62 ff. (PL 32. 1336 ff).
[49] *Ep.* 10. 1 (CSEL 34, 23).   [50] Ibid. 2, 3 (CSEL 34. 23–5).
[51] *Ep.* 13. 1 (CSEL 34. 30), tr. Parsons.   [52] *Ep.* 15. 1 (CSEL 34. 35).

is no time.[53] Augustine laments lack of time to Nebridius.[54] Although Augustine suffers from insomnia[55] and poor health,[56] he does not allege these as reasons for refusing to visit Nebridius. He says rather it would be unthinkable, *nefas*, a strong Latin word, to leave the friends with whom he was living.[57] Gaius will have to wait for a visit later on. Instead of the author himself, an anonymous 'brother' will deliver copies of Augustine's books to this convert from Manichaeism.[58] A colleague carries a letter to Antoninus.[59] The alacrity, therefore, with which Augustine visited Hippo to interview a possible recruit lends additional scope to his widening reputation, to his current interests, and to his proselytizing temperament.[60]

In 391 Augustine left Thagaste for Hippo for an interview with an aspirant to monastic life and in seach of another place to establish a monastery.[61] Nor does his projected establishment of a monastery at Hippo necessarily preclude or prejudice the case against an already existing one at Thagaste. As we noted above, Augustine was so busy at Thagaste that he might have felt the need to move to a place where he would be relatively unknown.

Today's distance between Thagaste and Hippo is some sixty miles on a modern motorway. Augustine would not have gone there, unless his lifestyle had already lent credibility to a monastic calling. He knew well that his reputation was spreading.[62] Many years later he will tell the congregation at Hippo of his prayers to attain salvation in a lowly ministry rather than to risk danger in an exalted one.[63] Studiously he avoided cities with an episcopal vacancy. Hippo had Bishop Valerius, so Augustine's visit was in the clear. His interview with a friend, a government official, was disappointing. Notwithstanding persistent good intentions, the friend's interest in monastic life had dwindled.[64] Meanwhile, Augustine attended a church service. Reluctantly, even somewhat forcibly, he was ordained a priest by Bishop Valerius.

[53] *Ep.* 18. 1 (CSEL 34. 44–5). [54] *Ep.* 14. 1 (CSEL 34. 32).
[55] *Ep.* 13. 1 (CSEL 34. 30). [56] See n. 49 above.
[57] Ibid. [58] *Ep.* 19 (CSEL 34. 46).
[59] *Ep.* 20. 1 (CSEL 34. 47). [60] *Vita* 3: 'confestim'.
[61] *Serm.* 355. 2 (Lambot, *SS*, 125). [62] Ibid.
[63] Ibid. In this sermon delivered at Hippo on 18 Dec. 425 we have an echo of the *Praeceptum* 370–1: '. . . quanto in loco superiore, tanto in periculo maiore uersatur'.
[64] *Vita* 3.

If his efforts to establish a monastery at Hippo were unsuccessful, can one possibly conjecture about Augustine's likely return to his native Thagaste? This appears to be a legitimate inference from his remark about entering the church at Hippo with only the clothes on his back.[65]

To recapitulate: while the case has recently been argued in favour of three levels of meaning for *seruus dei*, (1) Christians generally, (2) a select group of committed Christians or ascetics, and (3) monks,[66] these levels do not always reflect the latitude or ambivalence which are sometimes inherent in a particular text. In other words, the sense of *seruus dei*, *deo seruiens*, *frater*, and *sanctus* is seldom one-dimensional; there is no fixity of meaning in Augustine's early writings. It is sometimes unclear whether these terms possess the extended meaning of Christians who are brothers in the Lord or of men living a shared life.

Both the ambience of Thagaste and its activities thus allow a third-level interpretation of *seruus dei*: monk. Individuals there were involved in a quest for holiness. That this group was living under a single roof more than hints at their common purpose and suggests some sort of organizational structure. Nor is a *Rule* required in this instance any more than one would be required at Hippo during the years preceding Augustine's episcopal ordination. The discussions held at Thagaste, continued at Hippo and later published, presuppose a sense of fraternity. They further reveal an evident respect for Augustine's leadership and his intellectual labours. The subject-matter of these *Eighty-three Different Questions* moves far beyond philosophy. Their range of interest also reflects the upper-middle-class character which marked much early western monasticism. When Augustine refers to the group as 'brothers'[67] near the end of his life, we recall his use of the same word to describe men living in a monastery outside the walls of Milan: 'monasterium Mediolani plenum bonis fratribus extra urbis moenia'.[68] Both instances overreach the delineation of ordinary Christians or committed Christians. At that time, Augustine's understanding of *fratres*, a word which appears seven times in his

---

[65] *Serm.* 355. 2 (Lambot, *SS*, 125).
[66] Van der Lof, 'Threefold Meaning', 43–59 adheres in the main (pp. 54–5) to the position of Halliburton and Folliet.
[67] See n. 24 above.
[68] *Conf.* 8. 6. 15 (CCL 27. 122).

monastic *Rule*,[69] composed as some think *c.*397,[70] hardly excludes the third-level sense of monk. His intent and meaning with reference to the 'brothers' residing at Thagaste, therefore, need not be limited to a generalized expression of Christian fellowship or a group of ascetics.

The fact that none of the extant literature relating to Thagaste utilizes *monasterium* until 395 (we owe this citation to Paulinus of Nola in a letter to Alypius)[71] is no great matter. Augustine's vocabulary reveals his growing appreciation of this evolving phenomenon in the western Church. He tells us he knew nothing about the ascetic movement or monasticism until his kinsman Pontician told Alypius and himself the story of Antony's conversion.[72] The *Confessions*, which were composed anywhere between 397 and 401, shy away from the use of *monachus*.[73]

Debate about the type of *otium* enjoyed at Thagaste is now more solidly rooted in the sources.[74] One may wish to suggest that the sequence from *True Religion* 35. 65 need not accord with the life there. But Augustine's propensity for prayer, friendship, companionship, and his desire for God press one contemporary scholar, as we noted previously, to detect among these elements as

---

[69] *Praeceptum*: 'pauperum fratrum societas' 43; also 38, 180, 182, 232, 296, 309 (1 John 3: 15).

[70] Verheijen, *Augustine's Monasticism*, 45–52.

[71] *Ep*. 3 = Augustine, *Ep*. 24. 2, 6 (CSEL 34. 73–8). Paulinus had recently come from Spain via Rome to Nola in Campania. News of African monasticism had evidently spread quickly. Paulinus mentions 'monasteries' at Thagaste, Hippo Regius, and Carthage. See Lienhard, *Paulinus of Nola*, 60–9.
Within one year after his presbyteral ordination Augustine writes to Aurelius, bishop of Carthage, to thank him 'for allowing Brother Alypius to remain associated with us as an example to the brothers who wish to shun the anxieties of this world', *Ep*. 22. 1 (CSEL 34. 55). Here too (the year is 392) there is no mention of a 'monastery' as such. This, however, is consistent with Augustine's writing-habits at the time.

[72] *Conf*. 8. 6. 15 (CCL 27. 122): 'inde sermo eius (Ponticianus) deuolutus est ad monasteriorum greges et mores suaueolentiae tuae et ubera deserta heremi, quorum nos nihil sciebamus'.

[73] Lorié, *Spiritual Terminology*, 32 says that *monachus* 'is even absent from the *Confessions*'. Actually, it occurs once in reference to Antony of Egypt, *Conf*. 8. 6. 14 (CCL 27. 122).

[74] See n. 43 above. Also C. Mohrmann, 'Le rôle des moines dans la transmission du patrimoine Latin', *Études sur le latin des chrétiens*, 4 (Rome, 1977), 300: 'Pour saint Augustin l'*otium* philosophique de Cassiciacum devient l'*otium* théologique du jardin de Thagaste, puis la vie communautaire de l'évêque avec son clergé à Hippone (391).' Augustine was ordained a priest in 391, not a bishop.

early as the so-called vision at Ostia: '. . . a new note in
monasticism'.[75]

That chastity, of itself, does not make a monk is sufficiently
clear from the evidence of ascetical literature in the late fourth
century. Augustine's 'alienation' of family property and of his
personal possessions brought him closer to the gospel ideal of
Matt. 19: 21, the same text, he reminds us, which had so
profoundly influenced Antony of Egypt.[76]

'Augustine's ideal', Van der Meer maintains, 'was undoubtedly
a strictly monastic one. It was not the life in community, but sexual
continence and the renunciation of all personal property, that in
his view made the truly spiritual man.'[77] Such an assessment is
inadequate and is, for this reason, inapplicable to our present
context. Chastity, the surrender of property and possessions,
prayer, fasting, and reading of the Scriptures are all marks of the
ascetic. To these practices there must be added some emphasis
upon a life shared with others in the service of the Church. These
disciplines collectively are verifiable in varying degrees at Thagaste
where Augustine adds still another feature: respect for learning. It
comes as no surprise, therefore, that his monastic *Rule* will later
provide a library for the brothers.[78]

While F. Bolgiani has argued successfully that the ideal of
monastic life was the central theme of Augustine's conversion, this
is not to say that Augustine immediately became a monk. Bolgiani
spoke rather of the new convert's 'decisive and irreversible entry
upon the path of perfect ascesis'.[79] Alypius, Evodius, and
Augustine, we recall, have been described as 'a tight, almost
monastic group'[80] before they had left Milan. Meanwhile, neither
Monica's untimely death at Ostia nor the sojourn of nearly a year
in Rome failed to disrupt their plans. In fact, the protracted stay in
Rome consolidated these plans.[81]

It would obviously be anachronistic to impose Benedict's model

[75] See Ch. IV n. 3.   [76] *Conf.* 8. 12. 29 (CCL 27. 131).
[77] Van der Meer, *Augustine the Bishop*, 206.
[78] H. I. Marrou, *A History of Education in Antiquity* (New York, 1964), 443.
[79] Bolgiani, *Conversione*, 86: 'l'ingresso definitivo ed irreversibile sulla via di
una ascesi perfetta'. See also Ch. II n. 8.
[80] See Ch. IV n. 36.
[81] Recall the telling passage *Conf.* 9. 8. 17 (CCL 27. 142–3), which amounts to a
strong declaration of intent as to what the group would do once it had reached
north Africa. See pp. 43–4 above for an analysis of this text.

of a monk upon Augustine at Thagaste or later at Hippo, for that matter. Benedict was born some fifty years after Augustine's death. Augustine was an innovator; he was feeling his way along the paths of Christian asceticism. He was adapting first-hand observations of monastic life at Milan and Rome to fit his own personal needs as well as the requirements of the north African Church. We must, after all, allow Augustine the freedom to bring to his birthplace his own talented initiatives, notable gifts of intellect, distinctive traits of temperament, and depth of spirituality.

Experience comes first, its articulation afterwards. Conceptualizations ordinarily represent an attempt to encapsulate an experience after it has crystallized. Actually, we must wait until the year 407 for the bishop to furnish us with his conception of a monk.[82] Even then, his description of a monk will bear features which are characteristically his own.[83] The burden of this chapter, meanwhile, lends reinforcement to the opinion that Augustine had a genuine living experience of monastic life long before he ventured to offer a definition of it.

Unlike the situation in the eastern Empire, where monasticism had been flourishing for a century, the borderline between ascetic and monk was sometimes a thin one in the West during the latter part of the fourth century. But after Augustine, his friends, and his son had settled at Thagaste in the autumn of 388, others joined them in their quest for holiness: 'Indeed, some of the first monasteries in the West were these "lay monasteries" of sensitive pagans and Christians.'[84] To say that Augustine's family home possessed the accoutrements of Christian monasticism does not, it seems to me, either strain the existing evidence or overstate the case.

2. Presbyter at Hippo

Soon after Augustine's ordination to the presbyterate, Bishop Valerius honoured his resolve to remain a monk by giving him a garden within the Church property at Hippo.[85] Possidius tells us

[82] See A.-M. La Bonnardière, *Recherches de chronologie augustinienne* (Paris, 1965), 50, 52 for the date of *En. Ps. 132*.

[83] *En. Ps. 132*, § 6 (CCL 40. 1931) translated into English on p. 158 below.

[84] Brown, *Augustine*, 116. I am prepared to go further than the author will allow in his chapter, '*Seruus Dei*: Thagaste', 132-7.

[85] *Serm.* 355. 2 (Lambot, *SS*, 125); also *Vita* 5.

that the new presbyter wasted no time: 'The basic rule of this society was that no one should possess anything of his own, but that everything should be held in common and be distributed to each individual on the basis of need, as [Augustine] had formerly done after he returned to his native home from across the sea.'[86]

Here at Hippo for the first of many times during his life, Augustine quotes part of the verse from Acts 4: 32: 'one heart and one soul'.[87] So far as Augustine is concerned, the apostolic Jerusalem community will remain the model of both Christian and monastic life.[88] By far the greater number of citations from Acts 4: 32–5 pertain with equal force to the faithful: the ratio is roughly six to one.[89] From this perspective, therefore, distinction between laity and monks lies chiefly in the functional or practical order of living. Monks are laymen; monks do not marry. Marriage will later be described as 'a hill of lesser blessing', whereas continence, a greater blessing, is represented as a 'mountain'.[90] Both matrimony and celibacy are permanent features in the Christian landscape. 'Men and women who practise lifelong continence and are consecrated to virginity', the bishop will admonish, '. . . are not to regard marriage as evil.'[91] In point of fact, 'marriage with humility is better than virginity with pride'.[92] The Lucan ideal of Acts 4: 32–5 may thus be contextualized within the family or a formalized structure such as 'common life'.[93] This latter configuration was so appealing to Augustine that he later extended it to all his clerics.[94]

Meanwhile, he nowhere proposes a lay spirituality as such or a spirituality for monks: 'there is one commonwealth for all Christians'.[95] Holiness is equally incumbent upon everyone. Monastery and home simply offer different approaches to God. While utilizing various vectors of measurement on their journey towards God, clergy, laity, monks, and nuns minister to one another in the life of the Church as they build the Body of Christ and thus enrich the life of this world, *saeculum*.

Evodius and Severus follow Augustine to Hippo to live with him

---

[86] *Vita* 5.
[87] *En. Ps.* 4, §10 (CCL 38. 19).
[88] Verheijen, *Augustine's Monasticism*, 81, 95.
[89] *Règle* ii. 90–1.   [90] *Sanc. Virg.* 18. 18 (CSEL 41. 252).
[91] Ibid. (CSEL 41. 250–1).   [92] *En. Ps. 99* § 13 (CCL 39. 1402).
[93] The *Rule* 1. 7.   [94] *Sermm.* 355, 356 (Lambot, *SS* 123–43).
[95] *Op. Mon.* 25. 33 (CSEL 41. 580).

there. Alypius, as we have noted, will become bishop of Thagaste. Possidius is destined to become bishop of Calama, as Profuturus will become bishop of Cirta. Other unidentified persons also join this community. 'About ten men' later become bishops in the north African Church and these, in turn, 'established monasteries'[96]

It is for this monastery at Hippo that Augustine will compose his *Rule*.[97] Its precepts may thus be presumed to provide a fairly reliable index to daily life there. Augustine's 'occasional pieces', as Peter Brown calls them, regularly emerge from the crucible of experience. As with patristic writings generally, there is no divorce between life and teaching. Augustine was both the superior of this monastic community and its only priest. He may well have delegated duties of the former office to a confrère.

Ordination to the presbyterate immediately made an appreciable difference in Augustine's life. (It is interesting to speculate about the future direction of Thagaste, had Augustine remained there.) He soon requested release from his presbyteral obligations in order to study the Scriptures. 'How am I to take second place at the helm,' he asks Bishop Valerius, 'when I can hardly handle an oar?' The same letter reads: '. . . there is nothing in this life more taxing, more arduous, or more hazardous than the office of bishop, priest, or deacon.'[98]

Valerius, a Greek by birth, had met with difficulty preaching in Latin. Augustine was soon to mitigate this embarrassment. After six months' study of the Scriptures, he frequently assumed the task of preaching, and so distinguished himself in this ministry that he preached before the Plenary Council of Africa at Hippo on 3 December 393.[99] It comes as no surprise, therefore, when Augustine will later write to monks on the island of Capraria: 'Do not prefer your own monastic leisure, *otium*, to the needs of the Church.'[100] The future bishop will likewise represent Christ as knocking on the door of the contemplative's cell: 'Open to me, preach me to others. How shall I have access to people who have

---

[96] *Vita* 11: 'Nam ferme decem . . . et monasteria instituerunt.'
[97] This matter is discussed in Ch. VIII.
[98] *Ep.* 21. 1 (CSEL 34. 49–50).
[99] *Symb* (PL 40. 181–96).
[100] *Ep.* 48. 2 (CSEL 34. 138 AD 393: 'nec uestrum otium necessitatibus ecclesiae praeponatis . . .'.

actually shut their door to me, if no one opens the door? How shall they listen to me, if no one preaches?'[101]

Meanwhile, presbyteral duties in no way diminished Augustine's studious apostolate of the pen. In addition to *Sermons* and *Letters*, these years account for seven anti-Manichaean treatises, two anti-Donatist works, and an explanation of the Creed, referred to above and originally preached as a sermon. His *Commentary on the Lord's Sermon on the Mount*, two Commentaries on Romans, and still another on Galatians mark Augustine's early efforts at New Testament exegesis. That one of the Commentaries on Romans remained incomplete attests indirectly at least to the brisk pace of pastoral ministry at Hippo. Augustine finally found time to finish *Freedom of the Will*, which was begun several years earlier at Rome. Intermittent conversations with 'the brothers', initiated as soon as he returned to Thagaste, were faithfully recorded and will be published shortly after Augustine's episcopal ordination. Questions 51–65 probably range from the years 391–94/5 and testify to his study of the Bible immediately after priestly ordination. Questions 66–75 deal with Pauline themes, likewise indicating Augustine's renewed study of St Paul during the last two years of his presbyterate.[102] All these writings are bracketed by two treatises, one of which was begun at Milan. The other is Augustine's last work as a priest.[103] Their respective titles, *On Music* and *On Lying*, reveal the incredible shift in the direction of their author's life and thought. This last treatise has survived, even though its author gave orders for it to be destroyed.[104] Its circuitous composition[105] was possibly occasioned by Augustine's preoccupations with priestly ministry at the time.

As a monk–priest, Augustine inveterately combined intellectual activity with pastoral ministry. Common life at Hippo resonated with many religious and philosophical ideals from the world of late antiquity. The range of topics in the *Eighty-three Different Questions* spanned an interval of seven years, offering further

[101] *Tr. Jo.* 57. 4 (CCL 36. 471). Augustine is commenting upon the text from S. of S. 5: 2–3.
[102] Mosher, *Eighty-three Different Questions*, Eng. tr., FC 70. 18–20.
[103] For the chronological listing of these books and their author's mature reflections on each of them, see M. Bogan, *Saint Augustine: The Retractations*, Eng. tr., FC 60 (Washington, 1968), 45–118.
[104] *Retr.* 1. 27 (CCL 57. 88).
[105] Ibid. '(liber) et obscurus et anfractuosus . . .'.

proof (if any were needed) of Augustine's penchant for dialogue. Life together remained fundamentally fraternal and was inspired by the example of the apostles in the primitive Jerusalem community. Its social dimension was triggered as much by the requirements of Augustine's temperament as by the pastoral solicitude which was demanded by ministry in a servant-Church.

Whether Augustine was ordained bishop of Hippo in late 395 or 396 is uncertain.[106] Once again he will be changing his lifestyle owing principally to the demands of episcopal hospitality. The 'bishop's house'[107] will require a more open ambience than the lay monastery at Hippo could provide. House guests, travel, liturgical expectations of the laity, the ministry of preaching, allied pastoral duties, arbitration of civil and ecclesiastical cases in the lawcourt, all these would surely be inimical to the daily life of a monk. Yet Augustine in old age will describe the 'bishop's house' as a 'monastery of clerics'.[108] In this second monastery at Hippo life will be different; for one thing, there will be conversation at meals.[109] Augustine's monasticism reaches another turning-point: the clericalization of the monk. From the time he is obliged to relocate in the 'bishop's house', two monasteries will exist side by side, one for laymen, the other for clerics. The bishop, moreover, will soon establish at Hippo the first monastery for women in north Africa.[110] There will be two others for men, directed by the priests Leporius[111] and Eleusinus[112] respectively.

Just as he may be said to have clericalized the monk, with equal insistence Augustine will 'monasticize' the cleric. The bishop of Hippo will remain *un moine malgré tout*,[113] a monk in spite of everything.

---

[106] Augustine's signature appears for the first time in his own right at the end of the Acts of the Council of Carthage on 28 Aug. 397; see C. Munier, *Concilia Africae* A.345–A.525 (CCL 149), 49.

[107] *Serm.* 355. 2 (Lambot, *SS* 126).

[108] Ibid.

[109] *Vita* 22 (Pellegrino 122, 219 n. 15). In the bishop's house Augustine encouraged both reading and conversation at meals, whereas reading for the entire duration of the meal was customary in the lay monastery at Hippo.

[110] Gavigan, *Vita monastica* 30, 54–5.

[111] *Serm.* 356. 10 (Lambot, *SS* 138).

[112] Ibid. 15 (*SS* 142–3).

[113] Mandouze, *L'Aventure*, 165–242 offers excellent insights into Augustine's permanent attraction to monastic life.

Part Two

REGVLA SANCTI AVGVSTINI, *c.*397

VI

Eight Legislative Texts and a Letter

To unravel the entanglements of the textual labyrinth which constitutes the *Regula Sancti Augustini* requires the dexterity of a Theseus with the help of an Ariadne. Luc Verheijen has done this deftly and single-handedly in his meticulous study of 274 manuscripts containing 317 texts.[1] We shall observe how this task becomes all the more difficult because identification of Augustine as author of a monastic rule occurs for the first time in the *Rule* of Eugippius about one hundred years after Augustine's death. In like manner, we must wait more than a century and a half after the bishop of Hippo had died until an anonymous scribe identified Augustine as the author of the monastic rule which posterity has long associated with his name. One must take the route of philology and textual criticism, therefore, in order to explore further a number of eminently debatable issues. Fortunately, Verheijen's scholarship has neutralized the nomenclature in an effort to eliminate past prejudices and to minimize the ever-present risk of begging the question. Scholars have expressed hope that his terminology will become standardized.[2] For this reason, I have adopted it in its entirety. Accordingly, nine pieces (eight legislative documents and one letter) comprise the portfolio for the Augustinian *Rule*. Of these nine pieces, four are addressed to men:

(1) *Ordo Monasterii*: the *Regulations for a Monastery*.
(2) *Praeceptum*: the *Rule*.
(3) *Praeceptum longius*: the *Longer Rule*.
(4) *Regula recepta*: the *Later Version of the Rule*.

The remaining five pieces are addressed to women:

(5) *Obiurgatio*: the *Reprimand to Quarrelling Nuns*.
(6) *Regularis informatio*: the *Rule for Nuns*.

---

[1] *Règle* i. 17–24.
[2] S. Frank, *Franziskanische Studien*, 50 (1968), 382–8; R. J. Halliburton, *JTS* NS 19 (1968), 657–63; E. Colledge, *Medium Aevum*, 39 (1970), 328–32.

Table A. Texts Addressed to Men

(1) *Ordo monasterii*

Ante omnia, fratres carissimi,
diligatur deus, deinde et proximus . . .

. . . et nobis non parua erit laetitia
de uestra salute. Amen.

(2) *Praeceptum*

Haec sunt quae ut obseruetis praecipimus,
in monasterio constituti . . .

. . . orans ut ei debitum dimittatur
et in temptationem non inducatur.

(4) *Regula recepta*

(3) *Praeceptum longius*

TABLE B. Texts Addressed to Women

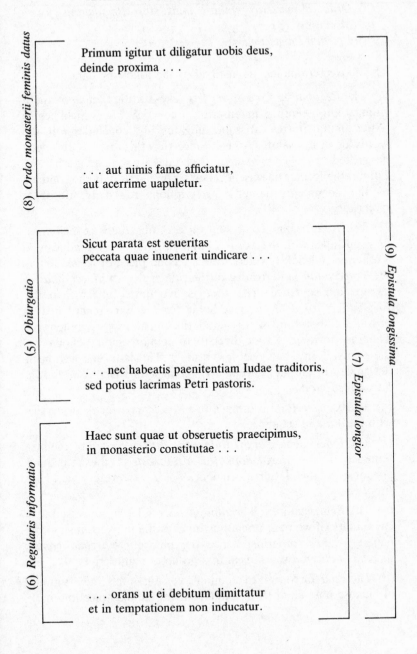

(8) *Ordo monasterii feminis datus*

Primum igitur ut diligatur uobis deus,
deinde proxima . . .

. . . aut nimis fame afficiatur,
aut acerrime uapuletur.

(5) *Obiurgatio*

Sicut parata est seueritas
peccata quae inuenerit uindicare . . .

. . . nec habeatis paenitentiam Iudae traditoris,
sed potius lacrimas Petri pastoris.

(6) *Regularis informatio*

Haec sunt quae ut obseruetis praecipimus,
in monasterio constitutae . . .

. . . orans ut ei debitum dimittatur
et in temptationem non inducatur.

(9) *Epistula longissima*

(7) *Epistula longior*

(7) *Epistula longior*: the *Longer Letter*.

(8) *Ordo monasterii feminis datus*: the *Regulations for a Monastery* (F).

(9) *Epistula longissima*: the *Longest Letter*.

The above terminology is justified by the following data:

(1) The *Regulations for a Monastery* takes its title *Ordo monasterii* from a ninth-century manuscript, Laon 328 *bis*, which begins 'Ante omnia, fratres carissimi, diligatur' and concludes with the words 'de uestra salute. Amen'. Since 1937 this text has also been designated *Disciplina monasterii*. Both titles are somewhat arbitrary. I prefer the former because it reflects more accurately the contents of the document, namely, prescriptions for daily life in a monastery.

(2) The *Rule* begins 'Haec sunt quae ut obseruetis praecipimus' and concludes with the words 'et in temptationem non inducatur'. Verheijen judiciously refers to this second piece of legislation as the *Praeceptum*, a derivative of the principal verb *praecipimus* in its opening sentence. The *Rule* is five times longer than the *Regulations for a Monastery*. Some few scholars regard it as a possible elaboration of this latter document or its supplement. There is, however, a wide diversity of opinion among scholars on the nexus, if any, between nos. 1 and 2. This latter has also been designated in the literature as *Regula ad seruos Dei*: *Rule for the Servants of God*.

(3) The *Longer Rule* combines the *Regulations for a Monastery* with the *Rule* in sequence.

(4) The *Later Version of the Rule* is the *Rule* preceded by the first sentence of the *Regulations for a Monastery*; the remaining portions of this latter document, §§ 2–11, were eventually suppressed.

(5) The *Reprimand to Quarrelling Nuns* is a letter addressed to a community of women. Its author rebukes the nuns for insubordination to their superior, hence the phrase *Obiurgatio contra sanctimonialium dissensionem* in a group of manuscripts.

(6) The *Rule for Nuns* is the feminine version of the *Rule*. A group of manuscripts, all of them letters, carries the identification-mark

. . . *et post increpationem earum* (i.e. *sanctimonialium*) *regularis informatio.*

(7) The *Longer Letter* consistently combines nos. 5 and 6.

(8) The *Regulations for a Monastery* (F) is generally the same as no. 1 (but in the feminine), except for some slight variations and some later additions to the text. Only § 11 of the masculine version is lacking.

(9) The *Longest Letter* combines a passage from no. 5 with the whole of no. 8 and a sizeable portion of no. 6.

Still closer inspection tells us that nos. 3, 4, 7, and 9 above are combinations of other pieces. This enables us to reduce the number of elements to five. Among these five, nos. 2 and 6, 1 and 8, are doublets. If the *Rule* is the original text, then the *Rule for Nuns* is simply its derivative in feminine form. If the *Rule for Nuns* is the original text, then the *Rule* is simply a transcription to the masculine gender. The same may be said for nos. 1 and 8, *Regulations for a Monastery*. In other words, the list of nine becomes a list of five, which, in turn, becomes a list of three.

Basically, therefore, three Latin texts comprise the portfolio for Augustine's Rule. They are:

no. 1 or no. 8: one is a transcription of the other; no. 2 or no. 6: one is a transcription of the other; no. 5: the *Reprimand to Quarrelling Nuns*. With respect to the transcriptions, the question of precedence remains, namely, which came first, the masculine or the feminine form?

We know regrettably little about the provenance of the above nine pieces. Circumstances of composition are unknown. Dates are, at best, a matter for conjecture. Finally, authors of the various transcriptions remain anonymous and their motives indeterminate. At the outset we face a twofold difficulty. On the one hand, there is the silence of Augustine himself, Possidius (his first biographer), and their contemporaries. On the other hand, there is a vacuum of historical evidence which surrounds the transmission of these texts.

The twentieth century has produced six critical editions: those by A. Goldbacher in 1911, P. Schroeder in 1926, D. De Bruyne in

1930, A. C. Vega in 1933, W. Hümpfner in 1943, and L. Verheijen in 1967.[3] This last scholar has furnished us with a vast assemblage of materials and a fairly exhaustive study. Even those researchers who are out of sympathy with some of Verheijen's conclusions nevertheless applaud the thoroughness of his research. A seasoned philologist, while disagreeing with the choice of two variant readings in the latest text of the *Rule*, yet assures us: 'Verheijen's knowledge of the MS tradition of the *Regula Sancti Augustini* is unrivalled and his exposition of the problems concerning the origin and relationship of the various pieces that constitute this important and extremely influential document of monastic history is as complete as the sources permit.'[4]

In order to stress their author's fondness for balanced phrases in parallel or in antithesis and to facilitate the task of reading the text aloud, as its author prescribes, the Latin and English texts of the *Regulations for a Monastery* and the *Rule* are set forth by cola and commata. Augustine endorsed the same technique, for example, when analysing the Epistles of St Paul, substituting, however, the Latin *membra* and *caesa* for the above Greek rhetorical terms.[5] While it is by no means a self-conscious document in the manner of Augustine's *magnum opus et arduum*, the *City of God*, the *Rule* reveals a generous measure of metrical clausulae. Distribution of accent and consonantal groupings generate sound patterns which carefully conform to rules governing rhetorical *cursus*. A skilled author is obviously at work in a transitional age when accentual rhythm was beginning to overtake metrical accent. It is one of the trials of a translator to try to capture these subtle and rhythmic variations. In the matter of Augustine's *Rule*, English translations have been generally inattentive to these features of Augustine's style. Both the Latin and the English texts, therefore, should be read aloud so as to perceive the musical tone of this monastic code with its variety of sound-effects.

Punctuation marks further delineate the sense, style, and meaning of the author. Such a format heightens the text's paratactic prose with its lapidary phrases. There is the additional

[3] See the '20th Century Critical Editions of the Rule' in the 'Select Bibliography' for the full listing.

[4] R. Arbesmann, 'The Question of the *Regula Sancti Augustini*', *AS* 1 (1970), 261.

[5] *Doc. Ch.* 4. 7. 11–13 (CCL 32. 123–5).

advantage of thus accentuating the author's generous use of antithesis, alliteration, and rhyme.[6] Rhetorical figures of sound abound throughout the original text, a trait which is indigenous to Latin as well as being the trademark of the author. Finally, the English translation reflects the musical rhythm and cadence of some clausulae, another distinguishing feature of the original Latin.

Still another impetus for the present translation is the conviction that the human voice itself conveys shades of meaning expressed in the original spoken Latin without serious detriment to the proprieties of Latin style and grammar. Preceptive features of the *Regulations for a Monastery* and the *Rule* require repetitive use of the subjunctive mood. While the hypotaxis mirrored by this mood is commonplace in Latin, modern English utilizes the human larynx for the same purpose. To transmit signals which are proper to these monastic texts without injury to the original, one may further rely upon the intonations of a reader's voice as the context may suggest.

The texts at hand become all the more difficult because Augustine seldom divorced feeling from thought. Although his *Sermons* and *Letters* exhibit this trait in a conspicuous manner, still many staccato statements in the *Rule* ought not to be construed as a sort of muscular Christianity. The bishop is legislating a lived-experience, as the story of his life and the short-lived history of Augustine's monasticism in north Africa amply demonstrate prior to the Arab conquest in the seventh century.

The author of the *Rule* literally urges: 'This little book is to be read to you once a week . . .' (8. 2). In the ancient world, silent reading was the exception. Prose and poetry, epistles too, were read aloud either by an interlocutor or by oneself. Augustine, for example, registered surprise when he came upon Ambrose reading silently in his study, no doubt owing to the brisk pace of the episcopal ministry in Milan.[7] Monks and nuns regularly listened to the Scriptures in a public setting; reading was also customary at mealtime.

---

[6] Augustine regularly exhibits 'une prédilection prononcée pour le style paratactique et antithétique, avec phrases courtes, structure rythmique, symétrie poursuivie jusqu'à la syllabe . . .'. See C. Mohrmann, 'Saint Augustin écrivain', *RA* 1 (1958), 51–2.

[7] *Conf.* 6. 3. 3 (CCL 27. 75–6). See B. M. W. Knox, 'Silent Reading in Antiquity', *Greek, Roman and Byzantine Studies*, 9 (1968), 421–35.

As we have already suggested, writing was tantamount to talking aloud. Virtually all Augustine's writings were, in fact, dictated.[8] For an author to set his thoughts directly in writing was considered a somewhat pedestrian occupation. Trained secretaries, *notarii* or *amanuenses*, usually performed this servile task. Both dictation by an author and the practice of reading aloud offered the listener a double warranty of pleasant sound effects. Familiarity with a text gradually sharpened one's auditory sense, thus making it more alert to sound and meaning. Nor was it necessary to await the pronouncements of the McLuhan era of the 1960s for the astute scholar to observe that there was a time long ago when the ear was favoured over the eye as the medium of communication. This said, however, one is well advised to heed the Italian adage, *traduttore traditore*.

---

[8] The subject-matter of the *Soliloquies* was so intimate and personal as not to lend itself to dictation: 'Nec ista dictari debent . . .'. Augustine is advised by 'Reason', his imaginary interlocutor, simply to assemble some notes on his reflections: 'Deinde quod inuenis paucis conclusiunculis breuiter collige', *Sol*. 1. 1 (PL 32. 869).

VII
Latin Texts and English Translations

Ordo monasterii

1. Ante omnia, fratres carissimi,
diligatur deus, deinde et proximus,[1]
quia ista sunt praecepta principaliter nobis data.

2. Qualiter autem nos oportet
5 orare uel psallere describimus:
id est, in matutinis dicantur psalmi tres:
sexagesimus secundus, quintus et octogesimus nonus;
ad tertiam prius psalmus unus ad respondendum
dicatur deinde antiphonae duae,
10 lectio et conpletorium;
simili modo sexta et nona;
ad lucernarium autem psalmus responsorius unus,
antiphonae quattuor, item psalmus unus responsorius,
lectio et conpletorium.
15 Et tempore opportuno post lucernarium,
omnibus sedentibus, legantur lectiones;
post haec autem
consuetudinarii psalmi ante somnum dicantur.
Nocturnae autem orationes,
20 mense Nouembri, Decembri, Ianuario et Februario,
antiphonae duodecim, psalmi sex, lectiones tres;
Martio, Aprili, Septembri et Octobri,
antiphonae decem, psalmi quinque, lectiones tres;
Maio, Iunio, Iulio et Augusto,
25 antiphonae octo, psalmi quattuor, lectiones duae.

3. Operentur a mane usque ad sextam,
et a sexta usque ad nonam uacent lectioni,
et ad nonam reddant codices
et postquam refecerint,
30 siue in horto, siue ubicumque necesse fuerit,
faciant opus usque ad horam lucernarii.

4 Nemo sibi aliquid suum uindicet proprium,
siue in uestimento, siue in quacumque re:
apostolica enim uita optamus uiuere.[2]

35 5. Nemo cum murmurio aliquid faciat,
ut non simili iudicio murmuratorum pereat.[3]

---

[1] Matt. 22: 37-40.   [2] Acts 4: 32.   [3] Num. 14: 1-37.

Regulations for a Monastery

1. Love God above all else, dearest brothers,
then your neighbour also,[1]
because these are the precepts
given us as primary principles.

2. We describe how we ought to pray or say the psalms.
Three psalms are to be said in the early morning hours:
the sixty-second, the fifth, and the eighty-ninth.
At Terce one psalm is to be said responsorially,
then two antiphons, the reading, and the closing prayer.
Do likewise at Sext and None.
At lamp-lighting, however,
one responsorial psalm is to be said,
four antiphons, another responsorial psalm,
the reading, and the closing prayer.
At a convenient time after lighting the lamps,
lessons are to be read with everyone seated.
Afterwards the customary psalms are to be said before sleep.
Night prayers consist of
twelve antiphons, six psalms, and three readings
in November, December, January and February;
in March, April, September, and October,
ten antiphons, five psalms, and three readings;
in May, June, July, and August,
eight antiphons, four psalms, and two readings.

3. Let them work from early morning till noon
and take leisure for reading from noon till three,
and at three o'clock return the books.
After some nourishment, they should work
in the garden or wherever necessary,
until the lighting of the lamps.

4. No one is to claim anything as his own,
whether clothing or whatever else;
we wish to live as the apostles did.[2]

5. No one is to do anything with a murmur,
so as not to perish from a similar judgement
as those who murmured.[3]

6. Fideliter oboediant,
patrem suum honorent post deum,
praeposito suo deferant sicut decet sanctos.

40   7. Sedentes ad mensam taceant, audientes lectionem.
Si autem aliquid opus fuerit,
praepositus eorum sit sollicitus.
Sabbato et dominica, sicut constitutum est,
qui uolunt uinum accipiant.

45   8. Si opus fuerit,
ad aliquam necessitatem monasterii mitti,
duo eant.
Nemo extra monasterium
sine praecepto manducet neque bibat;
50   non enim hoc ad disciplinam pertinet monasterii.
Si opera monasterii mittantur fratres uendere,
sollicite obseruent
ne quid faciant contra praeceptum,
scientes quia deum exacerbant in seruis ipsius;[4]
55   siue aliquid emant ad necessitatem monasterii,
sollicite et fideliter ut serui dei agant.

9. Otiosum uerbum apud illos non sit.
A mane ad opera sua sedeant.
Post orationes tertiae eant similiter ad opera sua.
60   Non stantes fabulas contexant,
nisi forte aliquid sit pro animae utilitate.
Sedentes ad opera taceant,
nisi forte necessitas operis exegerit,
ut loquatur quis.

65   10. Si quis autem non omni uirtute,
adiuuante misericordia domini,
haec conatus fuerit implere,
contumaci uero animo despexerit,

---

[4] Ps. 94: 7–10.

6. All are to obey with fidelity,
honour their father after God,
defer to their superior
in a manner worthy of holy men.

7. When seated at table,
they are to be silent and listen to the reading.
If, however, any need should arise,
the superior should take care of it.
Those who wish may have wine
on Saturdays and Sundays, as agreed upon.

8. If necessity requires sending someone
for anything needed by the monastery,
let two people go.
No one should eat or drink outside the monastery
without express permission to do so;
for this is not in keeping with the discipline of the monastery.
If brothers are sent to sell products of the monastery,
they should be solicitous
not to do anything contrary to what was directed,
realizing that they exacerbate God
as represented by his servants.[4]
Whenever they buy something needed by the monastery,
they are to transact the business
conscientiously and faithfully, as servants of God.

9. They should not engage in idle conversation.
They are to remain assiduously at work from early morning.
After Terce they should apply themselves
in like fashion to their respective tasks.
They ought not to stand around spinning tales,
except perhaps to talk to each other
about something useful to the soul.
They should keep silence while seated at work,
unless circumstances connected with the task
require one to speak.

10. Should anyone not make an effort
to fulfil these precepts
with all his strength
and the help of the Lord's mercy,

semel atque iterum commonitus,
70 si non emendauerit,
sciat se subiacere disciplinae monasterii
sicut oportet.
Si autem talis fuerit aetas ipsius,
etiam uapulet.

75 II. Haec autem in nomine Christi
fideliter et pie obseruantes,
et uos proficietis,
et nobis non parua erit laetitia
de uestra salute. Amen.

but should contumaciously disdain them—
if he does not mend his ways after one or two warnings—
let him realize that he must submit
to the discipline of the monastery.
Moreover, if his age admits of it,
he should also be whipped.

11. When you heed these observances
with fidelity and piety,
in the name of Christ,
you will make progress
and we shall experience no little joy
over your salvation. Amen.

Praeceptum[5]

I

1. Haec sunt quae ut obseruetis praecipimus
in monasterio constituti.

2. Primum, propter quod in unum estis congregati,
ut unianimes habitetis in domo[6]
5 et sit uobis anima una et cor unum in deum.[7]

3. Et non dicatis aliquid proprium,
sed sint uobis omnia communia,[8]
et distribuatur unicuique uestrum[9]
a praeposito uestro uictus et tegumentum,[10]
10 non aequaliter omnibus,
quia non aequaliter ualetis omnes,
sed potius unicuique sicut cuique opus fuerit.[11]
Sic enim legitis in Actibus Apostolorum,
quia 'erant illis omnia communia[12]
15 et distribuebatur unicuique sicut cuique opus erat'.[13]

4. Qui aliquid habebant in saeculo,
quando ingressi sunt monasterium,
libenter illud uelint esse commune.

5. Qui autem non habebant,
20 non ea quaerant in monasterio
quae nec foris habere potuerunt.
Sed tamen eorum infirmitati quod opus est tribuatur,
etiam si paupertas eorum, quando foris erant,
nec ipsa necessaria poterat inuenire.
25 Tantum non ideo se putent esse felices,
quia inuenerunt uictum et tegumentum,
quale foris inuenire non poterant.

---

[5] In two instances I have selected a reading which differs from Verheijen's critical edition. An ancient and a superior manuscript tradition, Augustine's thought expressed elsewhere on many occasions in many literary genres, and the inner logic of the immediate context, all compel me to choose *secari* (183) over *sanari*. I also prefer the singular form *pertinet* (198) over its variant in the plural, *pertinent*. See Arbesmann, 'The Question of the *Regula Sancti Augustini*', 253–4.
[6] Ps. 67: 7.   [7] Acts 4: 32a.   [8] Acts 4: 32b–c.   [9] Acts 4: 35.
[10] 1 Tim. 6: 8.   [11] Acts 4: 35.   [12] Acts 4: 32.   [13] Acts 4: 35.

Rule[5]

Chapter One

1.Here are the rules we lay down for your observance,
once you have been admitted to the monastery.

2. The chief motivation for your sharing life together
is to live harmoniously in the house[6]
and to have one heart and one soul seeking God.[7]

3. Do not call anything your own;
possess everything in common.[8]
Your superior ought to provide each of you[9]
with food and clothing,[10]
not on an equal basis to all,
because all do not enjoy the same health,
but to each one in proportion to his need.[11]
For you read in the Acts of the Apostles:
'They possessed everything in common',[12] and
'Distribution was made to each
in proportion to each one's need.'[13]

4. Those who owned anything in the world
should freely consent to possess everything in common
in the monastery.

5. Those who had nothing
should not seek in the monastery
possessions which were beyond their reach outside.
Allowance should be made for their frailty, however,
on the basis of individual need,
even if previous poverty
never permitted them to satisfy those needs.
But they should not consider their present good fortune
to consist in the possession of food and clothing
which were beyond their means elsewhere.

6. Nec erigant ceruicem,
quia sociantur eis
30 ad quos foris accedere non audebant,
sed sursum cor habeant[14]
et terrena uana non quaerant,
ne incipiant esse monasteria diuitibus utilia, non pauperibus,
si diuites illic humiliantur,
35 et pauperes illic inflantur.

7. Sed rursus etiam illi
qui aliquid esse uidebantur in saeculo
non habeant fastidio fratres suos
qui ad illam sanctam societatem
40 ex paupertate uenerunt.
Magis autem studeant,
non de parentum diuitum dignitate,
sed de pauperum fratrum societate, gloriari.
Nec extollantur, si communi uitae
45 de suis facultatibus aliquid contulerunt,
nec de suis diuitiis magis superbiant,
quia eas monasterio partiuntur,
quam si eis in saeculo fruerentur.
Alia quippe quaecumque iniquitas
50 in malis operibus exercetur
ut fiant,
superbia vero etiam bonis operibus insidiatur
ut pereant;
et quid prodest dispergere dando pauperibus
55 et pauperem fieri,
cum anima misera superbior efficitur
diuitias contemnendo, quam fuerat possidendo?

8. Omnes ergo unianimiter et concorditer uiuite,[15]
et honorate in uobis inuicem deum
60 cuius templa facti estis.[16]

II

1. Orationibus instate[17]
horis et temporibus constitutis.

---

[14] Col. 3: 1–2.   [15] Acts 4: 32; Rom. 15: 6.   [16] 2 Cor. 6: 16.   [17] Col. 4: 2.

6. Nor should they put their nose in the air
because they associate with people
they did not dare approach in the world.
Instead they should lift up their heart,[14]
and not pursue hollow worldly concerns.
Monasteries should not provide advantages
for the rich to the disadvantage of the poor.
Such would be the case if the rich become humble
and the poor become proud.

7. But on the other hand,
those who enjoyed some measure of worldly success
ought not to belittle their brothers
who come to this holy society
from a condition of poverty.
They should endeavour to boast
about the fellowship of poor brothers,
rather than the social standing of rich relations.
They are not to think well of themselves
if they have contributed to the common life
from their wealth.
Sharing their possessions with the monastery
ought not to become a greater source of pride
than if they enjoyed these goods in the world.
As a matter of fact,
every other vice produces evil deeds
with a view to doing evil,
but pride sets a trap for good deeds as well
with a view to destroying them.
What benefit is there in giving generously to the poor
and becoming poor oneself,
if the pitiful soul is more inclined to pride
by rejecting riches than by possessing them?

8. Live then, all of you, in harmony and concord;[15]
honour God mutually in each other;
you have become His temples.[16]

Chapter Two

1. Be assiduous in prayer[17]
at the scheduled hours and times.

2. In oratorio nemo aliquid agat
nisi ad quod est factum,
65 unde et nomen accepit;
ut si forte aliqui, etiam praeter horas constitutas,
si eis uacat, orare uoluerint,
non eis sit inpedimento,
qui ibi aliquid agendum putauerit.

70 3. Psalmis et hymnis cum oratis deum,
hoc uersetur in corde quod profertur in uoce.

4. Et nolite cantare, nisi quod legitis esse cantandum;
quod autem non ita scriptum est ut cantetur, non cantetur.

III

1. Carnem uestram domate
75 ieiuniis et abstinentia escae et potus,
quantum ualetudo permittit.
Quando autem aliquis non potest ieiunare,
non tamen extra horam prandii
aliquid alimentorum sumat, nisi cum aegrotat.

80 2. Cum acceditis ad mensam, donec inde surgatis,
quod uobis secundum consuetudinem legitur,
sine tumultu et contentionibus audite;
nec solae uobis fauces sumant cibum,[18]
sed et aures esuriant dei uerbum.[19]

85 3. Qui infirmi sunt ex pristina consuetudine,
si aliter tractantur in uictu,
non debet aliis molestum esse nec iniustum uideri,
quos facit alia consuetudo fortiores.
Nec illos feliciores putent,
90 quia sumunt quod non sumunt ipsi,
sed sibi potius gratulentur,
quia ualent quod non ualent illi.

---

[18] Matt. 4: 4.   [19] Amos 8: 11.

2. No one has any business in the prayer-room
apart from the particular purpose which it serves;
that is why it is called the oratory.
Consequently, if some wish to pray
even outside the scheduled periods,
during their free time,
they should not be deterred by people
who think they have some other task there.

3. When you pray to God in psalms and hymns,
the words you speak should be alive in your hearts.

4. Keep to the prescribed text when you sing;
avoid texts which are not suited for singing.

Chapter Three

1. To the extent that your health allows,
subdue your flesh
by fasting and abstinence from food and drink.
If anyone is unable to fast,
let him at least take no food between meals,
unless he is sick.

2. Listen to the customary reading
from the beginning to the end of the meal
without commotion or arguments.
Food is not for the mouth alone;[18]
your ears also should hunger for the Word of God.[19]

3. No one is to be annoyed,
nor should it seem to be unjust,
when a special diet is provided
for brothers whose health has been adversely affected
by their former status in life.
A different background
endows some people with greater physical strength.
These should not consider others fortunate
because they see concessions
granted to their brothers and not to themselves.
Let them be thankful rather that they have the strength
to endure what others cannot.

4. Et si eis, qui uenerunt
ex moribus delicatioribus ad monasterium,
95 aliquid alimentorum, uestimentorum, stramentorum,
operimentorum datur,
quod aliis fortioribus et ideo felicioribus non datur,
cogitare debent quibus non datur,
quantum de sua saeculari uita illi ad istam descenderint,
100 quamuis usque ad aliorum, qui sunt corpore firmiores,
frugalitatem peruenire nequiuerint.
Nec debent uelle omnes, quod paucos uident amplius,
non quia honorantur, sed quia tolerantur, accipere,
ne contingat detestanda peruersitas,
105 ut in monasterio, ubi, quantum possunt,
fiunt diuites laboriosi, fiant pauperes delicati.

5. Sane, quemadmodum aegrotantes necesse habent
minus accipere ne grauentur, ita et post aegritudinem
sic tractandi sunt, ut citius recreentur,
110 etiam si de humillima saeculi paupertate uenerunt,
tamquam hoc illis contulerit recentior aegritudo,
quod diuitibus anterior consuetudo.
Sed cum uires pristinas reparauerint,
redeant ad feliciorem consuetudinem suam,
115 quae famulos dei tanto amplius decet,
quanto minus indigent.
Nec ibi eos teneat uoluptas iam uegetos,
quo necessitas leuarat infirmos.
Illi se extiment ditiores,
120 qui in sustinenda parcitate fuerint fortiores;
melius est enim minus egere, quam plus habere.

IV

1. Non sit notabilis habitus uester,
nec affectetis uestibus placere sed moribus.

2. Quando proceditis, simul ambulate;

4. If food, clothes, a mattress, or blankets
are given to those who come to the monastery
from a more comfortable manner of life,
the more robust individuals,
to whom such things are not given
and who are on this account more fortunate, ought to recall
how much affluent people have altered their lifestyle
in order to embrace the present one, even though
the frugality practised by the stronger brothers
continues to elude them.
No one should desire the extras given to a few,
more out of tolerance than out of deference.
Deplorable disorder would occur,
if the monastery provided a setting,
to the extent that it is possible,
where the wealthy become workers,
while the poor become pampered.

5. Sick people necessarily take less food
so as not to aggravate their condition.
During convalescence they are to receive such care
as will quickly restore their health, even if they come
from the lowest level of poverty in the world.
Recent illness has afflicted them with the same frailty
which the wealthy possess from their previous manner of life.
When sick people have fully recovered,
they should return to their happier ways,
which are all the more fitting for God's servants
to the extent that they have fewer needs.
Food formerly necessary to remedy their illness
should not become a pleasure which enslaves them.
They should consider themselves richer,
since they are now more robust in putting up with privations.
For it is better to need less than to have more.

Chapter Four

1. Do not allow your clothing to attract attention;
seek to please not by the clothes you wear,
but by the life you live.

2. Whenever you leave the house, go together;

125 cum ueneritis quo itis, simul state.

3. In incessu, in statu, in omnibus motibus uestris
nihil fiant quod cuiusquam offendat aspectum,
sed quod uestram decet sanctitatem.

4. Oculi uestri,
130 et si iaciuntur in aliquam feminarum,
figantur in nemine.
Neque enim, quando proceditis,
feminas uidere prohibemini,
sed adpetere, aut ab ipsis adpeti uelle,
135 criminosum est.²⁰
Nec solo tactu et affectu, sed aspectu quoque,
adpetitur et adpetit concupiscentia feminarum.
Nec dicatis uos animos habere pudicos,
si habetis oculos inpudicos,
140 quia inpudicus oculus inpudici cordis est nuntius.
Et cum se inuicem sibi, etiam tacente lingua,
conspectu mutuo corda nuntiant inpudica,
et secundum concupiscentiam carnis
alterutro delectantur ardore,
145 etiam intactis ab inmunda uiolatione corporibus,
fugit castitas ipsa de moribus.

5. Nec putare debet qui in femina figit oculum
et illius in se ipse diligit fixum,
ab aliis se non uideri, cum hoc facit;
150 uidetur omnino, et a quibus se uideri non arbitratur.
Sed ecce lateat et a nemine hominum uideatur,
quid faciet de illo desuper inspectore
quem latere nihil potest?²¹
An ideo putandus est non uidere,
155 quia tanto uidet patientius, quanto sapientius?
Illi ergo uir sanctus timeat displicere,²²
ne uelit feminae male placere.
Illum cogitet omnia uidere,
ne uelit feminam male uidere.
160 Illius namque et in hac causa conmendatus est timor,
ubi scriptum est:
'Abominatio est domino defigens oculum.'²³

²⁰ Matt. 5: 28.   ²¹ Prov. 24: 12.

wherever you are going, stay together.

3. In your walk, posture, all external comportment,
do nothing to offend anyone who sees you.
Act in a manner worthy of your holy profession.

4. When you see a woman,
do not fix your eyes on her or any woman.
You are not forbidden to see women
when you are out of the house.
It is wrong, however, to desire women
or to wish them to desire you.[20]
Lust for women is mutually stimulated
not only by tender touches but by sight as well.
Make no claim to a pure mind when your eyes are impure;
an impure eye is the herald of an impure heart.
Unchaste hearts reveal themselves by exchanging glances
even without any words; people yield to lust
as they delight in their passion for each other.
Chastity takes to its heels, even though
their bodies remain unsullied by unchaste actions.

5. The man who directs his attention towards a woman
and enjoys her similar token of affection
should not think others fail to notice this mutual exchange.
He is certainly observed
even by persons he thinks do not see him.
But if his actions escape the notice of men and women,
what will he do about the One who keeps watch on high,
from whom nothing can be hidden?[21]
Is God therefore blind,
because he looks on with patience
proportionate to his wisdom?
The holy man should fear to displease God,[22]
lest he desire to please a woman sinfully.
So as not to look upon a woman in a sinful manner,
let him bear in mind that God sees everything.
Fear of the Lord is recommended in this matter too
where we read in the Scriptures:
'The Lord abhors a covetous eye.'[23]

[22] Prov. 24: 18.   [23] LXX Prov. 27: 20.

6. Quando ergo simul estis in ecclesia
et ubicumque ubi et feminae sunt,
165   inuicem uestram pudicitiam custodite;
deus enim qui habitat in uobis,
etiam isto modo uos custodiet ex uobis.[24]

7. Et si hanc de qua loquor oculi petulantiam
in aliquo uestrum aduerteritis, statim admonete,
170   ne coepta progrediatur, sed de proximo corrigatur.[25]

8. Si autem et post admonitionem iterum,
uel alio quocumque die, id ipsum eum facere uideritis,
iam uelut uulneratum sanandum prodat,
quicumque hoc potuit inuenire;
175   prius tamen et alteri uel tertio demonstratum,
ut duorum uel trium possit ore conuinci
et conpetenti seueritate coherceri.[26]
Nec uos iudicetis esse maliuolos, quando hoc indicatis.
Magis quippe innocentes non estis,
180   si fratres uestros, quos indicando corrigere potestis,
tacendo perire permittitis.
Si enim frater tuus uulnus haberet in corpore,
quod uellet occultare, cum timet secari,
nonne crudeliter abs te sileretur
185   et misericorditer indicaretur?
Quanto ergo potius eum debes manifestare,
ne perniciosius putrescat in corde?

9. Sed antequam aliis demonstretur,
per quos conuincendus est, si negauerit,
190   prius praeposito debet ostendi,

---

[24] 2 Cor. 6: 16.   [25] Matt. 18: 15.   [26] Matt. 18: 16–17.

6. Mutually safeguard your purity,
when you are together in church
and wherever women are present.
God, who dwells in you, will protect you
in this way too by your mutual vigilance.[24]

7. If you notice in any of your number
this roving eye referred to above,
immediately admonish the individual
and correct the matter as soon as possible,
in order to curb its progress.[25]

8. If, after this warning, you observe him
doing the same thing again or at any other time,
whoever happens to discover this must report the offender,
as if he were now a wounded person in need of healing.
But first, one or two others should be told
so that the witness of two or three may lend greater weight,
and the delinquent thus be convicted
and punished with appropriate severity.[26]
Do not consider yourselves unkind
when you point out such faults. Quite the contrary,
you are not without fault yourselves
when you permit your brothers to perish
because of your silence.
Were you to point out their misdeeds,
correction would at least be possible.
If your brother had a bodily wound
which he wished to conceal for fear of surgery,
would not your silence be cruel
and your disclosure merciful?
Your obligation to reveal the matter
is, therefore, all the greater
in order to stem the more harmful infection in the heart.

9. If he neglects to mend his ways
after such admonition,
he should first be reported to the superior,
before his behaviour is revealed to others
whose task it is to expose his failing
in the event of his denial,

si admonitus neglexerit corrigi, ne forte possit,
secretius correptus, non innotescere ceteris.
Si autem negauerit,
tunc nescienti adhibendi sunt alii,
195 ut iam coram omnibus possit,²⁷
non ab uno teste argui, sed a duobus uel tribus conuinci.²⁸
Conuictus uero, secundum praepositi, uel etiam presbyteri
ad cuius dispensationem pertinet arbitrium,
debet emendatoriam sustinere uindictam.
200 Quam si ferre recusauerit,
etiam si ipse non abscesserit,
de uestra societate proiciatur.²⁹
Non enim et hoc fit crudeliter, sed misericorditer,
ne contagione pestifera plurimos perdat.

205 10. Et hoc quod dixi de oculo non figendo
etiam in ceteris inueniendis, prohibendis,
indicandis, conuincendis uindicandisque peccatis,
diligenter et fideliter obseruetur,
cum dilectione hominum et odio uitiorum.

210 11. Quicumque autem in tantum progressus fuerit malum,
ut occulte ab aliqua
litteras uel quaelibet munuscula accipiat,
si hoc ultro confitetur,
parcatur illi et oretur pro illo;
215 si autem deprehenditur atque conuincitur,
secundum arbitrium presbyteri uel praepositi
grauius emendetur.

V

1. Vestes uestras in unum habete,
sub uno custode uel duobus uel quod sufficere potuerint
220 ad eas excutiendas, ne a tinea laedantur;
et sicut pascimini ex uno cellario,
sic induimini ex uno uestiario.
Et, si fieri potest, non ad uos pertineat,
quid uobis induendum pro temporis congruentia proferatur,

---

²⁷ 1 Tim. 5: 20.   ²⁸ Matt. 18: 16.   ²⁹ Matt. 18: 17.

so that, if possible, with a private correction,
the others may not become aware of his misconduct.
But if he denies the charge,
then the others are to be summoned without his knowledge
so that he can be accused in the presence of all,[27]
not by a single witness but by two or three.[28]
When convicted, he must submit
to the salutary punishment determined by
the judgement of the superior, or even that of the priest
whose authority embraces such matters.
If he refuses to submit to punishment
even if he is determined not to leave,
expel him from your society.[29]
Even this is not an act of cruelty but of mercy:
to prevent the contagion of his life
from infecting more people.

10. Diligently and faithfully, then,
attend to my words about suggestive glances at women.
Such advice holds also for detection, prevention, disclosure,
proof, and punishment of other offences,
with love for the person and hatred for the sin.

11. Whenever anyone has gone so far in misconduct
as to receive secretly from any woman
letters or small gifts of any kind,
if he confesses the matter freely,
pardon him and pray for him.
If, however, he is detected and proved guilty,
he is to be rather severely corrected
according to the judgement of the priest or the superior.

Chapter Five

1. Keep your clothes in one place
under the care of one or two,
or as many people as may be needed to air them out
and prevent damage from moths.
Just as a single storeroom furnishes your food,
so a single wardrobe should supply your clothing.
Pay as little attention as possible
to the clothes you receive as the season requires.

225 utrum hoc recipiat unusquisque uestrum quod deposuerat,
an aliud quod alter habuerat;
dum tamen unicuique, quod cuique opus est, non negetur.[30]
Si autem hinc inter uos contentiones et murmura oriuntur,
cum queritur aliquis
230 deterius se accepisse quam prius habuerat
et indignum se esse qui ita uestiatur,
sicut alius frater eius uestiebatur,
hinc uos probate quantum uobis desit
in illo interiore sancto habitu cordis,
235 qui pro habitu corporis litigatis.
Tamen si uestra toleratur infirmitas,
ut hoc recipiatis, quod posueritis,
in uno tamen loco, sub communibus custodibus
habete quod ponitis.

240 2. Ita sane, ut nullus sibi aliquid operetur,
sed omnia opera uestra in commune fiant,
maiore studio et frequentiori alacritate,
quam si uobis singuli propria faceretis.
Caritas enim, de qua scriptum est
245 quod 'non quaerat quae sua sunt', sic intelligitur,[31]
quia communia propriis, non propria communibus anteponit.
Et ideo, quanto amplius
rem communem quam propria uestra curaueritis,
tanto uos amplius profecisse noueritis;
250 ut in omnibus quibus utitur transitura necessitas,
superimineat, quae permanet, caritas.[32]

3. Consequens ergo est ut etiam si quis suis filiis,
uel aliqua necessitudine ad se pertinentibus,
in monasterio constitutis,
255 aliquid contulerit, uel aliquam uestem,
siue quodlibet aliud inter necessaria deputandum,
non occulte accipiatur,
sed sit in potestate praepositi,
ut, in re communi redactum,[33]
260 cui necessarium fuerit, praebeatur.[34]

4. Indumenta uestra

---

[30] Acts 4: 35.   [31] 1 Cor. 13: 5.   [32] 1 Cor. 13: 13.
[33] Acts 4: 32.   [34] Acts 4: 35.

Whether each of you receives what he had turned in
or what was worn by someone else is of little concern,
so long as no one is denied what he needs.[30]
If arguments and grumbling occur among you,
and someone complains
that he has received worse clothing than previously
and that it is beneath his dignity to be dressed
in clothes which another brother was wearing,
you thereby demonstrate to yourselves how deficient you are
in the holy and interior clothing of the heart,
arguing as you do about clothes for the body.
Even though one caters to your weakness
and you receive the same clothing,
you are to keep clothes
you are not wearing at the present time
in one place under common supervision.

2. In this way, let no one work for himself alone,
but all your work shall be for the common purpose,
done with greater zeal and more concentrated effort
than if each one worked for his private purpose.
The Scriptures tell us: 'Love is not self-seeking.'[31]
We understand this to mean:
the common good takes precedence over the individual good,
the individual good yields to the common good. Here again,
you will know the extent of your progress
as you enlarge your concern for the common interest
instead of your own private interest;
enduring love will govern all matters
pertaining to the fleeting necessities of life.[32]

3. Consequently, whenever anyone brings anything
to sons or relations who reside in the monastery,
an article of clothing,
or anything else that is considered necessary
the gift is not to be pocketed on the sly
but given to the superior as common property,[33]
so that it can be given to whoever needs it.[34]

4. The washing and cleaning of your clothes
may be done in the monastery or at the laundry.

secundum arbitrium praepositi lauentur,
siue a uobis, siue a fullonibus,
ne interiores animae sordes
265 contrahat mundae uestis nimius adpetitus.

5. Lauacrum etiam corporum,
cuius infirmitatis necessitas cogit, minime denegetur,
sed fiat sine murmure de consilio medicinae,
ita ut, etiam si nolit, iubente praeposito,
270 faciat quod faciendum est pro salute.
Si autem uelit, et forte non expedit,
suae cupiditati non oboediat.
Aliquando enim, etiam si noceat,
prodesse creditur quod delectat.

275 6. Denique, si latens est dolor in corpore,
famulo dei, dicenti quid sibi doleat,
sine dubitatione credatur;
sed tamen, utrum sanando illi dolori,
quod delectat expediat,
280 si non est certum, medicus consulatur.

7. Nec eant ad balneas,
siue quocumque ire necesse fuerit,
minus quam duo uel tres.
Nec ille qui habet aliquo eundi necessitatem,
285 cum quibus ipse uoluerit,
sed cum quibus praepositus iusserit, ire debebit.

8. Aegrotantium cura,
siue post aegritudinem reficiendorum,
siue aliqua inbecillitate,
290 etiam sine febribus, laborantium,
uni alicui debet iniungi,
ut ipse de cellario petat,
quod cuique opus esse perspexerit.

9. Siue autem qui cellario, siue qui uestibus,
295 siue qui codicibus praeponuntur,
sine murmure seruiant fratribus suis.

10. Codices certa hora singulis diebus petantur;
extra horam qui petierit, non accipiat.

The superior decides
how often your clothes are to be laundered,
lest an inordinate desire for clean clothes
inwardly stain your soul.

5. Nor shall the body be denied proper hygienic care
as standards for good health require.
Do this without grumbling,
following the advice of a physician.
In the event a brother is unwilling to comply
and the superior gives strict orders,
he shall do what has to be done for his health.
If a brother desires something which is harmful,
he ought not to satisfy his desire.
Desires are sometimes thought to be salubrious
when they are really injurious.

6. Whenever a servant of God says he is not feeling well,
take his word without hesitation,
even though the source of the pain is not apparent.
If uncertainty continues
whether or not the remedy he desires
would really make him better, consult a physician.

7. Whenever necessity requires a visit
to the public baths or any other place,
no fewer than two or three should go.
When someone has to leave the house, he ought to go
with companions designated by the superior,
not with persons of his own choosing.

8. Care of the sick, whether the convalescent
or those currently ill with any ailment,
even though they are not running a temperature,
shall be assigned to someone
who shall personally obtain from the storeroom
whatever he regards necessary for each individual.

9. Those responsible for food, clothing, or books
are to serve their brothers without grumbling.

10. Books are to be requested at a definite hour each day;
requests made at other times will be denied.

11. Vestimenta uero et calciamenta,
300 quando fuerint indigentibus necessaria,
dare non differant,
sub quorum custodia sunt quae poscuntur.

VI

1. Lites aut nullas habeatis,
aut quam celerrime finiatis,
305 ne ira crescat in odium,
et trabem faciat de festuca,[35]
et animam faciat homicidam.
Sic enim legitis:
'Qui odit fratrem suum homicida est.'[36]

310 2. Quicumque conuicio, uel maledicto,
uel etiam criminis obiectu, alterum laesit,
meminerit satisfactione quantocius curare quod fecit,
et ille qui laesus est, sine disceptatione dimittere.
Si autem inuicem se laeserunt,
315 inuicem sibi debita relaxare debebunt,[37]
propter orationes uestras,
quas utique, quanto crebriores habetis,
tanto saniores habere debetis.
Melior est autem qui, quamuis ira saepe temptatur,
320 tamen inpetrare festinat, ut sibi dimittat,
cui se fecisse agnoscit iniuriam,
quam qui tardius irascitur
et ad ueniam petendam difficilius inclinatur.
Qui autem numquam uult petere ueniam,
325 aut non ex animo petit,[38]
sine causa est in monasterio,
etiam si inde non proiciatur.
Proinde uobis a uerbis durioribus parcite;
quae si emissa fuerint ex ore uestro,
330 non pigeat ex ipso ore proferre medicamenta,
unde facta sunt uulnera.

3. Quando autem necessitas disciplinae,
minoribus cohercendis, dicere uos uerba dura conpellit,
si etiam in ipsis modum uos excessisse sentitis,

[35] Matt. 7: 3–5.   [36] I John 3: 15.   [37] Matt. 6: 12.   [38] Matt. 18: 35.

11. Those responsible for clothes and shoes
shall promptly honour the request for either
when anyone expresses the need.

Chapter Six

1. Either have no quarrels
or put an end to them as quickly as possible,
lest anger grow into hatred,
make timber of a splinter,[35]
and turn the soul into the soul of a murderer.
Thus you read:
'Anyone who hates his brother is a murderer.'[36]

2. Whoever has offended another
with insults or harmful words, or even a serious accusation,
must remember to right the wrong he has done
at the earliest opportunity.
The injured must remember to forgive
without further bickering.
If they have offended each other,
they shall mutually forgive their offences[37]
for the sake of your prayers.
The more frequent your prayers are,
the sounder they ought to be.
An individual who is prone to anger,
yet hastens to beg forgiveness
from someone he has consciously harmed,
is better than another who is less inclined to anger
and less likely to ask pardon.
An individual who absolutely refuses to ask pardon,
or does so without meaning it,[38]
is entirely out of place in the monastery,
even if he is not dismissed.
Spare yourselves the use of words too harsh.
If they have escaped your lips,
those same lips should promptly
heal the wounds they have caused.

3. Requirements of discipline may compel you
to speak harsh words to correct young people.
Even if you feel your criticism has been immoderate,

335 non a uobis exigitur, ut ab eis ueniam postuletis,
     ne apud eos quos oportet esse subiectos,
     dum nimia seruatur humilitas,
     regendi frangatur auctoritas.
     Sed tamen petenda uenia est ab omnium domino,
340 qui nouit etiam eos, quos plus iusto forte corripitis,
     quanta beniuolentia diligatis.
     Non autem carnalis, sed spiritalis
     inter uos debet esse dilectio.

VII

1. Praeposito tamquam patri oboediatur,[39]
345 honore seruato, ne in illo offendatur deus;
     multo magis presbytero, qui omnium uestrum curam gerit.

2. Ut ergo cuncta ista seruentur et,
   si quid seruatum non fuerit,
   non neglegenter praetereatur,
350 sed emendandum corrigendumque curetur,
     ad praepositum praecipue pertinebit;
     ita, ut ad presbyterum,
     cuius est apud uos maior auctoritas,
     referat, quod modum uel uires eius excedit.

355 3. Ipse uero qui uobis praeest,
     non se existimet potestate dominantem,[40]
     sed caritate seruientem felicem.[41]
     Honore coram uobis praelatus sit uobis,
     timore coram deo substratus sit pedibus uestris.
360 Circa omnes seipsum bonorum operum praebeat exemplum,[42]
     corripiat inquietos, consoletur pusillianimes,
     suscipiat infirmos, patiens sit ad omnes.[43]
     Disciplinam libens habeat, metum inponat.
     Et quamuis utrumque sit necessarium,
365 tamen plus a uobis amari adpetat quam timeri,
     semper cogitans deo se pro uobis
     redditurum esse rationem.[44]

4. Unde uos magis oboediendo,
   non solum uestri, uerum etiam ipsius miseremini,[45]

---

[39] Heb. 13: 17.   [40] Luke 22: 25–6.   [41] Gal. 5: 13.   [42] Titus 2: 7.

you are not obliged to ask their pardon;
too much attention to humility in their regard
would undermine their ready acceptance of your authority.
Instead, ask forgiveness from the Lord of all
who knows how generously you love
even those you may correct too harshly.
Your love for one another ought to be spiritual, not carnal.

Chapter Seven

1. Obey your superior as a father,[39]
always with the respect worthy of his position,
so as not to offend God in him.
Be especially obedient to the priest
who bears responsibility for all of you.

2. The superior has the principal task
of seeing to it that all these precepts are observed.
He should further provide
that infractions are not carelessly overlooked
but punished and corrected. He must refer
matters which exceed his competence and power
to the priest who has greater authority over you.

3. Your superior should regard himself to be fortunate
as one who serves you in love,[41]
not as one who exercises authority over you.[40]
Accord him the first place of honour among you,
but in fear before God
he shall lie prostrate beneath your feet.
Let him be a model of good deeds for everyone:[42]
he shall restrain the restless,
cheer the fainthearted, support the weak,
with patience towards all.[43]
He shall willingly embrace discipline and instil fear.
While both are necessary, he shall strive, nevertheless,
to be loved by you rather than feared, mindful always
that he will be accountable to God for you.[44]

4. By being obedient, you manifest more compassion
not only for yourselves, but also for him,[45]

[43] I Thess. 5: 14.   [44] Heb. 13: 17.   [45] Sir. 30: 24.

370 quia inter uos, quanto in loco superiore,
    tanto in periculo maiore uersatur.

VIII

1. Donet dominus,
   ut obseruetis haec omnia cum dilectione,
   tamquam spiritalis pulchritudinis amatores[46]
375 et bono Christi odore[47] de bona conuersatione flagrantes,[48]
   non sicut serui sub lege,
   sed sicut liberi sub gratia constituti.[49]

2. Ut autem uos in hoc libello
   tamquam in speculo possitis inspicere,
380 ne per obliuionem aliquid neglegatis,[50]
   semel in septimana uobis legatur.
   Et ubi uos inueneritis ea quae scripta sunt facientes,
   agite gratias domino bonorum omnium largitori.
   Ubi autem sibi quicumque uestrum uidet aliquid deesse,
385 doleat de praeterito, caueat de futuro,
   orans ut ei debitum dimittatur
   et in temptationem non inducatur.[51]

---

[46] Sir. 44: 6.   [47] 2 Cor. 2: 15.   [48] 1 Pet. 3: 16.
[49] Rom. 6: 14–22.   [50] Jas. 1: 23–5.   [51] Matt. 6: 12–13.

because the higher position among you
is all the more perilous.

Chapter Eight

1. The Lord grant you the grace
to observe these precepts with love
as lovers of spiritual beauty,[46]
exuding the fragrance of Christ[47]
in the goodness of your lives;[48]
you are no longer slaves under the law,
but a people living in freedom under grace.[49]

2. These precepts should be read to you once a week,
so that you will see yourselves
in this little book as in a mirror
and not neglect anything through forgetfulness.[50]
When you find yourselves doing what has been written here,
thank the Lord, the giver of all good gifts.
However, if anyone of you realizes
that he has failed on a specific point,
let him be sorry for the past, safeguard the future,
and continue to pray for his offences to be forgiven,
and that he not be led into temptation.[51]

Obiurgatio

. . . Augustinus in domino salutem.

1. Sicut parata est seueritas peccata quae inuenerit uindicare, ita non uult caritas quod uindicet inuenire. Haec causa fecit ut ad uos non uenirem, cum meam praesentiam quaereretis, non ad pacis uestrae gaudium sed ad dissensionis uestrae augmentum. Quomodo enim contemnerem et impunitum relinquerem, si, et me praesente, tantus uester tumultus existeret, quantus, me absente, etsi oculos meos latuit, tamen aures meas uestris uocibus uerberauit? Nam fortassis etiam maior esset uestra seditio in praesentia mea, quando necesse esset uobis non concedi quod in perniciosissimum exemplum, contra sanam disciplinam, quod uobis non expedit, petebatis, ac sic non quales uolo inuenirem uos et ipse inuenirer a uobis qualem non uolebatis.[52]

2. Cum ergo scribit Apostolus ad Corinthios dicens: Testem deum facio super animam meam quia parcens uobis nondum ueni Corinthum, non quia dominamur fidei uestrae, sed cooperatores sumus gaudii uestri,[53] hoc etiam ego dico uobis quia parcens uobis non ad uos ueni. Peperci etiam mihi, ne tristitiam super tristitiam de uobis haberem,[54] et elegi non exhibere faciem meam uobis, sed effundere cor meum deo pro uobis, et causam magni periculi uestri, non apud uos uerbis, sed apud deum lacrimis agere,[55] ne conuertat in luctum guadium meum quo soleo gaudere de uobis et inter tanta scandala, quibus ubique abundat hic mundus, aliquantulum consolari, cogitans copiosam congregationem et castam dilectionem et sanctam conuersationem uestram et largiorem gratiam dei quae data est uobis, ut non solum nuptias carnales contemneretis, uerum etiam eligeretis societatem in domo unanimes habitandi,[56] ut sit uobis anima una et cor unum in deum.[57]

3. Haec in uobis bona, haec dei dona considerans, inter multas tempestates, quibus ex aliis malis quatitur, cor meum solet utcumque requiescere. Currebatis bene. Quis uos fascinauit? Suasio illa non est ex deo qui uocauit uos. Modicum fermenti[58]— nolo dicere quod sequitur. Hoc enim magis cupio et oro et hortor,

---

[52] 2 Cor. 12: 20.   [53] 2 Cor. 1: 23–4.   [54] Phil. 2: 27.   [55] Lam. 2: 19.
[56] Ps. 67: 7.   [57] Acts 4: 32.   [58] Gal. 5: 7–9, 3: 1.

Reprimand to Quarrelling Nuns

. . . Augustine sends greetings in the Lord.

1. As severity is ready to punish the faults it may discover, so love is reluctant to discover the faults it must punish. This is my reason for not visiting you when you requested me to come. Instead of rejoicing in your peace, my presence would only have heightened your dissension. How could I make light of it or leave it unpunished if there were to be, in my presence, a tumult as great as that which, in my absence, beat upon my ears with your words, even though my eyes did not see it? Perhaps your rebellion would have been more serious, had I been present. There would be no choice granted me in this matter. Your demands were at variance with your own best interests and they set a dangerous precedent for sound discipline. I should not have found you as I desire, and you would have found me such as you do not desire.[52]

2. The Apostle wrote the following words to the Corinthians: 'I appeal to God and stake my life upon what I am going to say. It was out of consideration for you that I did not after all come to Corinth. Do not think we are dictating the terms of your faith; we are working with you for your own happiness'.[53] I send you the same message: I stayed away 'out of consideration for you'. I have thereby taken consideration of myself too so as to spare myself 'sorrow upon sorrow' from you.[54] I chose not to show my face to you but to pour out my heart to God for you and to plead this perilous case of yours, not in words before you but in tears before God.[55] Here is my plea: may he not turn into grief the great joy I usually experience over you and the little comfort I take in the thick of scandals which infest this world. Your large community, your chaste love, the holiness of your lives, the more than generous grace of God which enables you not only to renounce marriage but also to choose 'living together in harmony under the same roof',[56] so as to have 'one heart and one soul seeking God',[57]—these thoughts have been my measure of consolation.

3. When I reflect upon these blessings of yours, these gifts of God, my heart usually finds some rest from the many other evils which disturb it. 'You were running well; who was it bewitched you? Whatever persuasion he used, it did not come from God who is calling you. A little leaven . . .'.[58] I refuse to finish the sentence.

ut ipsum fermentum reuertatur in melius, non tota massa, sicut paene iam fecerat, conuertatur in peius. Si ergo repullulastis sanum sapere,[59] orate ne intretis in temptationem,[60] ne iterum in contentiones, aemulationes, animositates, dissensiones, detractiones, seditiones, susurrationes.[61] Non enim sic plantauimus et rigauimus hortum dominicum in uobis,[62] ut spinas istas metamus ex uobis.[63] Si autem adhuc uestra tumultuatur infirmitas, orate ut eruamini de temptatione.[64] Quae autem conturbant uos, si adhuc uos conturbant, nisi se correxerint, portabunt iudicium, quaecumque illae fuerint.[65]

4. Cogitate quid mali sit ut, cum de Donatistis in unitate gaudeamus, interna schismata in monasterio lugeamus. Perseuerate in bono proposito, et non desiderabitis mutare praepositam, quam in monasterio illo habendo, per tam multos annos perseuerantes, uos et numero et aetate creuistis, quae uos mater non utero sed animo suscepit. Omnes enim quae illuc uenistis, ibi eam, aut sanctae praepositae sorori meae seruientem, placentem, aut etiam ipsam praepositam quae uos susciperet, inuenistis. Sub illa estis eruditae, sub illa uelatae, sub illa multiplicatae, et sic tumultuamini ut uobis eam mutetis, cum lugere debueratis si eam uobis mutare uellemus. Ipsa est quam nostis, ipsa est ad quam uenistis, ipsa est quam per tot annos habendo creuistis. Nouum non accepistis nisi praepositum. Aut si propter illum quaeritis nouitatem et in eius inuidia contra matrem uestram sic rebellastis, cur non potius hoc petistis ut uobis ipse mutetur? Si autem hoc exhorretis, quia noui quomodo eum in Christo uenerabiliter diligatis, cur non potius illud?

In uobis namque regendis sic praepositi rudimenta turbantur, ut magis uelit uos ipse deserere, quam istam ex uobis famam et inuidiam sustinere, ut dicatur non uos aliam quaesituras fuisse praepositam, nisi ipsum coepissetis habere praepositum. Tranquillet ergo deus et componat animos uestros. Non in uobis praeualeat opus diaboli,[66] sed pax Christi uincat in cordibus uestris,[67] nec

[59] Phil. 4: 10.   [60] Matt. 26: 41.   [61] 2 Cor. 12: 20.   [62] 1 Cor. 3: 6–9.
[63] Jer. 12: 13.   [64] 2 Pet. 2: 9, Ps. 17: 30.   [65] Gal. 5: 10.
[66] 1 John 3: 8.   [67] Col. 3: 15.

Indeed, this is my desire, my prayer, my exhortation: that the leaven itself will turn back towards a better course, instead of the whole lump, as it nearly had done, turning to a worse course. If sound wisdom has blossomed afresh in you,[59] pray that you may be spared the test,[60] and fall not again into quarrelling and jealousy, angry tempers and personal rivalries, backbiting, general disorder, hushed comments about one another.[61] For we have not planted and watered the Lord's garden in you[62] only to reap these thorns from you.[63] If your weakness, however, still stirs up a tempest, pray to be delivered from the test.[64] The women who are unsettling your minds, if they persist in this matter, whoever they are, they will bear judgement unless they change their behaviour.[65]

4. When we rejoice over unity with the Donatists, consider what a misfortune it is to mourn internal schism in the monastery. Stand firm in your good resolution and you will no longer desire the removal of your superior. By having her in that monastery you have persevered and grown for so many years in numbers and in age; she has borne you as a mother, not in her womb but in her mind. When all of you came there you found her either serving the holy superior, my sister, in an acceptable manner, or welcoming yourselves after she had become superior herself. She guided your early training; she supervised your taking of the veil; you saw your numbers increase and now you are on the verge of riot for us to remove her. If I took the initiative in this matter, you ought to lament my action. You know her firsthand, you first came to her, your numbers have increased all these years with her leadership.

The priest-superior is your only new official. If you are seeking the removal of your Mother on his account and jealousy for him is the reason for rebellion against her, why not request his transfer instead? If such a thought terrifies you, for I know the extent of your love and reverence for him in Christ, why are you not equally horrified at the thought of asking for her removal? The priest-superior's efforts to guide you are so thwarted that he has greater reason for leaving you than for putting up with the invidious reputation you establish. People say that you would not have sought another superior, were it not for the fact that he became your priest-superior.

May God, therefore, calm and compose your minds! Do not allow the work of the devil to gain the upper hand among you.[66] 'May the peace of Christ conquer in your hearts'.[67] Do not blush

dolore animi, quia non fit quod uultis, uel quia pudet uoluisse quod uelle non debuistis, erubescendo curratis in mortem, sed potius paenitendo resumatis salutem, nec habeatis paenitentiam Iudae traditoris,[68] sed potius lacrimas Petri pastoris.[69]

[68] Matt. 27: 3-5.   [69] Matt. 26: 75.

with shame and rush headlong to death because you are upset with the failure to fulfil your wishes, or because you are ashamed of your wish for something you ought not to have wished for. Instead, recover your salvation by repentance, not the repentance of Judas the traitor,[68] but the tears of Peter the shepherd.[69]

Rule for Nuns*

Chapter One

1. Here are the rules we lay down for your observance, once you have been admitted to the monastery.

2. The chief motivation for your sharing life together is to live harmoniously in the house,[70] and to have one heart and one soul seeking God.[71]

3. Do not call anything your own; possess everything in common.[72] Your superior ought to provide each of you[73] with food and clothing,[74] not on an equal basis to all, because all do not enjoy the same health, but to each one in proportion to her need.[75] For you read in the Acts of the Apostles: 'They possessed everything in common',[76] and 'Distribution was made to each in proportion to each one's need'.[77]

4. Those who owned anything in the world should freely consent to possess everything in common in the monastery.

5. Those who had nothing should not seek in the monastery possessions which were beyond their reach outside. Allowance should be made for their frailty, however, on the basis of individual need, even if previous poverty never permitted them to satisfy those needs. But they should not consider their present good fortune to consist in the possession of food and clothing which were beyond their means elsewhere.

6. Nor should they put their nose in the air because they associate with people they did not dare approach in the world. Instead they should lift up their heart,[78] and not pursue hollow worldly concerns. Monasteries should not provide advantages for the rich to the disadvantage of the poor. Such would be the case if the rich become humble and the poor become proud.

7. But on the other hand, those who enjoyed some measure of worldly success ought not to belittle their sisters who come to this holy society from a condition of poverty. They should endeavour

---

* This translation presents the basic masculine text as in time adapted for nuns through changes of grammatical gender and the substitution of feminine vocabulary, for example, 'sister' for 'brother', but stripped of later interpolations which recent textual criticism disallows.

[70] Ps. 67: 7.   [71] Acts 4: 32a.   [72] Acts 4: 32b–c.   [73] Acts 4: 35.
[74] I Tim. 6: 8.   [75] Acts 4: 35.   [76] Acts 4: 32.   [77] Acts 4: 35.
[78] Col. 3: 1–2.

to boast about the fellowship of poor sisters, rather than the social standing of rich relations. They are not to think well of themselves if they have contributed to the common life from their wealth. Sharing their possessions with the monastery ought not to become a greater source of pride than if they enjoyed these goods in the world. As a matter of fact, every other vice produces evil deeds with a view to doing evil, but pride sets a trap for good deeds as well with a view to destroying them. What benefit is there in giving generously to the poor and becoming poor oneself, if the pitiful soul is more inclined to pride by rejecting riches than by possessing them?

8. Live then, all of you, in harmony and concord;[79] honour God mutually in each other; you have become his temples.[80]

Chapter Two

1. Be assiduous in prayer[81] at the scheduled hours and times.

2. No one has any business in the prayer-room apart from the particular purpose which it serves; that is why it is called the oratory. Consequently, if some wish to pray even outside the scheduled periods, during their free time, they should not be deterred by people who think they have some other task there.

3. When you pray to God in psalms and hymns, the words you speak should be alive in your hearts.

4. Keep to the prescribed text when you sing; avoid texts which are not suited for singing.

Chapter Three

1. To the extent that your health allows, subdue your flesh by fasting and abstinence from food and drink. If anyone is unable to fast, let her at least take no food between meals, unless she is sick.

2. Listen to the customary reading from the beginning to the end of the meal without commotion or arguments. Food is not for the mouth alone;[82] your ears also should hunger for the Word of God.[83]

3. No one is to be annoyed, nor should it seem to be unjust, when a special diet is provided for sisters whose health has been adversely affected by their former status in life. A different background endows some people with greater physical strength.

[79] Acts 4: 32; Rom. 15: 6.   [80] 2 Cor. 6: 16.   [81] Col. 4: 2.
[82] Matt. 4: 4.   [83] Amos 8: 11.

These should not consider others fortunate because they see concessions granted to their sisters and not to themselves. Let them be thankful rather that they have the strength to endure what others cannot.

4. If food, clothes, a mattress, or blankets are given to those who come to the monastery from a more comfortable manner of life, the more robust individuals, to whom such things are not given and who are on this account more fortunate, ought to recall how much affluent people have altered their lifestyle in order to embrace the present one, even though the frugality practised by the stronger sisters continues to elude them. No one should desire the extras given to a few, more out of tolerance than out of deference. Deplorable disorder would occur, if the monastery provided a setting, to the extent that it is possible, where the wealthy become workers, while the poor become pampered.

5. Sick people necessarily take less food so as not to aggravate their condition. During convalescence they are to receive such care as will quickly restore their health, even if they come from the lowest level of poverty in the world. Recent illness has afflicted them with the same frailty which the wealthy possess from their previous manner of life. When sick people have fully recovered, they should return to their happier ways, which are all the more fitting for God's servants to the extent that they have fewer needs. Food formerly necessary to remedy their illness should not become a pleasure which enslaves them. They should consider themselves richer, since they are now more robust in putting up with privations. For it is better to need less than to have more.

Chapter Four

1. Do not allow your clothing to attract attention; seek to please not by the clothes you wear, but by the life you live.

2. Whenever you leave the house, go together; wherever you are going, stay together.

3. In your walk, posture, all external comportment, do nothing to offend anyone who sees you. Act in a manner worthy of your holy profession.

4. When you see a man, do not fix your eyes on him or any man. You are not forbidden to see men when you are out of the house. It is wrong, however, to desire men or to wish them to desire

you.[84] Lust for men is mutually stimulated not only by tender touches but by sight as well. Make no claim to a pure mind when your eyes are impure; an impure eye is the herald of an impure heart. Unchaste hearts reveal themselves by exchanging glances even without any words; people yield to lust as they delight in their passion for each other. Chastity takes to its heels, even though their bodies remain unsullied by unchaste actions.

5. The woman who directs her attention towards a man and enjoys his similar token of affection should not think others fail to notice this mutual exchange. She is certainly observed even by persons she thinks do not see her. But if her actions escape the notice of men and women, what will she do about the One who keeps watch on high, from whom nothing can be hidden?[85] Is God therefore blind, because he looks on with patience proportionate to his wisdom? The holy woman should fear to displease God,[86] lest she desire to please a man sinfully. So as not to look upon a man in a sinful manner, let her bear in mind that God sees everything. Fear of the Lord is recommended in this matter too where we read in the Scriptures: 'The Lord abhors a covetous eye'.[87]

6. Mutually safeguard your purity, when you are together in church and wherever men are present. God, who dwells in you, will protect you in this way too by your mutual vigilance.[88]

7. If you notice in any of your number this roving eye referred to above, immediately admonish the individual and correct the matter as soon as possible, in order to curb its progress.[89]

8. If, after this warning, you observe her doing the same thing again or at any other time, whoever happens to discover this must report the offender, as if she were now a wounded person in need of healing. But first, one or two others should be told so that the witness of two or three may lend greater weight, and the delinquent thus be convicted and punished with appropriate severity.[90] Do not consider yourselves unkind when you point out such faults. Quite the contrary, you are not without fault yourselves when you permit your sisters to perish because of your silence. Were you to point out their misdeeds, correction would at least be possible. If your sister had a bodily wound which she

---

[84] Matt. 5: 28.   [85] Prov. 24: 12.
[86] Prov. 24: 18.   [87] LXX Prov. 27: 20.
[88] 2 Cor. 6: 16.   [89] Matt. 18: 15.   [90] Matt. 18: 16–17.

wished to conceal for fear of surgery, would not your silence be cruel and your disclosure merciful? Your obligation to reveal the matter is, therefore, all the greater in order to stem the more harmful infection in the heart.

9. If she neglects to mend her ways after such admonition, she should first be reported to the superior, before her behaviour is revealed to others whose task it is to expose her failing in the event of her denial, so that, if possible, with a private correction, the others may not become aware of her misconduct. But if she denies the charge, then the others are to be summoned without her knowledge so that she can be accused in the presence of all,[91] not by a single witness but by two or three.[92] When convicted, she must submit to the salutary punishment determined by the judgement of the superior, or even that of the priest whose authority embraces such matters. If she refuses to submit to punishment, even if she is determined not to leave, expel her from your society.[93] Even this is not an act of cruelty but of mercy: to prevent the contagion of her life from infecting more people.

10. Diligently and faithfully, then, attend to my words about suggestive glances at men. Such advice holds also for detection, prevention, disclosure, proof, and punishment of other offences, with love for the person and hatred for the sin.

11. Whenever anyone has gone so far in misconduct as to receive secretly from any man letters or small gifts of any kind, if she confesses the matter freely, pardon her and pray for her. If, however, she is detected and proved guilty, she is to be rather severely corrected according to the judgement of the priest or the superior.

Chapter Five

1. Keep your clothes in one place under the care of one or two, or as many people as may be needed to air them out and prevent damage from moths. Just as a single storeroom furnishes your food, so a single wardrobe should supply your clothing. Pay as little attention as possible to the clothes you receive as the season requires. Whether each of you receives what she had turned in or what was worn by someone else is of little concern, so long as no one is denied what she needs.[94] If arguments and grumbling occur

---

[91] 1 Tim. 5: 20.   [92] Matt. 18: 16.   [93] Matt. 18: 17.   [94] Acts 4: 35.

among you, and someone complains that she has received worse clothing than previously and that it is beneath her dignity to be dressed in clothes which another sister was wearing, you thereby demonstrate to yourselves how deficient you are in the holy and interior clothing of the heart, arguing as you do about clothes for the body. Even though one caters to your weakness and you receive the same clothing, you are to keep clothes you are not wearing at the present time in one place under common supervision.

2. In this way, let no one work for herself alone, but all your work shall be for the common purpose, done with greater zeal and more concentrated effort than if each one worked for her private purpose. The Scriptures tell us: 'Love is not self-seeking'.[95] We understand this to mean: the common good takes precedence over the individual good, the individual good yields to the common good. Here again, you will know the extent of your progress as you enlarge your concern for the common interest instead of your own private interest; enduring love will govern all matters pertaining to the fleeting necessities of life.[96]

3. Consequently, whenever anyone brings anything to daughters or relations who reside in the monastery, an article of clothing, or anything else that is considered necessary, the gift is not to be pocketed on the sly but given to the superior as common property,[97] so that it can be given to whoever needs it.[98]

4. The washing and cleaning of your clothes may be done in the monastery or at the laundry. The superior decides how often your clothes are to be laundered, lest an inordinate desire for clean clothes inwardly stain your soul.

5. Nor shall the body be denied proper hygienic care as standards for good health require. Do this without grumbling, following the advice of a physician. In the event a sister is unwilling to comply and the superior gives strict orders, she shall do what has to be done for her health. If a sister desires something which is harmful, she ought not to satisfy her desire. Desires are sometimes thought to be salubrious when they are really injurious.

6. Whenever a servant of God says she is not feeling well, take her word without hesitation, even though the source of the pain is not apparent. If uncertainty continues whether or not the remedy she desires would really make her better, consult a physician.

[95] 1 Cor. 13: 5.   [96] 1 Cor. 13: 13.   [97] Acts 4: 32.   [98] Acts 4: 35.

7. Whenever necessity requires a visit to the public baths or any other place, no fewer than two or three should go. When someone has to leave the house, she ought to go with companions designated by the superior, not with persons of her own choosing.

8. Care of the sick, whether the convalescent or those currently ill with any ailment, even though they are not running a temperature, shall be assigned to someone who shall personally obtain from the storeroom whatever she regards necessary for each individual.

9. Those responsible for food, clothing, or books are to serve their sisters without grumbling.

10. Books are to be requested at a definite hour each day; requests made at other times will be denied.

11. Those responsible for clothes and shoes shall promptly honour the request for either when anyone expresses the need.

Chapter Six

1. Either have no quarrels or put an end to them as quickly as possible, lest anger grow into hatred, make timber of a splinter,[99] and turn the soul into the soul of a murderer. Thus you read: 'Anyone who hates his brother is a murderer'.[100]

2. Whoever has offended another with insults or harmful words, or even a serious accusation, must remember to right the wrong she has done at the earliest opportunity. The injured must remember to forgive without further bickering. If they have offended each other, they shall mutually forgive their offences[101] for the sake of your prayers. The more frequent your prayers are, the sounder they ought to be. An individual who is prone to anger, yet hastens to beg forgiveness from someone she has consciously harmed, is better than another who is less inclined to anger and less likely to ask pardon. An individual who absolutely refuses to ask pardon, or does so without meaning it,[102] is entirely out of place in the monastery, even if she is not dismissed. Spare yourselves the use of words too harsh. If they have escaped your lips, those same lips should promptly heal the wounds they have caused.

3. Requirements of discipline may compel you to speak harsh words to correct young people. Even if you feel your criticism has

[99] Matt. 7: 3–5.   [100] 1 John 3: 15.   [101] Matt. 6: 12.
[102] Matt. 18: 35.

been immoderate, you are not obliged to ask their pardon; too much attention to humility in their regard would undermine their ready acceptance of your authority. Instead, ask forgiveness from the Lord of all who knows how generously you love even those you may correct too harshly. Your love for one another ought to be spiritual, not carnal.

Chapter Seven

1. Obey your superior as a mother,[103] always with the respect worthy of her position, so as not to offend God in her. Be especially obedient to the priest who bears responsibility for all of you.

2. The superior has the principal task of seeing to it that all these precepts are observed. She should further provide that infractions are not carelessly overlooked but punished and corrected. She must refer matters which exceed her competence and power to the priest who has greater authority over you.

3. Your superior should regard herself to be fortunate as one who serves you in love,[104] not as one who exercises authority over you.[105] Accord her the first place of honour among you, but in fear before God she shall lie prostrate beneath your feet. Let her be a model of good deeds for everyone;[106] she shall restrain the restless, cheer the fainthearted, support the weak, with patience towards all.[107] She shall willingly embrace discipline and instil fear. While both are necessary, she shall strive, nevertheless, to be loved by you rather than feared, mindful always that she will be accountable to God for you.[108]

4. By being obedient, you manifest more compassion not only for yourselves,[109] but also for her, because the higher position among you is all the more perilous.

Chapter Eight

1. The Lord grant you the grace to observe these precepts with love as lovers of spiritual beauty,[110] exuding the fragrance of Christ[111] in the goodness of your lives;[112] you are no longer slaves under the law, but a people living in freedom under grace.[113]

---

[103] Heb. 13: 17. [104] Gal. 5: 13. [105] Luke 22: 25–6.
[106] Tit. 2: 7. [107] 1 Thess. 5: 14. [108] Heb. 13: 17.
[109] Sir. 30: 24. [110] Sir. 44: 6. [111] 2 Cor. 2: 15.
[112] 1 Pet. 3: 16. [113] Rom. 6: 14–22.

2. These precepts should be read to you once a week, so that you will see yourselves in this little book as in a mirror and not neglect anything through forgetfulness.[114] When you find yourselves doing what has been written here, thank the Lord, the giver of all good gifts. However, if anyone of you realizes that she has failed on a specific point, let her be sorry for the past, safeguard the future, and continue to pray for her offences to be forgiven, and that she not be led into temptation.[115]

---

[114] Jas. 1: 23–5.   [115] Matt. 6: 12–13.

Part Three

DISPUTED QUESTIONS

VIII
A Historical Overview

THE Abbé Migne's collection of Greek and Latin texts written by the Church Fathers and edited in the last century has been unfairly described as the *cloaca maxima* (main sewer) of ancient Rome.[1] As distasteful as this metaphor is, it does apply with special aptness to the vast infrastructure of 274 manuscripts which together constitute the dossier for the Augustinian Rule. I am fully aware of this deep and extensive underground, not unlike Schliemann's Troy or the catacombs of Saint Sebastian. Such matters, however, pertain to the specialist. I deliberately adopt, instead, a shorthand technique which, admittedly, fails to convey the many intricacies of the textual evidence. Also, the boundaries here laid down do not extend beyond the death of Isidore of Seville in 636, except when necessary. The same is generally true with reference to the fate of the Augustinian Rule during the Carolingian Renaissance, the Gregorian Reforms, and the burgeoning of monasticism during the early Middle Ages. Here is subject matter for another book.

Allowing for these limitations, three sources may be said to comprise the basic portfolio for Augustine's Rule:

(1) *Regulations for a Monastery*
(2) The *Rule*
(3a) *Reprimand to Quarrelling Nuns*: *Letter* 211. 1–4
(3b) *Rule for Nuns*: *Letter* 211. 5–16

The first of these is a monastic code which takes its name, *Regulations for a Monastery*, from a ninth-century manuscript, Laon 328 *bis*. This document appears to have emerged originally from an Augustinian milieu, for it resonates with the North African Father's teaching.[2] The second document in the dossier is widely acknowledged to be the original *Rule* of Saint Augustine.

---

1 E. Schwartz, 'Christliche und jüdische Ostertafeln', *Abhandlungen der Königlichen Gesellschaft der Wissenschaften zu Göttingen*, phil.-hist. Kl., NF 8, no. 6 (1905), 67 n. 1.
2 This matter will be reviewed in Appendix II.

Table C. *Basic Portfolio for Augustine's* Rule

Ante omnia, fratres carissimi,
diligatur deus, deinde et proximus . . .

⎤ *Regulations for a Monastery*

. . . et nobis non parua erit laetitia
de uestra salute. Amen.

Haec sunt quae ut obseruetis praecipimus . . .

⎤ *Rule*

. . . et in temptationem non inducatur.

Sicut parata est seueritas
peccata quae inuenerit uindicare . . .

⎤ *Reprimand to Quarrelling Nuns Letter 211. 1–4*

. . . sed potius lacrimas Petri pastoris.

Haec sunt quae ut obseruetis praecipimus . . .

⎤ *Rule for Nuns Letter 211. 5–16*

. . . et in temptationem non inducatur.

The third text, *Letter* 211. 1–4: *Reprimand to Quarrelling Nuns*, is today generally recognized as genuine. However, its authenticity has been contested by one scholar for stylistic reasons.[3] Finally, *Letter* 211. 5–16: *Rule for Nuns*, will receive special attention in the middle section of this historical survey.

These brief identifications should help to reduce the confusion that necessarily besets an attempt to familiarize oneself with the literature relating to the Rule(s) of St Augustine. Since different terminology is employed by different scholars, identification of documents is by no means uniform, even when the same text is being described. A glossary of terms thus becomes a virtual necessity. The threat of confusion inherent in the welter of material that has resisted standardization through the centuries is increased by statements or queries, written or vocal, such as the following: 'Augustine's *Rule* is a rule for women; adaptation for men was a later development.' 'Everyone knows that Augustine's *Rule* was originally a letter.' 'The famous *Letter to Nuns* was probably but not certainly by Augustine.' 'The *Rule* of Augustine is really a product of the eleventh or twelfth century.' 'Did the bishop compose a *Rule* after all?' 'Is the text we read today the same as the original, or have there been interpolations?'

Both these questions possess some validity. For example, the bishop of Hippo nowhere in his prodigious literary output refers to a monastic rule. Possidius possibly alludes to one, but if he does, that bit of evidence by this first of Augustine's biographers and his friend of some forty years is at best indirect (some would say oblique), and is inconclusive.[4] Furthermore, no contemporary of the bishop nor any acknowledged public figure in the succeeding generation names Augustine as author of such a document. Yet the impact of the so-called 'Augustinian Rule' was felt 'some ten years after the death of St Augustine'.[5] Oddly enough, while writers in Gaul, Italy, and Spain attested to two documents subsequently designated as the *Regulations for a Monastery* and

---

[3] Verheijen's responses to these objections, first raised in 1948 by W. Hümpfner, are satisfactory as far as they go. While further study of this question is desirable, I believe such an investigation would likewise favour Augustine's authorship of *Letter* 211. 1–4. See *Règle* ii. 204–5 and more recently 'La Règle de saint Augustin: L'état actuel des questions (début 1975), *Augustiniana*, 35 (1985) 245–7.

[4] See n. 22 below.

[5] C. Lambot, 'La Règle de saint Augustin et saint Césaire', *RB* 41 (1929), 339: 'quelques dix ans après la mort de s. Augustin'.

the *Rule*, respectively, those in north Africa, the homeland of Augustine, maintained a stony silence. And though these non-African authors borrowed generously from both the documents just noted, there is, except in Eugippius, as we shall indicate below, no mention of Augustine's name by any of these writers in connection with either of them or with any monastic rule. Any suspicion of 'plagiarism' on the part of these borrowers is, of course, wide of the mark. There frankly was no need for them to acknowledge derivative material. Writings of fellow Christians were in those days regarded as common property, a patrimony which could be handily appropriated by a later Christian writer in the interests of edification.

We shall presently note that the earliest designation of Augustine as author of a monastic code is provided by the recently authenticated *Rule* of Eugippius about one hundred years after Augustine's death in 430. We are later indebted to a single, unidentified scribe from the late sixth or early seventh century for further documentary evidence designating the bishop of Hippo as author of a monastic rule. The oldest extant manuscript, Paris, Bibliothèque Nationale, lat. 12634, contains the rubric 'Explicit Regula Sancti Augustini Episcopi'. Here for the second time in history, as far as the existing evidence allows, what was designated by its author as a *libellus* is now called the *regula* of St Augustine. Fs. 9–20 contain the *Regulations for a Monastery* and the *Rule* in that order. Both texts are separated by an *Amen*. The *Rule* begins on the same line with no *incipit*. It concludes with the explicit just noted above. Fs. 21–77 contain varied samples of monastic texts. Apart from the integral text *The Thought of Novatus the Catholic on Humility and Obedience and Trampling Pride Underfoot*, the remaining pieces are excerpts of uneven length from a wide compass of monastic literature, specifically:

(1) the Rule of the Holy Fathers;
(2) the Rule of the Master;
(3) the Rule of St Basil, translated by Rufinus;
(4) the Rule of St Pachomius, translated by Jerome;
(5) Cassian's *Conferences* and *Institutes*.
(6) Jerome's *Letter* 125 to Rusticus the monk.[6]

Since Augustine's authorship of the text in question is in this

---

[6] *Règle* i. 111–14.

instance restricted to the pen of an anonymous scribe, the resources of philology and textual criticism must be drawn upon to pursue the matter further. Here we are assisted by a scholar whose lifelong researches have included a careful scrutiny of 274 manuscripts containing 317 relevant texts which, in various combinations, transmit both masculine and feminine forms of the *Rule*.[7] It is no wonder then that 'the effort to determine the origin and authenticity of these documents has been one of the most complex investigations in the modern study of Patristic literature'.[8]

The Augustinian Rule fared no better in later printed editions than it did in the labyrinthine network of the earlier manuscripts. The *editio princeps* of the *Omnia Opera Sancti Augustini*, published at Basel in 1506, embraced three texts bearing the title *Regula Sancti Augustini*. In 1529 Erasmus of Rotterdam, the new editor, instructed the publisher, J. Froeben, to assign two of these texts to the final part of the volume reserved for the *spuria*. No one seems ever to have contested the appropriateness of Erasmus' decision to retire the document designated *Regula Prima* or *Regula Consensoria*.[9] Its authenticity had long been called into question, and properly so: Jordan of Quedlinburg (Saxony), for example, had argued against Augustine's authorship as early as the fourteenth century.[10] Nor, as far as we know, did any of Erasmus' contemporaries make serious objection to his designation of the *Regula Secunda* (= *Regulations for a Monastery*) as similarly spurious. Such was not the case, however, with respect to his appraisal of the so-called *Regula Tertia* (= the *Rule*). In his judgement, this document 'was probably written for women, not men',[11] in particular, for a convent of nuns at Hippo where Augustine's sister had been the superior. Though indisputably an authentic product of Augustine's pen, the *Regula Tertia* was in all probability nothing more than a transcription of *Letter* 211. 5–16 into the masculine form for the use of monks. This 'censure of Erasmus' did not sit well with the many communities of men who

---

[7] Ibid. 17–24.   [8] *RB 1980*, 61.

[9] The text appears in *Règle* ii. 7–9. C. J. Bishko, 'The Date and Nature of the Spanish "Consensoria monachorum",' *American Journal of Philology*, 69 (1948), 337–95 suggests a 7th-c. Hispanic origin.

[10] R. Arbesmann and W. Hümpfner, *Jordani de Saxonia Liber Vitasfratrum* (New York, 1943). See the Introduction, lxxvi–lxxvii.

[11] Erasmus, *D. Aurelii Augustini Hipponensis episcopi omnium operum primus tomus* (Basel, 1528), 591–2.

regarded the *Rule* as the touchstone of their common life, nor did
it go unchallenged in the field of scholarship.[12] Accordingly, there
have been periodic attempts to 'reclaim' the *Regulations for a
Monastery* and to counter the 'censure of Erasmus' with the
proposal that *Letter* 211. 5–16 itself was a later transcription of the
already existing masculine *Rule* into the feminine form, which was
evidently appended as a postscript to *Letter* 211. 1–4.

Research on the Augustinian Rule these past thirty years has
concentrated, *inter alia*, upon the following areas: (1) the matter of
authorship, (2) its intended audience, and (3) its date of
composition. A veritable explosion in Augustinian studies took
place during the middle fifties. Writing at that time of seismic
change in Augustinian scholarship, Henri Marrou employed
generally acceptable terms when he said of 'the famous text of the
Rule called St Augustine's Rule' that it 'does not appear to be
wholly from the actual hand of the great bishop (we touch upon a
very disputed question), but it certainly springs from his circle of
influence, and sets out the ideal which he himself tried to
practise'.[13] As in any area of research, it takes time for newly
discovered patristic data to become assimilated by other scholars
and still longer for these fruits of scholarship to reach a level of
general interest. Even allowing for such a time-lag, however, it is
somewhat surprising to read in 1983: 'Three rules were attributed
to St. Augustine (d. 430), but none of them is authentic.'[14] A
publication of the middle seventies concluded: 'The document
which has passed under this name since the eleventh century was
not actually composed by St Augustine of Hippo in the early fifth
century. He may have written down some principles of life for
small communities of men and women; or the early rules may be
the work of a slightly later age, perhaps of the sixth century.'[15]
This latter remark calls immediately for a few comments.

[12] *Règle* ii. 24–70 surveys these opinions with the author's usual thoroughness.
[13] H. I. Marrou, *Saint Augustine and his Influence through the Ages* (New York, 1957), 155–6.
[14] See the article 'Rules' by J.T. Lienhard in *A Dictionary of Christian Spirituality*, ed. by Gordon S. Wakefield (London, 1983), 341.
[15] C. Brooke, *The Monastic World 1000–1300* (New York, 1974), 125. For a detailed critique of this volume in connection with the *Rule* see A. Zumkeller, 'Ursprung und spirituelle Bedeutung der Augustinusregel: Eine notwendige Richtigstellung zu dem Werk Christopher Brooke's "Die grosse Zeit der Klöster

First of all, one can no longer declare in such an apodictic manner that Augustine did not compose a *Rule*. Secondly, it is incorrect to speak of the eleventh century as the period when this legislative piece was first attributed to him. We have already noted that the oldest extant manuscript of the *Rule*, Paris, BN lat. 12634, dated by Lowe as of late sixth- or early seventh-century origin, explicitly identified Augustine as its author.[16] Thirdly, to suggest 'a slightly later age, perhaps the sixth century', flies in the face of textual and stylistic evidence. Caesarius of Arles availed himself of this text as early as *c*.512. It had, therefore, been in circulation during the late fifth century. Obvious differences, moreover, exist between the Latinity of the early fifth century and the sixth century. Fifty years ago Dom Morin pointed out that the Latinity of the *Regulations for a Monastery* belonged to a time earlier than that of St Benedict. The same can be said of the *Rule*. Fourthly, it is gratuitous, in the light of research these past thirty years, to propose that the north African bishop 'may have written down some principles of life for small communities of men and women'. Such a statement reveals unfamiliarity with both the history of western monasticism in late antiquity and the history of scholarship. But this is to anticipate our story. For the moment, I wish to focus on a more fundamental question.

1. Authorship of the *Rule*

When Augustine wrote his *Retractations* near the end of his life, he reviewed ninety-three of his works (comprising 232 'books') and was prevented from a like review of his *Letters* and *Sermons* only by his death.[17] In an addendum to his biography of Augustine, Possidius likewise furnished an *Indiculus* of 1,030 works. This list of Possidius' included many *Sermons* and *Letters*.[18] The objection

1000–1300" (deutsch: Freiburg, 1976). Ordens-Korrespondenz', *Zeitschrift für Fragen des Ordenslebens*, 19 (1978), 287–95.

[16] *Règle* i. 111–13.

[17] *Retr.* 2. 67 (CCL 57. 142–3).

[18] A. Wilmart, 'Operum S. Augustini elenchus a Possidio eiusdem discipulo Calamensi episcopo digestus', *Misc. Agost.* ii. 149–233. D. L. Ludwig, *Der sog. Indiculus des Possidius: Studien zur Enstehungs—und Wirkungsgeschichte einer spätantiker Augustin—Bibliographie* (Göttingen, 1984) argues against Possidius' authorship of this *Indiculus* by suggesting that its composition dates from a generation or so after his death. Ludwig's thesis thus contradicts the evidence of the

is sometimes raised: why is there no mention of the *Rule* in either the list of Augustine himself or that of his biographer? Incidentally, we should note at once that, since both listings are incomplete, the *Rule* is not their only omission. Also, to argue that the bishop has no corrections to make to the *Rule* is not helpful, because he does include in his list at least two other works not subjected by himself to emendation or correction, namely, the *Reply to Felix the Manichee* and *The Nature of Good*.[19]

Most significantly, it is legitimate to ask how Augustine could regard the *Rule* as a composition destined for publication in the same manner as his other writings. Both the *Rule* of Eugippius, it will be pointed out, and an anonymous scribe affixed the title *Regula* to this monastic piece, which had been designated by its author as a *libellus*, a 'little book' or pamphlet. Unlike his *libri*, *sermones*, and *epistulae*, the *Rule* was hardly destined for a wider reading public. When Possidius concludes his *Indiculus* with the comment that Augustine composed his writings 'for the instruction of souls',[20] could he possibly be revealing that he had it in mind to include in his list only didactic and pastoral works deserving of public notice, those destined for readers beyond the pale of a particular monastery? The *Rule* is, after all, basically a domestic document which was designed for a single house. There is no provision in the text for establishing other foundations and no mention of any connection with any other monastery. For this reason, its strictly intramural features do not fit the specification 'books, sermons, and letters' given by Augustine in the final paragraph of his *Retractations*. The silence, therefore, of both this latter work and Possidius' *Indiculus* does not jeopardize the authenticity of the *Rule*. Augustine and his first biographer have merely made the matter of authorship all the more puzzling for posterity.

Elsewhere Possidius possibly offers a hint regarding the authorship of the *Rule* in his citation of Acts 4: 32–5. Augustine cites

---

manuscript tradition. For a résumé of her position see 202–3. In the event that Ludwig's thesis should eventually gain acceptance among scholars, the point I am making still stands. The selective nature of the *Indiculus* helps to explain its failure to include the *Rule*.

[19] *Retr.* 2. 8, 9 (CCL 57. 97).
[20] Wilmart, 'Elenchus', 208: '. . . ad instructionem animarum fecit libros, tractatus, epistolas . . .'.

Acts 4: 32–5 in whole or in part some eighty-two times, fourteen of which include v. 35b.[21] In all patristic literature, the sequence 32b + 32c + 35b is found only twice: in the biography of Augustine by Possidius (ch. 4) and in the first chapter of the *Rule* (6–15). The verses as quoted in the aforesaid sequence would, accordingly, be:

32b Do not call anything your own,
32c but possess everything in common,
35b let there be distribution to each one on the basis of need.

Though striking, this coincidence in manner of citation does not, of itself, authenticate Augustine's authorship. But it remains, at least, powerfully suggestive. Actually, reaction to this surprisingly significant scriptural find of Verheijen, has been mixed. Some scholars say that Verheijen is safe in drawing from it the inference he does; others maintain that he is over-confident in his conclusion.[22] Might it not have been, say those who object, that the author of the *Rule* read Possidius rather than that Possidius read the *Rule*? On the other side of the question, one might also ask: since Augustine was fairly fond of citing this text from Acts, why is it found only in the pertinent passage of the *Rule* in the identical sequence in which it is found in Possidius? Once again, the elusive data of internal criticism must be examined with care. More than one inference is admissible.

We noted earlier that the oldest manuscript of the *Rule*, Paris, BN lat. 12634, which dates from the late sixth or early seventh century, actually identifies Augustine of Hippo as its author. Villegas and de Vogüé have correctly identified southern Italy, more precisely the region of Naples as its original home. They assign the manuscript itself to c.600.[23] The explicit or identification-tag at the end of the *Rule* furnishes evidence which should not be minimized, even though a later scribe assigns the

---

[21] *Règle* ii. 89–95, where Verheijen has consulted the card-index of the *Vetus Latina* as far as the Venerable Bede. Near Eastern literature and the Greek Fathers were likewise examined.

[22] For two different perspectives on this matter see Halliburton, *JTS* NS 19 (1968), 661: '. . . *on this evidence alone* [original emphasis] it would be hard to claim St. Augustine as the author of the *Praeceptum*'; R. Arbesmann, *AS* 1 (1970), 260: 'Verheijen is quite justified, it seems to us, in seeing in this striking parallel a close connection between the text of the *Rule* and Augustine's monastery of lay-monks at Hippo.'

[23] See n. 27 below.

very same text to Cassian.[24] In this instance we can safely infer an error on the part of the copyist because a random and limited sampling from a listing of fourteen manuscripts, preserved prior to the year AD 1000, both contains the *Rule* and explicitly assigns it to Augustine.

Paris, BN lat. 12634	6th/7th c.
Reims 392	9th c.
Lambach 31	9th c.
Munich, clm 28118	9th c.
Vatican, Palatine 211	9th c.
Paris 2826	9/10 c.
Turin G V 7	9/10th c.
Escorial a I 13	10th c.

While other approaches to this question of authorship must be explored, thus far these particular attributions to Augustine furnish the best available evidence to support his authorship.

Meanwhile let us employ another vector of measurement: examination of the *testimonia* from late antiquity. Borrowings from the text of the *Rule* turn out to be plentiful here. Although they provide no direct help in the matter of authorship, these *testimonia* present us with a tentative chronology, indicating a time-frame which, in turn, squares comfortably with Augustine's floruit, AD 354–430. In Gaul, for example, Caesarius of Arles utilized the *Regulations for a Monastery* and the *Rule* 'for about two-thirds'[25] of his *Rule for Nuns* (which existed in two versions, *c*.512 and 534); Caesarius' *Rule for Monks* (*c*.524) likewise depended heavily on both of the aforementioned documents. Elsewhere chs. 14–23 of the *Regula monasterii Tarnantensis* incorporated virtually all the *Rule* attributed to Augustine. Its likely date of composition ranges approximately from 551 to 573.[26] The manuscript tradition yields at least six different spellings for the otherwise uncertain site of this monastery, which was located in south-eastern Gaul.

In Italy, as we noted earlier, the recently authenticated *Rule* of

---

[24] *Règle* i. 128–9. Laon 328 *bis*, a 9th-c. manuscript, concludes thus: 'Explicit Regula Cassiani feliciter'.

[25] M. McCarthy, *The Rule for Nuns of St. Caesarius of Arles: A Translation with a Critical Introduction* (Washington, DC, 1960), 10.

[26] F. Villegas, 'La "Regula Monasterii Tarnantensis": Texte, sources et datation', *RB* 84 (1974), 62.

Eugippius assimilated the whole of the *Regulations for a Monastery* and the *Rule*.[27] Here, in fact, what had been designated by its author as a *libellus* is designated for the first time by the explicit of Eugippius' *Rule* as a *regula*.

In two respects Augustine's and Benedict's *Rules* bear some resemblance: their oldest extant manuscripts (for Benedict, Hatton 48, *c*.700, from Worcester, now preserved in the Bodleian Library, Oxford), date from approximately a century and a half to two centuries after their respective author's death. Secondly, the earliest external evidence of Benedict's authorship dates from Paul the Deacon, *c*.786/7, more than two hundred years after Benedict had died. (Scholars are a long way from consensus in these matters.) Augustine fares better in this regard: the *Rule* of Eugippius, abbot of the Lucullanum monastery near Naples, furnishes the earliest written attestation for Augustine's authorship of a monastic rule *c*.530, about one hundred years after the bishop of Hippo had died. About a dozen references to this latter text are listed in the *Rule* of Benedict.[28] In connection with this fact, it is appropriate that we take note of a modern assessment which states: 'While the *RB* (Rule of Benedict) remains primarily in the tradition of Egypt as mediated by Cassian and the *RM* (Rule of the Master), the second most important influence upon it is that of Augustine, whose humaneness and concern for fraternal relationships have contributed to the *RB* some of its best known and most admired qualities.'[29]

In Spain, Eutropius, bishop of Valencia (*c*.590), revealed a faint echo of the *Regulations for a Monastery* and the *Rule* in his letter on the *Harsh Treatment of Monks and the Dissolution of Monasteries*.[30] The anonymous *Rule* of St Paul and St Stephen in northern Spain likewise utilized the *Rule*.[31] Leander of Seville and his younger brother, Isidore (in his *Rule for Monks*) drew upon a feminine form of both the *Regulations for a Monastery* and the

[27] F. Villegas and A. de Vogüé, *Eugippii Regula*, CSEL 87 (Vienna, 1976), 3–16 incorporates the whole of the *Ordo Monasterii* and *Praeceptum*; cf. ibid., pp. vii–xiii.

[28] R. Hanslik, *Benedicti Regula*, CSEL 75 (Vienna, 1960), 170 lists fourteen citations of Augustine's *Rule*. See also Lienhard, 'Index of Reported Patristic and Classical Citations, Allusions and Parallels in the *Regula Benedicti*', *RB* 89 (1979), 236–9 for the wider impact of Augustine's writings upon Benedict's *Rule*.

[29] *RB 1980*, 64.

[30] L. Verheijen, 'La "Regula Sancti Augustini"', *VC* 7 (1953), 55–6.

[31] J. E. M. Vilanova, *Regula Pauli et Stephani* (Montserrat, 1959).

Rule,[32] which is, as far as we know, the first appearance of the feminine version in textual history.

It should be noted that early evidence for the feminine form of the Augustinian Rule is confined to Spain. More about this matter later. Isidore of Seville is usually regarded as the last of the Church Fathers in the West. Therefore, by the end of the patristic era, the diffusion of this monastic code credited to the bishop of Hippo is amply documented. One scholar, for example, has referred to the 'Augustinian invasion'[33] of southern Europe during the first half of the sixth century. The Vandal incursions into northern Africa were greatly responsible for the exodus from that region of many monks who, very likely, carried the Augustinian Rule with them to Italy, Gaul, and Spain. The same invasions help explain the silence of north Africa with regard to Augustine's *Rule*. Recall that the Vandals were actually besieging Hippo as its beloved bishop lay dying.

While the *Rule* of Eugippius and the oldest extant manuscript of the *Rule* expressly name Augustine, and while a large number of ancient texts derive either directly or indirectly from the *Rule*, it seems inadvisable to exaggerate this external evidence. Thus it is that we are obliged to rely so much upon the tenuous data of internal evidence as a tool in researching the history of the *Rule*. The volume of evidence from this direction is by no means slender.

It has been proposed, for example, that the use of Scripture in the text of the *Rule* offers another strong suasion in favour of Augustine's authorship.[34] Accordingly, when the bishop of Hippo has already five times cited Titus 2: 7 in other connections,[35] namely regarding the duty of good conduct as being incumbent upon all who exercise pastoral ministry in the church (*Serm.* 46. 4. 9) and upon bishops in particular (twice: *Letters* 121.1, 126. 8), regarding Aaron in his role as levite (*Quest. in the Hept.* 2, q. 119), and regarding the conduct of clerics (*Serm.* 355. 1)—is a sixth

[32] Verheijen, ' "Regula" ' 47–54; A. C. Vega, *El 'De Institutione Virginum' de San Leandro de Sevilla* (Escorial, 1948); Isidore, *Regula Monachorum* (PL 83. 867–94).

[33] A. de Vogüé, 'Saint Benoît et son temps: Règles italiennes et règles provençales au vi^e siècle', *Regulae Benedicti Studia*, 1 (1972), 188–9.

[34] T. van Bavel, 'Parallèles, vocabulaire et citations bibliques de la "Regula Sancti Augustini": Contribution au problème de son authenticité', *Augustiniana*, 9 (1959), 12–77.

[35] A.-M. La Bonnardière, *Biblia Augustiniana: Les Épîtres aux Thessaloniciens, à Tite et à Philémon* (Paris, 1964), 39, 44.

citation of the same verse in the *Rule* (7. 3) to be considered a mere coincidence? Or is there some discernible reason, such as is suggested by the fact that all six of these uses of Titus 2: 7 occur in contexts treating of church leadership? While this verse lends itself to such usage, how legitimate is the inference that this sixth instance of its use ought to be associated with the bishop of Hippo? This much can be said: such an ensemble of quotations of the verse in explanation of a pastoral office in the church does not appear in any Latin author before Augustine.[36] This invites the double conclusion that the composition of the *Rule* does not pre-date Augustine and that its composition lies comfortably within the boundaries of Augustine's floruit.

More persuasive still is the annexation of the phrase *in deum* in the second paragraph of the *Rule* (5), to the words *anima una et cor unum* of Acts 4: 32. This addition, moreover, is found for the first time in the writings of Augustine and was used by him twenty-eight times, a dozen of these occurring in a monastic context.[37] One may argue similarly in reference to the use of Heb. 13: 17 in the penultimate chapter of the *Rule* (7. 1, 3). The citations of Sir. 30: 24 at the end of ch. 7 (7. 4), and of 2 Cor. 2: 15 and Rom. 6: 14 in the penultimate paragraph of the *Rule* (8. 1) have parallels, also, in other undisputed writings of Augustine which orchestrate a distinctive monastic theme.[38]

Only one scriptural passage employed in the *Rule* presents some resistance to this sort of comparison. In closing with the words *non inducatur* (387), the *Rule* echoes Matt. 6: 13. But in other quotations of or allusions to that verse of Matthew, Augustine regularly uses some form of *infero*.[39] How explain the bishop's preference for *inferre* over *inducere* in his fairly frequent recourse to this final petition of the Lord's Prayer in these other places in his writings? Do we have here a parallel to the preference exhibited in the first chapter of the *Rule* when the quoting of Acts 4 appears in the pattern 32b + 32c + 35b?

On the basis of the above biblical citations, perhaps all one would wish to say is that the text attributed to the bishop of Hippo

[36] Van Bavel, 'Parallèles', 65–6, 74.
[37] Id., ' "Ante omnia" et "in Deum" dans la "Regula Sancti Augustini" ', *VC* 12 (1958) 162–5.
[38] Id., 'Parallèles', 67–70.
[39] Id., 'Inferas—Inducas: A propos de Mtth. 6, 13 dans les œuvres de saint Augustin', *RB* 69 (1959), 348–51.

by Eugippius and an unknown scribe in late antiquity certainly could not have existed before Augustine. Just how far one chooses to draw inferences on the authenticity of the *Rule* from the data presented here is discretionary. Cumulatively, however, these biblical passages present strong suasions in favour of Augustine's authorship.

In addition to the above biblical citations there are some five hundred parallels, with uneven and varying demonstrative force, between the *Rule* and writings of the Augustinian corpus acknowledged to be authentic.[40] As in the case of the Scriptures, here again there are striking verbal and conceptual similarities. The many parallels converge toward a harmonious whole in which the patterns of thought and language are often identical. It would be simply too facile to propose that an unnamed *alter ego* profoundly immersed in Augustine's thought and rhetorical style could have written the *Rule*. Such a claim would be just as extravagant as the argument that the document was a forgery. Overwhelmingly, internal evidence goes counter to both these extremes.

A final item of internal evidence can be invoked in support of Augustine's having written the *Rule*. It is impressive to learn that the word *emendatorius* is 'strictly Augustinian'.[41] No less than six uses of the word are cited from undisputed works of Augustine; a seventh occurs in the *Rule* (199). To date, the word-index to Augustine's writings now stored on data loggers at the Computer Centre of Würzburg University has listed one additional citation. No matter, these listings are sufficient to corroborate Augustine's authorship of the *Rule*: there is apparently no listing for *emendatorius* prior to Augustine. Apart from uses of this word attributed to him, the only others cited are single uses by each of two monastic texts which clearly derive from the *Rule*, namely, the *Tarnantensian Rule*, 18 (PL 66. 985) and Isidore of Seville's *Rule for Monks*, 18 (PL 83. 887).[42] This use of *emendatorius* would seem to furnish irrefutable evidence for Augustine's authorship of the *Rule*.

To recapitulate: first of all, the silence of both Augustine and his

---

[40] Id., 'Parallèles', 16–73. See also *Règle* ii. 187–95 for a review of 35 parallels between the *Praeceptum* and Augustine's *De opere monachorum*.

[41] Verheijen, *Nouvelle approche*, 316.

[42] J.-M. Clément, *Lexique des anciennes règles monastiques occidentales* (Steenbrugge, 1978), i. 402–3.

biographer regarding the *Rule* in no way undermines its authenticity as a work of Augustine. Secondly, the sequence of verses, Acts 4: 32b + 32c + 35b, both in the *Rule* and in Possidius' *Vita* offers a strong suasion in favour of Augustine's authorship, even though the argument based on it remains inconclusive. Thirdly, the oldest extant manuscript names Augustine, as does the *Rule* of Eugippius; these attributions constitute the best external evidence of his authorship thus far. Fourthly, *testimonia* drawn from patristic writings of Gaul, Italy, and Spain firmly situate the text as the earliest monastic rule of western origin (except possibly for the *Regulations for a Monastery*) and, chronologically, as being wholly consonant with the dates of Augustine's pastoral ministry. Fifthly, a phalanx of textual and philological parallels from Augustine's uncontested writings clears the field in favour of the legitimacy of the bishop's title as a monastic legislator. Conceptual motifs found in these parallels, moreover, confirm this conclusion. Finally, the neologism *emendatorius* (199) offers incontrovertible evidence that Augustine of Hippo is properly credited as being the author of the monastic rule which bears his name.

2. Addressed to Men, to Women, or to Both?

Any discussion of the Augustinian Rule must raise the further question of its audience. To whom was this document addressed: to men, to women, or to both? Opinion remains divided, possibly because the issues at first appear to be so intractable, but in equal likelihood because scholars have not taken time to assimilate the vast and complex literature on the subject. Four approaches to these questions are available: (1) a critical reading and comparison of the *Rule* itself with undisputed affinities in Augustine's life and writings, (2) a study of the manuscript tradition and of the data supplied by ancient *testimonia*, (3) an examination of the evidence of textual criticism, and (4) a review of the history of scholarship as it has reflected the above data.

What Does the Text Say?

Turning, therefore, directly to the text of the *Rule*, let us sift the internal evidence in this matter of the author's public. Was Augustine writing for men, for women, or for both? At least seven passages in the text have been thought to suggest a feminine environment. This surmise was challenged as long ago as the late seventeenth century, yet it resurfaces still in popular literature on the subject.[43]

The first passage thought to support this impression is the one in which the *Rule* says: 'Do not allow your clothing to attract attention; seek to please not by the clothes you wear but by the life you live' (4. 1). Needless to say, affectation in matters of clothing and singularity of dress are by no means an exclusively feminine prerogative. Men can be just as fastidious in such matters as women and equally inclined to fussiness about their outward appearance. In the sixth century, for example, when Dorotheos of Gaza urged his monks to take proper care of their clothing, he cited the following as a violation among the brothers: 'when one could wear a shirt a week or two, to want to wash it every day and so, by constant washing, wear it out too quickly and always asking for new'.[44]

A second argument maintains that a feminine setting is suggested for the *Rule* by the sequence 'exuding the fragrance of Christ in the goodness of your lives' (8. 1). Scholars, including Erasmus, have detected here a reference to perfume and seek further support for their argument in the ensuing simile of the mirror, where the author says: 'you will see yourselves in this little book as in a mirror' (8. 2). Actually, both the metaphor and the simile derive, respectively, from 2 Cor. 2: 15 and Jas. 1: 23–5, and St Paul and St James were hardly writing for an exclusively female public. Furthermore, Augustine employs the image of a mirror at least nine other times.[45] As for the metaphor relating to 'the fragrance of Christ', it occurs in two other monastic texts addressed to men as well as in two letters posted to Paulinus of Nola and his wife.[46]

A third proposal contends that Augustine envisaged a religious community composed only of women when he said: 'The washing and cleaning of your clothes may be done in the monastery or at the laundry' (5. 4). Incidentally, the *Rule* of Pachomius, § 69,

---

[43] For the full documentation from the *Quodlibeta Regularia* of Eustace of St Ubaldo, see *Règle* ii. 66–8.

[44] Eric P. Wheeler, *Dorotheos of Gaza: Discourses Sayings, Cistercian Studies*, 33 (Kalamazoo, 1977), 107.

[45] Van Bavel, 'Parallèles', 70–1.

[46] Ibid. 69. To van Bavel's list of citations I add *Ep.* 83, 5 (CSEL 34. 391).

provides for soiled clothing to be laundered outside the monastery. Can one really not conceive of Augustine mandating men to be responsible for soiled laundry? To put it another way, must washing clothes be construed as unseemly work for men? On this basis alone, one might equally well discredit St Bernard's advice to his monks: 'Be as eager to wash the dishes as you are to eat what is on them.' Moreover, Augustine is the only Church Father in the East or West to leave us a distinct treatise on the subject of work.

A fourth citation centres on the *Rule*'s prohibition of 'letters . . . or small gifts of any kind' (4. 11). But the *Rule* of St Benedict (ch. 54), a document addressed to men, contains the same prohibition.

A fifth interpretation, citing the admonition of the *Rule* that members of the religious community leave the house 'together . . . (and) stay together (4. 2) . . . with companions designated by the superior, not with persons of one's own choosing' (5. 7), sees these passages as stemming from an over-protective concern for women. But the law of companionship, 'no fewer than two or three', is an injunction derived from the words of the Lord recorded in the Gospel.

A sixth viewpoint says that the reciprocal roles assigned to lay superior (*praepositus*) and priest (*presbyter*) in the *Rule* imply that the latter functioned as chaplain of the community, which from this state of dependence would seem to have been made up of women. But a letter of Epiphanius to Bishop John of Jerusalem, along with other evidence, attests to the distinct roles for each person in monasteries of men. Once again, the inference that the *Rule* was written solely for women is invalidated.

A final contention, stating that the *Rule*'s 'common purpose' (5. 2) points to the feminine character of the community, is seen to be baseless. This same principle is stressed as fundamental to an understanding of Augustine's views in most of his statements concerning monasticism.

The Manuscript Tradition and Evidence from Late Antiquity

The senior member of the manuscript family, Paris, BN lat. 12634, has many precious relations. We shall mention only a few. The head of the second family, Munich, clm 28118, is dated as being from the ninth century; its original home was the Benedictine abbey of St Maximin at Trier. This second family tree carries the

Rule, but it does not include the *Regulations for a Monastery*. A third family, transmitting the *Rule for Nuns*, Escorial a I 13, dates back to the tenth century. These family relationships, with their variety of stemmata, indicate that the *Rule* and the *Rule for Nuns* clearly developed along independent lines. The manuscript tradition demonstrates not only the antiquity of the *Rule for Nuns* but also that it is derivative in character.

Sound criteria of textual criticism 'leave hardly any doubt'[47] that the *Rule for Nuns* is an adaptation of the *Rule* addressed to monks. More precisely, the eleventh- or twelfth- century manuscript Rheinau (Zürich) 89, from the former Benedictine Abbey of Rheinau in Switzerland, contains the *Incipit*: 'Here begins the Preface to the Rule of the blessed Augustine which he composed for nuns.'[48] The manuscript also has the *Explicit*: 'Here ends the Preface.'[49] In other words, this manuscript does not present *Letter* 211. 1–16 as a single unit or composite piece. The break between §§ 1–4 and §§ 5–16, that is, between the Preface (= *Praefatio*) and the *Rule for Nuns* is clear-cut, so much so, indeed, that another *Incipit* follows immediately, stating: 'Here begins the Rule for Nuns published by the blessed Augustine.'[50] The text concludes with the simple rubric: 'Expl(icit).'[51] Verheijen has produced a diplomatic text of Rheinau (Zürich) 89, which anticipates by a century all but one member of this family of manuscripts, namely, Escorial a I 13, dating from the tenth century.[52] Until 1967, the best critical text of *Letter* 211. 1–16 was that edited by Goldbacher.[53] He could not have known the importance of Florence, B.C. II II 459, a manuscript formerly assigned to the fourteenth century, which is now dated as being of the late twelfth or early thirteenth century. Moreover, as we shall indicate below, the number of manuscripts available to Goldbacher was necessarily limited at that time, whereas Verheijen based his critical edition upon both a wider range and a superior quality of manuscripts. We shall return to the significance of Verheijen's superior critical edition for the light it sheds on the question of Augustine's original text. Meanwhile, the conclusion is inescapable that Verheijen's text of *Letter* 211. 1–4 'not only represents a marked improvement over

---

[47] Arbesmann, 'Question of the *RSA*', 253.   [48] Règle i. 49.
[49] Ibid. i. 53.   [50] Ibid.   [51] Ibid. 66.
[52] Ibid. 40–5.
[53] Goldbacher, *S. Augustini Epistolae*, 4 (CSEL 57, Vienna, 1911), 356–71.

Goldbacher, but may safely be presumed to come as close as humanly possible to the original'.[54]

Late sixth- and early seventh-century Spain also furnishes data which support the aforementioned conclusion that Augustine addressed his *Rule* originally to men. When St Leander of Seville (d. 600) addressed his sister, the nun Florentina, in his *Education of Nuns*, he borrowed from the Augustinian *Rule for Nuns*. Furthermore, in his *Rule for Monks*, Leander's younger brother Isidore, relied upon a feminine adaptation of the *Regulations for a Monastery* (its first appearance in recorded history as far as we know), as well as on the *Rule for Nuns*. Verheijen has proved that this feminine adaptation used by Leander and Isidore antedates Fructuosus of Braga by about fifty years and renders untenable the attribution to him of the transcription of the *Rule for Nuns*.[55]

Briefly, then, independent developments among the masculine and feminine forms of the Augustinian Rule as attested to in the manuscript tradition, the composite character of *Letter* 211. 1–16, which was challenged for the first time by Verheijen, and data on the relationship of texts drawn from Leander and Isidore of Seville, all suggest derivation of the *Rule for Nuns* from a masculine original.

A word of caution is in order. Transcription from the feminine to the masculine or from the masculine to the feminine frequently entailed more than a predictable change from *famulus dei* to *famula dei*, from *praepositus* to *praeposita*, more even than the adaptation *pater/mater*, *frater/soror*, or vice versa. Borrowers in succeeding generations felt the need to fill out the compressed idiom which resulted from the preceptive force of Augustine's style. Interpolations and accretions proliferated. The textual critic can easily become lost in a labyrinth of some thirty monastic Rules which appeared in the west from the fourth to the ninth centuries, to say nothing of citations of the *Rule* documented both in Church Councils and other monastic writings. In the cases of Leander and Isidore of Seville above, for example, the utmost skill is required to tease out the various borrowings and to determine the direction of a particular transcription, whether a change occurred from *frater* to *soror*, or the other way round. A considerable winnowing process takes place only gradually as the accretions of later

---

[54] Arbesmann, 'Question of the *RSA*', 246.
[55] Verheijen, 'La "Regula Sancti Augustini"', 47–54.

generations are identified and accounted for in so vast a network of monastic literature, before attempting to reconstruct as close an approximation as is possible to Augustine's original text.

Survey of an Opinion

As recently as 1974 we read: '. . . and in a famous letter, probably but not certainly by him (Augustine), a community of women whose holiness had been called in question were told how such a life should be led. From this letter stemmed the later developments to which the name "The Rule of St. Augustine" came to be attached.'[56] This assessment does not square with the facts.

To begin with, the authenticity of *Letter* 211. 1–4 was questioned for the first time in 1948.[57] Such doubt is confined to a single scholar. One could just as well call into question the authorship of *Letter* 210, the authenticity of which, to the best of my knowledge, has never been challenged. It anticipates the issues of *Letter* 211 and renders the latter more intelligible. We have also noted previously Caesarius of Arles's use of Augustine's *Rule*, thereby indicating its existence soon after Augustine's death. Such evidence appreciably weakens the hypothesis that the *Rule for Nuns* preceded this ancient text, even though Lambot himself—for reasons we shall presently note—resolutely argued for an original feminine form. We have also observed that Leander and Isidore of Seville utilized a feminine adaptation of the *Rule* in the late sixth and early seventh centuries. Still, the antecedent antiquity of a masculine version appears to be unassailable.

The cumulative textual evidence briefly reviewed above indicates the adaptation of the feminine form from the masculine, rather than the opposite. How then shall we account for the persistence of this opposite view among scholars?

In a letter to the Abbot of the Augustinian Canons at Chamouzey in Les Vosges, *c.*1120, Gaultier, bishop of Maguelonne, debited St Norbert with the opinion that the Augustinian Rule was written for women. Hearsay, *sicut audiuimus*, was the basis for Gaultier's remarks.[58] In that same letter, the bishop faulted St Norbert for imposing upon the Canons Regular the strict

---

[56] Brooke, *Monastic World*, 21.   [57] See n. 3 above.

[58] *Règle* ii. 20. Gaultier wrote: 'We are surprised, however, that . . . he (Norbert) accepted our *Rule*, which he claims was addressed to women, not to ourselves. This is what we were told (*sicut audiuimus*).'

Regulations for a Monastery, the authenticity of which he challenged. Here, for the first time, is recorded that opinion which gained wide currency in the Late Middle Ages and has remained virtually invincible until the present century, although the claim for authenticity continued to be made at intervals. The idea that the *Rule for Nuns* was Augustine's original text is met with a second time about forty years after the foundation of the Premonstratensians. And again, as in the case of Gaultier, the account relates to the *Regulations for a Monastery*. In 1156 the author of this account, identified as Irungus of Saint-Emmeram (once a member of Cluny but now a Cistercian), sent to Adelspach in Bavaria a text in the form of a dialogue, which at one point says:

> *Clu.* 'Why do you maintain that their [the Premonstratensians'] Rule was written for women?'
>
> *Cis.* 'The Prologue of the same Rule.'
>
> *Clu.* 'Their Rule has no Prologue.'
>
> *Cis.* 'Because they dropped it and changed the feminine form into the masculine.'[59]

By that time the Premonstratensians had, in fact, dropped the *Regulations for a Monastery*, which had been mistakenly equated with *Letter* 211. 1–4: *Reprimand to Quarrelling Nuns*.

At approximately the same time and in a letter to Abelard, the famous Héloïse lamented her community's having to follow St Benedict's *Rule* because the Church Fathers had not written one for women. It is possibly worthwhile to inquire here whether the words *apud Latinos* of that lament implied that Héloïse was familiar with eastern monasticism, for example, in the tradition of St Basil, whose *Longer* and *Shorter Rules* were followed by both sexes.[60] At any rate, it never occurred to her that the *Rule* acknowledged by the Canons Regular of St Augustine could have been a transcription from the feminine to the masculine form. Moreover, she asks Abelard (1079–1142) to compose a Rule fittingly adapted to the needs of her community, and in answering he also appeared to be unfamiliar with any ancient Rule for women. In the course of replying to Héloïse's request Abelard twice named Augustine before quoting from the *Longer Rule*.[61]

---

[59] Ibid.

[60] Ibid. ii. 21 n. 1. Héloïse wrote: 'Actually among the Latins (*apud Latinos*), women as well as men follow the one *Rule* of blessed Benedict.'

[61] *Letter* 8 (PL 178. 292–3). The sentence from the *Rule* (3. 1) reads: 'To the

He declares that Augustine established monasteries for clerics and wrote a Rule for them. In his second reference to Augustine, however, Abelard cites a sentence that appears in identical form in the feminine version of the *Rule*. Here is a prominent philosopher and man of letters, charged at one time with ignorance of the Church Fathers, who wrote the *Sic et Non* as a manifesto of his familiarity with ancient Christian writers. Yet he is unacquainted with an Augustinian Rule for women.

Jordan of Quedlinburg (Saxony), *c.*1300–80, knew of three masculine texts: *Regulations for a Monastery*, the *Rule*, and the *Regula Consensoria*. Jordan eliminated the last-named document from the second edition of his *Liber Vitasfratrum*. Concluding, on grounds of style, that Augustine could not have been its author, he came to regard it as a translation of St Basil.[62] The silence of Jordan and of his mentor, Henry of Friemar *c.*1245–1340, on any Augustinian Rule for women may be construed as indicative of their unfamiliarity with any feminine form of the *Rule*. Chauvinistic and sometimes uncritical though these two authors were in matters relating to Augustine and the origins of the Augustinian Hermits, there is no known evidence to suggest that either of them had cause to suppress information about a feminine version. Each, with his own distinctive mode of exaggeration, sought to vindicate in the strongest terms the claim of the Augustinian Hermits to be the original monastic descendants of Augustine, thus needlessly initiating a long-standing controversy with the Canons Regular of St Augustine on the matter (which controversy was somewhat ameliorated only by papal intervention in the year 1484). But nowhere in this long and searching debate is there any mention of the *Rule* as existing at any time in the feminine form. The range of Henry of Friemar's acquaintance with monastic tradition should be noted. Entrusted by his Order with many important tasks, he had travelled widely in Germany, France, and Italy.[63]

While the argument *ex silentio* is, admittedly, an elusive one, it

---

extent that your health allows, subdue your flesh by fasting and abstinence from food and drink.' The sentence from the *Regulations for a Monastery*, § 7 (in col. 292): 'Sabbato tantum et Dominica, sicut consuetudo est, qui volunt vinum accipiant', varies slightly from Verheijen's reconstruction of the original text.

[62] Arbesmann–Hümpfner, *Liber Vitasfratrum*, Introduction, p. lxxvii.

[63] R. Arbesmann, 'Henry of Friemar's "Treatise on the Origin and Development of the Order of Hermit Friars and its True and Real Title"', *Augustiniana*, 6 (1956), 37–145.

is appropriate to ask how really intelligible is the silence of these learned Augustinian Hermits and that of Héloïse and Abelard as well?

When preparing the *editio princeps* of Augustine's writings, Desiderius Erasmus dismissed the *Regulations for a Monastery* as unworthy of Augustine because of its rather pedestrian contents and plain style. The *Rule*, however, he credited to the bishop of Hippo, since its texture, style, and inspiration were inescapably Augustinian. The great humanist, himself an Augustinian Canon at one time, ventured the suggestion that this monastic code 'was *probably* [emphasis mine] written not for clerics but for women'.[64] According to Erasmus, allusions to a mirror and perfume in ch. 8 of the *Rule* were likely indications that women were its author's intended audience. This objection, we noted above, was satisfactorily answered as long ago as the late seventeenth century.[65]

Erasmus' opinion, voiced by himself as only probable, became crystallized, however, and was later perpetuated by the authority of Robert Cardinal Bellarmine (1542–1621). Noting that *Letter* 211 was directed 'not to men but to women' and that Augustine's *Retractations* made no mention of the *Rule*, this famous Jesuit theologian and historian rejected the authenticity of the *Rule* bearing Augustine's name.[66] However, in all this he leant heavily on the authority of Erasmus, without offering any critical evaluation of his own.

At that time, moreover, scholarly opinion on the matter was somewhat tentative. There were notable exceptions. The Church historian Caesar Baronius (1538–1607) maintained the priority of the masculine version, although he believed, erroneously, that it was written for clerics rather than for monks.[67] Knowing both versions, Francis Suarez, the Spanish Jesuit (1548–1617), considered Augustine to be the author of both and judged the masculine version to be the older of the two.[68]

Within the same century, Ange Le Proust of the Hermits of St Augustine (d. 1697), was well aware of the relationships between

[64] See n. 11 above.
[65] See n. 43 above.
[66] Bellarminus, *De scriptoribus ecclesiasticis* (Lyons, 1613), 98. See *Règle* ii. 32–3 for the text.
[67] Baronius, *Annales ecclesiastici* 4 (Rome, 1600), 647. See *Règle* ii. 30–1.
[68] Suarez, *De religione*, tract. 9 (Lyons, 1625), 368–9. See *Règle* ii. 31–2.

Caesarius of Arles's *Rule for Nuns*, on the one hand, and both the *Regulations for a Monastery* and the *Rule*, on the other. Three Augustinian Canons, Alain Le Large (1697), Eusebius Amort (1747), and Augustine Ristl (1750), likewise knew of Caesarius' dependence upon the other two texts.[69] Obviously then the dependency of Caesarius' *Rules* upon a masculine model had already been long recognized. Knowledge of this fact, nevertheless, failed to enter the mainstream of scholarship on the history of monastic Rules until C. Lambot again brought it to attention in 1929.

Twentieth-Century Scholarship

In that year, C. Lambot rediscovered the close connection prevailing between the composite elements of the *Regulations for a Monastery* and the *Rule*. However, on the basis of internal evidence Lambot insisted that Augustine's *Rule* derived from the *Rule for Nuns*.[70] One year later, D. De Bruyne suggested the thesis that St Benedict himself had composed the *Regulations for a Monastery*; the *Rule*, he said, was a transcription from the feminine original of Augustine.[71] Both texts, according to De Bruyne, were the basis for the life of Benedict's first community at Subiaco, a thesis which, incidentally, was overturned by Dom Morin when he proved that the *Liturgy of the Hours* in use at Vivarium, Cassiodorus' foundation in southern Italy, was identical with that of the *Regulations for a Monastery*.[72]

Pierre Mandonnet proposed in 1937 that the *Regulations for a Monastery* was written by Augustine for his lay monks at Thagaste and that the *Rule* was a further elucidation of the earlier code, drafted specifically for Augustine's new monastery at Hippo after his ordination to the presbyterate in 391. Accordingly, Mandonnet argued that *Letter* 211. 5–16, the *Rule for Nuns*, should be seen as a transcription of the *Rule* to the feminine form.[73] Once again, in 1941, Lambot none the less insisted that internal evidence made it

[69] Ibid. 64–5.

[70] C. Lambot, 'La Règle de saint Augustin et saint Césaire', *RB* 41 (1929), 333–41.

[71] D. de Bruyne, 'La première règle de saint Benoît', *RB* 42 (1930), 316–42.

[72] G. Morin, 'L'ordre des heures canoniales dans les monastères de Cassiodore', *RB* 43 (1931), 145–52.

[73] P. Mandonnet, *Saint Dominique* (Paris, 1937), ii. 142–8.

clear that Augustine's original monastic code was written for women.[74] Unfortunately for Lambot, the range of palaeographical materials available in 1941 was much more restricted than it is today. Basically, Lambot's contention at that point in time was that the transcription from the feminine form to the masculine was so inept as to be unworthy of Augustine; presumably there was a later redactor. Lambot reached this conclusion by comparing seven textual variations common to the *Rule* and to the *Rule for Nuns*. But the number of manuscripts consulted by Verheijen furnished him with a far broader base and, hence, a more secure foundation for establishing sound critical editions of all three texts in question by drawing clearer lines of transmission among them after delineating their dependent and independent relationships. In one case at least, widely accepted consensus on the dating of Florence, B.C. II II 459 gave Verheijen a further advantage by enabling him better to estimate its importance.

On the other hand, Gustave Bardy, a knowledgeable interpreter of Augustine wrote in 1948:

The majority of historians . . . believe that the text commonly called the Rule of St. Augustine is a letter, or the final draft of a letter—designated Letter 211—originally addressed to women religious about the year 423, and adapted much later to accommodate the requirements of monasteries of men. This second conclusion, the most important for us, is likewise the most difficult to accept. Evidence from antiquity and most of the authorities favour the chronological priority of the masculine Rule.[75]

Some two decades of research had since that time strengthened Bardy's assessment of the problem when, some twenty-five years after Lambot, in 1967 Luc Verheijen made a close comparison of the *Rule* and the *Rule for Nuns* on the basis of thirty-three textual variations. By reason of the superiority of Verheijen's critical edition, however, only two of Lambot's seven passages were common to the comparisons made by Verheijen.[76] We shall discuss one of them:

[74] C. Lambot, 'Saint Augustin a-t-il rédigé la Règle pour moines qui porte son nom?' *RB* 53 (1941), 41–58.
[75] G. Bardy, *Saint Augustin: L'homme et l'œuvre* (7th edn.; Paris, 1948), 161–2, n. 2.
[76] *Règle* ii. 74–80. The original Latin of the passage cited on p. 146 from the *Rule for Nuns* will be found in Verheijen's diplomatic text, *Règle* i. 61.

Rule	*Rule for Nuns*
(5. 2): In this way, let no one work for himself alone, but all your work shall be for the common purpose, done with greater zeal and more concentrated effort than if each one worked for his private purpose.	In this way, let no one work for herself alone, *whether it be clothing or bedding, whether it be undergarments or outer garments, or covering for the head*, but all your work shall be for the common purpose, done with greater zeal and more concentrated effort than if each one worked for her private purpose.

Lambot had suggested that the above sequence from the *Rule for Nuns* (rendered in italics) is integral to the original text. Verheijen, however, argues that the issue at hand was storage of clothes in a single wardrobe, and also their care and supervision, not their production. Contextually, the meaning is unmistakably clear. The text envisages a monastery, not a dress-making establishment. Accordingly, the words in italics above represent a later interpolation by someone who wished to adapt the text into the feminine form. Here I should remark that the interpolation (fourteen words in all) introduces a somewhat jarring note into the flow of the Latin text.

In 1923, Goldbacher, on whom Lambot relied, had utilized six manuscripts of the *Longer Letter*, three manuscripts of the *Longer Rule*, and one manuscript of the *Rule* to establish his critical text of *Letter* 211. 1–16.[77] Verheijen's 1967 edition employed twenty-two manuscripts.[78]

Two manuscripts are particularly important here: Rheinau (Zürich) 89 and Escorial a I 13. Analysis of this matter would take us too far afield. I mention only two significant results of Verheijen's research: (1) the unity of *Letter* 211. 1–16 was then for the first time vigorously challenged, and (2) to a high degree of probability, the *Regulations for a Monastery* and the *Rule* were determined to have been transcribed into the feminine form in Spain during the late sixth and early seventh century.

To sum up: isolated passages from Augustine's *Rule* hardly encourage, much less endorse, the conclusion that this document was directed initially towards a group of women. This is seen to be

[77] CSEL 57. 356.
[78] *Règle* i. 35.

the case when these texts are examined both in their immediate context and within the larger context of the entire Augustinian corpus. Twentieth-century scholarship has seesawed back and forth, with variations, between opposite sides of the question. Mandonnet's work initially earned a limited acceptance, but may yet prove to have been genuinely prophetic in the long run. History often undermines our 'certainties'. Lambot thought his insistence upon a feminine original, first in 1929 and again in 1941, was justified by his careful use of scholarly methods. Yet his use of internal criticism proceeded in a veritable vicious circle. But the circle has since been broken. By his strength as a textual critic, Verheijen has furnished the fullest documentation of the sources presently available. Verheijen showed that both masculine and feminine forms of the *Rule* developed along distinct lines: the masculine version morphologically and chronologically preceded its feminine counterpart. Such is surely what we learn from the ancient *testimonia* and the history of the manuscripts. In addition, it appears to be no longer possible to regard *Letter* 211. 1–16 as a unified structure. We shall presently discuss Verheijen's latest suggestion that the nuns at Hippo were possibly in possession of the feminine transcription of Augustine's *Rule* before they received *Letter* 211. 1–4.

Very briefly, then, sound criteria of textual criticism point to the chronological precedence of Augustine's *Rule* over the *Rule for Nuns*. Regrettably, much secondary literature has failed to catch up with recent research in these areas. For whatever reasons, few scholars have assimilated and digested Verheijen's findings. Although opinion still remains divided, the case for an original feminine version is weak indeed.

The suitability of Augustine's *Rule* for both sexes must, in any case, be acknowledged as one of its distinctive features. If one accepts Verheijen's textual criticism, an original text in the masculine allowed for grammatical changes of gender and the substitution of such words as *praeposita*, *famula*, and *soror* for their masculine counterparts. Whether the transcription into the feminine was actually made by Augustine himself or by some other person matters little, except to the historian. Whether, in fact, the text was transcribed from a feminine original to the masculine matters equally little, except to the historian. In either instance, we possess a single monastic code admirably tailored for both sexes. The bishop of Hippo, therefore, unlike Caesarius of Arles, stands alone in the history of early western monasticism as one whose legislative text does duty equally well for both men and women. There is, indeed, irony latent in the thought that this could be true of a man whose views on women are pilloried as prejudicial and woefully short-sighted.

3. Date(s) of Composition

A few scholars are of the opinion that the *Rule* was written by Augustine some time after his ordination to the presbyterate, when he established a monastery at Hippo in the garden near the church there. The earliest possible date of composition, therefore, would be 391. W. Hümpfner suggests a date no later than 393, on the basis of Augustine's use of *induco* instead of *infero* in the allusion to the Lord's Prayer which concludes the *Rule*.[79] Van Bavel lessens the force of this suggestion by citing *induco* in a like context from Augustine's *Letter* 177. 4 (dated 416).[80] However, in view of the numerous citations from the Dominical prayer throughout the bishop's writings, a single use of *induco* is hardly decisive. In some respects the argument here resembles that based on the sole occurrence of Acts 4: 32*b* + 32*c* + 35*b* in the *Rule* (1. 3). A more flexible opinion is offered by Mandonnet, who maintains that the *Rule* was drafted some time after Augustine's transfer to Hippo, beginning with 391 but before his episcopal ordination in late 395 or early 396.[81]

A. Zumkeller introduces a second time-frame when he suggests that the *Rule* was written after Augustine's episcopal ordination.[82] Van Bavel argues persuasively that the contents of the *Rule* require 'a certain theological maturity'.[83] A somewhat later dating would, on this account, appear to be more likely. Some five hundred parallel passages from the Augustinian corpus prompt van Bavel to opt for the closing years of the fourth century as the probable time of composition. Dom Sanchis likewise suggests that

[79] W. Hümpfner, 'Die Mönchsregel des heiligen Augustinus', *AM* 250. See also Arbesmann–Hümpfner, *Liber Vitasfratrum*, Introduction, p. lxxviii by Hümpfner.

[80] Van Bavel, 'Inferas–Inducas', 351.

[81] Mandonnet, *Saint Dominique*, ii. 135 ff. thought that Augustine addressed the *Regulations for a Monastery* to the lay monks at Thagaste *c*.388 and the *Rule* some time after his ordination to the presbyterate at Hippo in 391.

[82] Zumkeller, *Mönchtum*, 329.   [83] Van Bavel, 'Parallèles', 75.

the evolution of two basic Augustinian motifs, monastic poverty and brotherly love, lends greater credibility to a later dating.[84] Van Bavel, Sanchis, and Verheijen all claim that the *Rule* was written for the community of lay monks, the first of Augustine's two monasteries at Hippo. The cautious and deliberate latitude of opinion allowed for by these three scholars need not detain us. The date ± 397 does justice to their distillation of the internal evidence. Merlin was of the opinion that Augustine, already a bishop, wrote the *Rule* before leaving his monastery of lay monks to take up residence at the *domus episcopi*.[85] This would be before 28 August 397, when Augustine's signature appears for the first time in his own right as successor to Bishop Valerius.[86] Verheijen nuances this date further by suggesting that the *Rule* could well have been written after Augustine had settled in as the bishop of Hippo. He offers the hypothesis that the *Rule* antedates Augustine's *Answer to Faustus* and proposes 397 as the likely date of composition.[87] Spectators on the sidelines are quick to observe that many writings of Augustine date from the closing years of the fourth century, the best known being of course the *Confessions*, generally dated 397–400. To say nothing of his sermons, Augustine dictated thirty-three books and long letters during the years 395–410. His middle years were extraordinarily prolific.[88] But then he seems always to have been *l'homme engagé*. Surely there was time for the *Rule* as well.

L. Cilleruelo[89] and J. Morán,[90] who identify recalcitrant monks at Carthage as its intended recipients, adopt a third time-frame for the composition of the *Rule*. These were the same monks to whom Augustine, *c.*400 addressed his treatise *The Work of Monks*. This treatise was written by Augustine in response to a request made by Bishop Aurelius of Carthage, urging him to counter the arguments

[84] D. Sanchis, 'Pauvreté monastique et charité fraternelle chez saint Augustin: Le commentaire augustinien de Actes 4, 32–5 entre 393 et 403', *Studia Monastica*, 4 (1962), 7–33.
[85] N. Merlin, *Saint Augustin et la vie monastique* (Albi, 1933), 27.
[86] CCL 149. 49.
[87] Verheijen, *Augustine's Monasticism*, 48–51. The hypothesis is not convincing. See J. Gavigan's comments in *AS* 11 (1980), 229–30.
[88] Brown, *Augustine*, 278.
[89] L. Cilleruelo, 'Nota sobre la fecha de composición de la Regula Augustini', *Archivo agustiniano*, 55 (1961), 257–61.
[90] J. Morán, 'Notas sobre el monacato agustiniano', *Ciudad de Dios*, 175 (1962). 535–47.

that had arisen between those monks who chose to support themselves by manual labour and others who preferred to live solely on the alms of the faithful. Seeing it as a further effort on the part of Augustine to control the behaviour of these refractory monks, Cilleruelo situates the *Rule* c.401/2.

Some writings of the bishop (notably *Correction and Grace* and *The Gift of Perseverance*) suggest a fourth and final alternative time of composition. These writings were addressed by Augustine to Valentine and the monks at Hadrumetum, which is modern Sousse in Tunisia. Two issues were at stake here: (1) Augustine's well-known insistence on the necessity of grace and (2) the allegedly superfluous role of the superior. There were monks at Hadrumetum who challenged the first of these matters and favoured the second. According to A. C. Vega,[91] A. Sage,[92] and A. Manrique,[93] it was probably this *cause célèbre* which prompted Augustine to compose the *Rule* near the end of his life. Its appearance at such a late date would explain how the *Rule* failed to be included in Augustine's *Retractations*, a fate identical with that of some other works dealing with the same controversy among these quarrelsome monks. In further support of this view, Sage pointed out that the 'doctrinal density'[94] of the penultimate paragraph of the *Rule* also relates to the latter years of Augustine's life. In that paragraph, the word *gratia* occurs for the only time in the entire work (namely, in ll. 376–7: *non sicut serui sub lege, sed sicut liberi sub gratia constituti*), although the first words of the paragraph, *Donet dominus*, have already introduced the same theme.

Needless to say, profoundness of theological thought or its compactness are by no means narrowly limited to Augustine's late years only. Such 'doctrinal density' appears in early writings as well. For instance, one need not await the time after Augustine's letter to Boniface in 418, when the Pelagian controversy had reached its peak, to find in Augustine's writings the maturity of thought manifest in this final portion of the *Rule*. Specifically,

[91] A. C. Vega, 'Notas histórico-críticas en torno a los orígenes de la Regla de San Agustín', *Boletín de la Real Academia de la Historia*, 152 (1963), 13–94.

[92] A. Sage, *La Règle de saint Augustin commentée par ses écrits* (Paris, 1961), 263.

[93] A. Manrique, *La vida monástica en San Agustín* (El Escorial–Salamanca, 1959), 454–64.

[94] Sage, *La Règle*, 263.

echoes of Rom. 6: 14 appear in Augustine's fourfold division of
history (in his *Eighty-three Different Questions*), into periods *ante
legem, sub lege, sub gratia, in pace*,[95] with a bipolar synthesis of the
same division implied in the contrast *sub lege constituti, nondum
sub gratia*. Augustine's *Eighty-three Different Questions* is a
cumulative presentation of some discussions held with lay monks at
Thagaste and Hippo as early as 388, though their publication did
not come about until the year 395/6. Another instance of the *sub
lege–sub gratia* antithesis appears in the treatise or sermon (the
genre is unclear) *Continence*, sometimes assigned to the year
395.[96] Furthermore, in the *Rule* itself, 'density' is by no means
limited to the final chapter. Its overall contents are an instance of
multum in paruo. The prescriptions of the *Rule*, moreover, convey
the distinct impression of having been the end-result of just such
prolonged discussions as those previously observed to have taken
place among the lay monks at Thagaste and Hippo. Besides,
economy of expression is virtually guaranteed by the inherent
qualities of Latin, especially as rendered by a good literary
craftsman. The compression evidenced in the language of the *Rule*
may be ascribed equally well to Augustine's habitual practice of
composition by dictation.

From such a late dating of the *Rule* would accrue, it is true, the
triple advantage that the silence concerning the *Rule* in *Sermons*
355 and 356, in the *Retractations*, and in Possidius' *Indiculus* would
thus be more intelligible. As noted earlier, however, the last two
of these three works possess other lacunae. And monastic rules as
such did not fall within the purview of the *Retractations*, since the
intramural features of the *Rule* either eliminated or at least greatly
narrowed the chances for its subsequent notice by Augustine or his
biographer in that regard. The silence of *Sermons* 355 and 356 can
also be explained otherwise than by a late date of composition. To
argue that the *Rule* was addressed either to the monks at
Hadrumetum or to the members of the *domus episcopi* at Hippo
establishes both a limiting and an arbitrary dichotomy. There is a
third alternative, namely, the supposition that the *Rule* was

[95] *Diu. QQ* 66. 3 (CCL 44A. 154).
[96] *Cont.* 3. 8–9 (CSEL 41. 148–51). La Bonnardière, 'La date du *De continentia
de saint Augustin*', *REA* 5 (1959), 121–7 suggests 416–18 as its time of
composition. D. Faul, 'The Date of the *De Continentia* of St. Augustine', *SP* 6
(1962), 374–82 dates the work *c.*426. The matter remains unsettled.

destined for Augustine's first community of lay monks at Hippo.
On this supposition, *Sermons* 355 and 356 would understandably
make no mention of the *Rule*, which was a non-clerical document.
As those sermons portray it, the scandal involving the priest
Januarius pertained to a monastery of clerics, not to one of monks.
Recourse to the *argumentum ex silentio* requires explanation of all
possible options.

A lack of discernment similar to that just noted besets Sage in
his efforts to assign a late date to the *Rule* by focusing upon the
'principal duty of the superior (*praepositus*) as one who corrects
his monks'.[97] It is true that Abbot Valentine, who was superior of
the community, did correct his monks, but the *Rule* (7. 2) provides
a broader scope of action for the priest (*presbyter*), whose
authority over the religious community exceeds that of the
superior. Therefore, to propose a chronological proximity between
the procedures reflected in Augustine's *Correction and Grace* and
the prescriptions detailing exercise of authority by a *praepositus* or
presbyter within the community (as articulated in ch. 7 of the *Rule*)
is not particularly persuasive.

4. Date of the *Rule for Nuns*

A time of composition has also been proposed for the feminine
version of the *Rule*. Verheijen had earlier suggested that the *Rule
for Nuns* was transcribed at Hippo or, at least, for the use of the
nuns there.[98] In other words, *Letter* 211. 1–4 (*Reprimand to
Quarrelling Nuns*) and §§ 5–16 (*Rule for Nuns*) were previously
thought by Verheijen and others to be linked in logical sequence
to this domestic dispute. More recently, however, Verheijen has
nuanced his opinion still further. He now feels that in the
Reprimand to Quarrelling Nuns (§ 2) the associating of Acts 4: 32a
with Ps. 67: 7 is an indication that the nuns were first in possession
of a feminine version of the *Rule*.[99] On that understanding, the
nexus between Acts 4: 32a and Ps. 67: 7 in the *Rule* itself (I. 2)
establishes the basis for the same juxtaposition of these texts in the
bishop's subsequent *Reprimand to Quarrelling Nuns*. If, as
Verheijen thinks, the nuns did already possess the feminine form

[97] Sage, *La Règle*, 263.
[98] Verheijen, *Règle* ii. 202.
[99] Id. *Augustine's Monasticism*, 70.

of the *Rule*, the later *Reprimand*, delivered by Augustine in his transparent epistolary manner, would have had even additional impact and meaning.

The usual date assigned to *Letter* 211. 1–4 has been 423. But the reading *de Donatistis* (§ 4) instead of *de deo natis* is no doubt the correct one, thereby suggesting a date closer to the Council of Carthage in 411 which, politically at least, sounded the death-knell of Donatism. With good reason the long-standing date 423 for *Letter* 211. 1–4 is pushed back. Augustine's contrast between schism in the community of nuns and his rejoicing over unity with the Donatists hardly allows an interval of more than ten years after the event. The transcription of the *Rule for Nuns* then lies somewhere between 397 and 423.

In sum, then, four periods in Augustine's life furnish possible dates for the composition of his *Rule*. A margin of dates for each period is defensible. Such variety of opinion among scholars does not impute ignorance so much as it reveals a discerning use of internal evidence.

Few scholars have claimed Augustine's early years at Hippo between 391 and his episcopal ordination in 395/6 as the time of composition for the *Rule*. While the last of the four time-frames (426–d. 430), Augustine's old age, is attractive to other scholars, it appears to have lost much ground in the wake of recent research. The third time-frame, 401/2, in connection with the unruly monks near Carthage, is doubtfully sustainable for the same reasons and has never gained wide currency among scholars. Barring more convincing evidence to the contrary, *c.*397 seems to be a more likely time of composition for Augustine's *Rule*.

Caveat lector: Verheijen's strengths as a textual critic have shown that the sequence of the *Reprimand to Quarrelling Nuns* and the *Rule for Nuns* in the manuscript tradition is quite fortuitous. To conclude, then, on the slender base of textual evidence alone that the *Rule for Nuns* was composed for the use of those nuns among whom Augustine's sister had served as superior before her death raises as many questions as answers. Who is responsible for the transcription? The nuns themselves? A single hand or an interested group? We frankly do not know. It seems fair to ask further whether transcription into the feminine form occurred during Augustine's lifetime. Nor is the earliest appearance of the *Rule for Nuns* in the textual history during the late sixth and early seventh century in Spain particularly illuminating on these issues. That the feminine version of Augustine's *Rule* derives from the masculine is the most some scholars may wish to say.

IX
Augustine as Monk–Bishop

EXCEPT for the sudden dismissal of his concubine and a subsequent short-lived liaison with another woman, there was for Augustine throughout the years we are considering an almost predictable coherence of action. So perceptive a man could scarcely have been unmoved by the contrast between his personal incapacity for continence and the resolve of his concubine to stay chaste the rest of her life. Surrender of sexuality, property, and power was an outcome of Augustine's restless search for another lifestyle during his two unsettled years as a professor of rhetoric at Milan. And once he found this lifestyle, he had to share it with others. No wonder the triple renunciation of Rom. 13: 13 and the single renunciation of Matt. 19: 21, with their invitation to follow Christ, stirred so deeply within his heart.

Both the rhetorical and, to a much greater extent, the philosophical traditions, as old as Isocrates and Plato, respectively, served as an anvil upon which Augustine gradually forged his thinking on monasticism. At Milan and shortly afterwards at Cassiciacum the sounds of the hammer were heard distinctly as these malleable metals were yielding gradually to the design of Augustine's mind. There was, to be sure, a certain congruity of vocation between the philosopher and the monk. Long before at the age of eighteen, Cicero's *Hortensius* had introduced the young Augustine to the themes of wealth and wisdom. Ten years of teaching rhetoric had prepared the ground for his fertile listening to Ambrose and his reading of the Scriptures. While Augustine's philosophical interests gradually abated in favour of the Bible, he could never part company with such treasures as wisdom, contemplation, and beauty. Within the philosophical quarries of late antiquity there were many genuinely ascetic and religious raw materials. While every quarry actually begins at bedrock, the observer begins to take notice only with what is visible to the eye.

From the time Pontician told Alypius and Augustine the story of Antony of Egypt, a monastic paradigm provided an impetus to the immediate and future direction of their lives. But Augustine was necessarily selective in his assimilation and adaptation of such a paradigm to his own time, temperament, place, and circumstances. Three titles from among his early writings tell part of the story. His unquenchable thirst for God was revealed in the *Soliloquies*. *The Ways of the Catholic Church and the Manichaeans* furnished positive proof of Augustine's love for Christ, people, and the Church. Seven years thereafter of uninterrupted living with ascetics both at Thagaste and Hippo finally begot the *Eighty-three Different Questions* and answers for 'the brothers', as he affectionately called them. Augustine's monastic manner of life was in full view from the time of his early days at Thagaste. This is not to say there were no further modifications or developments. Yet in all of this, Augustine could never forsake completely many components in the Classical heritage any more than Jerome could ignore the style of Cicero. And in the long run some of the richest intellectual refinements of Graeco-Roman thought, designed by men for men in an all-male world, would no longer be restricted to men but would also become the preserve of women. Here it is worth recalling that grammatical gender chiefly distinguishes Augustine's *Rule* from his *Rule for Nuns*, in addition to the appropriate change of such words as *pater/mater*, *frater/soror* wherever necessary in the text. Unlike Caesarius of Arles in the next generation, who felt the need to draft two different texts for both sexes, Augustine's *Rule* stands alone, so far as I am aware, in the entire history of western monasticism as the single legislative text which does double duty since it met the needs of both men and women.

Although altered appreciably, the nexus between the individual and the common good, a debt Augustine owed chiefly to Stoic thought, gradually gave shape to the tension which held together, in a sometimes delicate equilibrium, the practical details of day-to-day living which are found in chs. 2–7 of his monastic *Rule*. A criterion for calibrating this tension between the common and the individual good predictably resurfaced in Augustine's *Rule* and was thereby transformed from its political and ethical heritage in Graeco-Roman antiquity into a norm for measuring the distance between selfishness and love.

At the heart of the *Rule* as well as within the heart of Plotinian metaphysics one hears undertones, resonating at a still deeper level, between the one and the many, unity and multiplicity. That

its second sentence should sound four notes for unity is a
deliberate stroke of its author:

Primum, propter quod *in unum* estis congregati ut *unianimes* habitetis in
domo et sit vobis anima *una* et cor *unum* in deum (1. 2).

As so often in Augustine, the alchemy of Acts 4: 32–5 and 2 Cor.
6: 16 yielded wondrous effects by the conclusion of this same first
chapter. Also latent therein is Augustine's capacity for forming
friendships and his refusal to forsake entirely the utopian Greek
ideal of sharing possessions, both of which contributed towards his
outright rejection of Plotinian individualism. But it was the
doctrine of the Incarnation and a personal God, punctuated by the
Christian virtues of love and humility, that radically altered his
thinking. Porphyry's arrangement of the *Enneads*, it will be
remembered, concluded with the phrase: 'the flight of the alone to
the Alone', a sentiment as attractive to Augustine as it was
fundamental to any intelligible grasp of Plotinian thought. With
the full force of his Trinitarian theology Augustine gradually
enriches and enlarges Plotinus' concepts of unity and multiplicity.
Only in the company of others could he long for, desire, search,
find, and love the beauty which he established as the goal for all
adherents of his monastic *Rule*.

By annexing *in deum* to the Lucan *anima una et cor unum* of
Acts 4: 32, Augustine's contemplative bent of mind and unquiet
heart were relentlessly impelled in the company of others by his
ardent desire for God. 'After you have found him,' he urges, 'you
must continue to seek him.'[1] Although his personal and pastoral
life mirrored such indefatigable single-mindedness and single-
heartedness, Augustine was never a monk such as he described in
his treatise, *The Work of Monks*. Nor was he a monk in the
manner of his contemporaries Cassian and Jerome. The bishop of
Hippo would nuance still further Jerome's facile comments to
Paulinus of Nola:

If you wish to exercise the office of priest, if the burden or the honour of
the episcopacy happens to delight you, then live in the cities and the towns
and make the salvation of others benefit your own soul. But if you wish to
be what you are called, a monk—that is, one who is alone—what are you
doing in the cities, which are assuredly not the dwelling of those who are
alone, but of the many?[2]

---

[1] *En. Ps. 104*, §3 (CCL 40. 1537), 'inuentus quaerendus'.
[2] *Ep.* 58. 5 (CSEL 54. 533).

While his intellectual labours at Thagaste added a new dimension to western monasticism, Augustine's enforced ordination at Hippo in 391 did not deter him from his resolve to remain a monk. Bishop Valerius honoured his determination by giving Augustine a garden for a building-site on the church grounds to set up a monastery. Just as one ought not to be too restrictive when applying the term *monasterium* to Thagaste, so also one ought not to impose other contemporary or later meanings of *monachus* upon Augustine himself. The conception of a monk which he articulated in his *Commentary on Ps. 132*, § 6 possessed both originality and legitimacy:

> The Greek μόνος means 'one', but not 'one' in any sense. A man in a crowd is one, but he can be called 'one' only in association with many others. He cannot be called μόνος, that is, 'one alone'. The Greek μόνος means 'one alone'. Therefore, μόνος, that is, 'one alone' is correct usage for those who live together in such a way as to make one person, so that they really possess, as the Scriptures say, 'one heart and one soul' (Acts 4: 32)—many bodies but not many souls, many bodies but not many hearts.

At first sight Augustine's interpretation of *monachus* appears to be somewhat forced. Such a description, however, discloses at once the eschatological dimension of both ecclesial and monastic life. As he is strengthened and sanctified by the Holy Spirit, the monk exemplifies the ideals of Acts 4: 32, at the same time deepening his solidarity with Christ and his Church on their way to the Father. Two distinctive features of Augustine's thought are worthy of mention: (1) its Trinitarian base, and (2) the felicitous balance between its eschatological and incarnational currents. On the less speculative side, Augustine could readily adjust the flexibility of such a description to fit his own circumstances. Yet as Bishop of Hippo, he consistently fostered monastic life in the more conventional sense which dissociated it from the fulfilment of pastoral obligations.

If the dating of Augustine's *Rule c.*397 adopted by Verheijen, van Bavel, Sanchis, and others is acceptable, then its non-clerical character as a document designated for laypersons of both sexes becomes evident also on these grounds, apart from the actual wording of the text itself. On this account, it is reasonable to ask to what extent such a monastic code was appropriate for clerics and priests who were engaged in ministry. While one can readily combine the concept of fraternity which was so fundamental at Thagaste with the apostolic witness so strongly emphasized at Hippo and derived from the early Jerusalem community, could one at the same time so readily blend these same two components (fraternal and communal witness to Acts 4: 32–5), with the energetic pastoral outreach which so significantly marked almost half of Augustine's eventful life? *Sermons* 355 and 356 in the sunset of his life amply demonstrate Augustine's accomplishment in doing precisely this by further insisting that his clergy do the same. A recently discovered letter written by Augustine deplores the crass misconduct of Antoninus, bishop of Fussala, in matters of poverty. Although he had been Augustine's second and ill-fated choice as bishop for the inauguration of a new episcopal see, Antoninus flagrantly ignored everything he had learned in Augustine's monastery at Hippo, where he had lived since boyhood.[3]

Barring another hypothesis as to its origin, the *Rule* was addressed (1) either to the monastery in the garden, *intra ecclesiam*, at Hippo, (2) or to monks in the environs of Carthage, (3) or to Abbot Valentine and his community at Hadrumetum. While the last two hypotheses have met with the least favour among scholars, our fragmented data indicate that its prescriptions were directed towards non-clerics at one of these three north African sites. Its addressees, in fact, were referred to twice as 'servants of God', whereas 'holy man' occurred once and 'brothers' was used six times; the seventh was a citation from 1 John 3: 15. A priest served as spiritual director whose additional tasks sometimes required his meting out discipline. On both textual and historical grounds, therefore, some may wish to question the suitability of Augustine's *Rule* as a guide for men and women whose chief concern extends to pastoral ministry in the Church.

For thousands of adherents to this monastic code this issue is far from being narrowly academic today. I have argued elsewhere on behalf of Augustine's *Rule* for persons engaged in apostolic work

---

[3] In one of the recently discovered letters, *Ep.* 20*, 28 (CSEL 88. 109), Augustine writes to Fabiola in Rome with reference to Bishop Antoninus: 'Tu quippe in hoc saeculo quaeris deum, ille in ecclesia quaerit hoc saeculum.'

and ministry.[4] To this end the *Rule* demonstrated remarkable effectiveness during the early Middle Ages.[5] As to its function during Augustine's lifetime, the history of the late fourth and fifth centuries maintains a stony silence. Similar lack of evidence for a monastic code to guide the bishop's clerical community from the date of his episcopal ordination in 395/6 suggests that Acts 4: 32–5 constituted, in effect, its basic rule of life. Such clearly is the message of *Sermons* 355 and 356.

Finally, Augustine's monastic writings reflect a wide range of firsthand experience. His *Rule*, for example, was chiefly the product of a direct experience in the first of his two monasteries at Hippo during the years 391–5. *The Work of Monks* responded forthrightly to the disorderly conduct of antinomian monks in the environs of Carthage. A deep-rooted national schism which had enveloped some of the bishop's blood relations was largely responsible for his reflections on the meaning of *monachus* in his *Commentary on Ps. 132*. Still another intramural situation was unveiled with Augustine's detailed disclosure of the personal holdings of his clerics in the matter of property. Here are no musings of an armchair theologian; here is no romanticization of common life; here is no utopian exegesis of Acts 4: 32–5. Augustine's vocabulary is that of a seasoned practitioner. His monastic writings bear comparison with the best of the autobiographical passages from his talented pen.

In the light of this study, then, the following observation by L. Th. Lorié requires some adjustment: 'Augustine . . . should be considered to be the father of a western spirituality, a western mysticism of a catholic Christian type, or, if a special label is wanted, of an ecclesiastical or clerical type, not specifically monastic.'[6] While this statement is both deserving and defensible, it is at the same time deficient, because it ignores Augustine's personal fidelity to a monastic ideal, his significant achievement as a monastic legislator for both men and women, his promotion of monasteries in a traditional sense (that is, devoid of pastoral responsibilities), his steady insistence on monasticizing his local clergy and his portrait as a monk-bishop drawn by Possidius. Lorié goes on to conclude: 'Of Augustine it may be said that he became a monk when later generations began to see him as such, and make

---

[4] Lawless, 'Enduring Values', 59–78.   [5] Brooke, *Monastic World*, 125.
[6] Lorié, *Spiritual Terminology*, 162–3.

him their model.'[7] Lorié seems to take for granted as normative Benedict's model of monasticism. Augustine died fifty years before Benedict was born. When he conceives of 'the monastic tradition' as 'a given method', 'a school',[8] Lorié evidently has in mind Benedict, Cassian of Marseilles, and possibly other representatives of Gallic monasticism such as Abbot Honoratus of Lérins, Hilary, or Caesarius of Arles. Augustine, meanwhile, demonstrates cogently that other vectors of measurement are available for determining the variety of experiences which the monastic inclination or impulse will reflect. Its boundaries need not be limited to a particular school or method. Augustine's persevering response to a monastic calling, as he conceived of it in his own terms and in his daily life, is possibly the most underrated facet of his personality.

[7] Ibid. 163.
[8] Ibid.

APPENDICES

Appendix I

Regula recepta: Later Version of the *Rule*

Most people are generally familiar with the version of the *Rule* which begins with the opening sentence of the *Regulations for a Monastery*:

> Love God above all else, dearest brothers,
> then your neighbour also,
> because these are the precepts
> given us as primary principles.

There follows immediately:

> Here are the rules we lay down for your observance,
> once you have been admitted to the monastery.

From the early twelfth century, §§ 2–11 of the *Regulations for a Monastery* have been detached from § 1 with its initial words: 'Love God above all else . . .'. Eventually, this sonorous first sentence circulated in many manuscripts as the opening sentence of Augustine's *Rule*. Properly speaking, it does not belong in the *Rule*. In the first place, such is the evidence of the manuscript tradition and, in the second place, serious doubts exist in the minds of some scholars whether or not Augustine ever composed the sentence.

A word of explanation as to how this transfer took place is appropriate. One account of why and how this occurred stems from Eusebius Amort, who suggested in 1747 that the Canons of Springirsbach found the austerities of the *Regulations for a Monastery* too severe for a northern European climate and petitioned for exemption from its requirements. To this end, Pope Gelasius II, on 11 August 1118, granted a dispensation from those monastic regulations which hindered the exercise of pastoral ministry.[1] Recent research attributes the separate existence of the *Rule* in the form preceded by the first section of the *Regulations for a Monastery* to Yves of Chartres (d. 1115), an opinion which appears to be preferable.[2] The earliest manuscripts attesting to this form of the Augustinian Rule are of French or English origin. Except for its famous first sentence, one might say that thereafter the text of the *Regulations for a Monastery* became effectively suppressed. Arbesmann correctly observes: 'On the whole, the period during which the prescriptions of the *Regulations for a*

---

[1] Verheijen, *Règle* ii. 117–20.   [2] Ibid. 212–13.

Monastery were actually practised as a norm of monastic life was rather brief.'[3] That the *Regulations for a Monastery* and the *Rule* became bifurcated and went separate ways is, therefore, a medieval development in the history of these texts.

[3] R. Arbesmann, 'Question of the *Regula Sancti Augustini*', 249.

Appendix II

Ordo monasterii: Current State of Research

A ninth-century manuscript, Laon 328 *bis*, confers the title *Ordo monasterii* (*Regulations for a Monastery*) upon a text which begins 'Ante omnia, fratres carissimi, diligatur' . . . and concludes with the words 'de uestra salute. Amen'. Since 1937 the same text has also been designated *Disciplina monasterii*. Both titles are arbitrary.[1] I prefer the former because it reflects more accurately the contents of this document, namely, regulations for daily life in a monastery.

This monastic text immediately sets forth the New Testament command to love. There follows a sudden leap of thought to a detailed description of what we currently call *Liturgy of the Hours*, the first of its kind in western monastic literature. Directives for the work schedule, spiritual reading, personal and communal poverty, avoidance of murmuring, and religious obedience constitute the basic components of monastic life. Regulations relating to food, wine, silence, extramural comportment, and punishment for offences round out the text. Its final sentence urges fidelity to these observances in the name of Christ.

A brief survey of twentieth-century scholarship on the question of authorship reveals the following spectrum of opinion. Casamassa,[2] De Bruyne,[3] Vega,[4] and Sage[5] reject Augustinian authorship. Manrique maintains that Augustine probably knew and approved of this document, but that it was not the product of his pen.[6] Luc Verheijen allows partial but extremely limited authorship to Augustine.[7] His opinion is sensitively nuanced, as we shall note below.

Cilleruelo believes that Augustine could have composed the *Ordo*

---

[1] Mandonnet, *Saint Dominique*, ii. 130–1. With good reason Arbesmann, 'Question of the *RSA*', 240 objects to Mandonnet's abandoning the long-standing term *Ordo Monasterii*.

[2] A. Casamassa, 'Note sulla *Regula Sancti Augustini*', *Sanctus Augustinus, Vitae spiritualis magister*, 1 (Rome, 1959), 357–89. Edited posthumously by A. Trapè.

[3] De Bruyne, 'La première règle de saint Benoît', 316–42.

[4] Vega, *La Regla de San Agustín*, 7.

[5] Sage, *La Règle*, 256–7; also 259.

[6] Manrique, *Vida monástica*, 472–5.

[7] Verheijen, 'Remarques sur le style de la "Regula Secunda" de saint Augustin. Son rédacteur', *AM* 255–63. Also *Règle* ii. 125–74.

monasterii.[8] Hümpfner[9] esteems the work to be genuine. Bardy[10] cautiously accepts the research of Mandonnet[11] in favour of Augustine. Zumkeller declares the issue to be unsettled.[12]

Gavigan, Hackett, and Ladner assume a guarded posture in this matter of authorship and it seems best to cite their opinions. J. Gavigan claims that this text 'appears, in fact, to take its origin from Augustinian monasteries for lay-monks. Arguments to the contrary are not convincing. We find no fundamental contradiction between the spirit of the OM and works of Augustine universally acknowledged as genuine. A study of the manuscript tradition leads to the same conclusion.'[13] M. B. Hackett rightly observes: 'Augustine may not have written the *Ordo Monasterii* for his first monastery at Thagaste, or indeed for any of his later foundations, although it is difficult to see on what grounds, apart from stylistic reasons which of themselves are not entirely conclusive, his authorship can safely be rejected.'[14] This same sensitive scholarship is reflected in the viewpoint of G. B. Ladner: 'If the *Ordo Monasterii* is not by Augustine himself, it did, however, almost certainly originate in his age and in an Augustinian milieu.'[15]

1. The Question of Authorship

The *Regulations for a Monastery* consists of 379 words, roughly one-fifth the length of Augustine's *Rule*. Verheijen's critical edition furnishes a superior text with eleven sections. This erudite Dutch scholar suggests Augustine's direct hand in §§ 1 and 11, its initial and final sentences. Verheijen further proposes Alypius, Bishop of Thagaste, as the author of the intervening §§ 2–10. Athanase Sage acknowledged with reluctance the possibility that Augustine knew only its conclusion, § 11.

Verheijen derives his hypothesis for Alypian authorship of §§ 2–10 upon (1) the *couleur juridique* of this document, and (2) the fact that Alypius was a lawyer. A comparison of Augustinian and Alypian texts would, according to Verheijen, tilt the scales in favour of the bishop of Thagaste. But it is doubtful whether the few passages taken down by *notarii* as pronouncements of Alypius at the Council of Carthage in 411

[8] Cilleruelo, *El monacato*, 62–73.
[9] Arbesmann–Hümpfner, *Liber Vitasfratrum*. See Introduction, p. lxxviii.
[10] Bardy, *Saint Augustin*, 161–2.
[11] Mandonnet, *Saint Dominique*, ii. 121–48.
[12] Zumkeller, *Das Mönchtum*, 330–1.
[13] Gavigan, *Vita monastica*, 34 n. 50.
[14] M. B. Hackett, 'The Rule of St. Augustine and Recent Criticism', *The Tagastan*, 20 (1958), 48.
[15] Ladner, *The Idea of Reform*, 357–8.

would furnish a sufficient quantity of material for a productive comparative study of Augustine and Alypius.[16]

Besides, Augustine, like Alypius, was educated with a view to a career in the civil service: 'Moreover, my studies which were called honourable were directed to the study of law, so that I might excel at it.'[17] He describes the orientation of his lectures thus: 'I sold a skill at speech designed for victories at court.'[18] In anticipation of the resolve to resign from his teaching post at Milan, Augustine says: 'Thus youths who did not meditate on your law, or on your peace, but on foolish lies and court quarrels, would no longer prise from my mouth weapons for their madness.'[19] At the acme of success as a teacher, he writes: 'I have plenty of friends, and if I do not rashly attempt too much, at least a governorship may be granted me.'[20]

There are other considerations too. First of all, legal and rhetorical education was virtually the same except for apprenticeship. Secondly, Alypius had studied under Augustine both at Thagaste and at Carthage.[21] Thirdly, when composing house-regulations a non-lawyer would instinctively employ legal-sounding phrases or expressions.[22] The *Regulations for a Monastery* express the language of the Roman *iuris consulti* whom Quintilian credits with a *summus circa uerborum proprietatem labor*.[23] It is this *uerborum proprietas* to which a professor of rhetoric, like Augustine, would adhere. There is nothing in this monastic code that would contradict Augustine's authorship. In addition, as I have demonstrated elsewhere,[24] the composition of this simple piece of monastic literature is quite graceful.

That the *Regulations for a Monastery* overlap with Augustine's floruit is beyond dispute. Caesarius of Arles, for example, made generous use of the text in his *Rule for Nuns*.[25] Caesarius did not borrow from Augustine's *Rule for Nuns*: he used the *Longer Rule*, that is, the combination of *Regulations for a Monastery* and Augustine's *Rule*. Furthermore, the *Liturgy of the Hours* in vogue at Vivarium at the time of Cassiodorus (484/90–590?) shows clear dependence upon the monastic office in the *Regulations for a Monastery*, likewise attesting to the latter's antiquity.[26] Similarly, the manuscript tradition also links, however tenuously, what

---

[16] Arbesmann, 'Question of the RSA', 260–1.
[17] *Conf.* 3. 3. 6 (CCL 27. 39).
[18] Ibid. 4. 2. 2 (CCL 27. 40).
[19] Ibid. 9. 2. 2 (CCL 27. 133).
[20] Ibid. 6. 11. 19 (CCL 27. 87).
[21] Ibid. 6. 7. 11, 6. 9. 14 (CCL 27. 80–3).
[22] See Rudolf Lorenz's review of Verheijen's *La Règle de saint Augustin* in *Zeitschrift für Kirchengeschichte*, 80 (1969), 263–8, esp. 267.
[23] *Institutio Oratoria* 5. 14. 34.
[24] G. Lawless, '*Ordo Monasterii*: Structure, Style, and Rhetoric', *Augustinianum*, 22 (1982), 469–91.
[25] McCarthy, *Rule for Nuns of St. Caesarius*, 128.
[26] Morin, 'L'ordre des heures canoniales', 145–52.

is probably the oldest monastic code in the West with Augustine. Paris, BN lat. 12634 situates the *Regulations for a Monastery* immediately before the text of Augustine's *Rule*. While there is no *explicit* to separate the two texts, they are separated by an *Amen*. There follow on the same lines the opening words of Augustine's *Rule*, with no *incipit*. This oldest manuscript of the *Rule*, we noted earlier, concludes with the words: 'Explicit Regula Sancti Augustini Episcopi'.[27]

It should be pointed out that Paris, BN lat. 12634 also contains a miscellany of several extracts from the monastic legislation of Pachomius (translated by Jerome), Basil (translated by Rufinus), the *Rule of the Master*, and others. While the association of the *Regulations for a Monastery* with Augustine's *Rule* indisputably derives from late antiquity and remains unbroken in one of the three manuscript families that have transmitted Augustine's *Rule*, it could be that such an association, in the first instance, is after all quite fortuitous. We simply do not know.

2. *Locus originis*

The sequence of the psalms in § 2 of the *Regulations for a Monastery* has been thought to preserve the order of psalms for Matins at Bethlehem, 50–62–89 (as found in Cassian, *Institutes* 3. 6), thereby suggesting a north African origin for this monastic code as a consequence of Bishop Alypius' visit to Jerome *c.*395. But the sequence of psalms in the *Regulations for a Monastery* is 62–5–89. To account for this discrepancy in the numeration of the psalms, Verheijen ascribes to Cassian a possible slip of memory in the latter's recollection of Matins introduced at Bethlehem not only by inverting the sequence to read 62–50–89, but further by substituting Ps. 5 for Ps. 50.[28] There is, however, no historical evidence that such is the case. In fact, the sequence from 62: 2 'de luce', through 5: 4, 5 'mane', towards the 'vespere' of 89: 6 is both more coherent and logical. It is just as likely that the author of the *Regulations for a Monastery* simply deemed the sequence 62–5–89 more natural to the unfolding of a single day in the life of a monk.[29] To attribute to Cassian any such lapse of memory apropos of Ps. 50 is seemingly gratuitous.

No one will deny the eastern influences which helped to shape the *Liturgy of the Hours* in this oldest western monastic code. Silence during work-hours, the pivotal role of the *pater*, likewise indicate traces of eastern influence. Alypius, as we just observed, had visited Jerome in Bethlehem and very likely brought back to Thagaste some of these features of eastern monasticism. But Augustine had also become acquainted with Egyptian and Basilian coenobitism during his extended

---

[27] See Ch. VIII n. 6.   [28] *Règle* ii. 136.
[29] P. F. Bradshaw, *Daily Prayer in the Early Church* (London, 1981), 125.

sojourns in Milan and Rome. He referred, for example, to manual labour as 'an eastern custom'.[30] We noted earlier from Augustine's account of eastern coenobitism and his familiarity with monasteries in Milan and Rome how deeply impressed he was with the way of life he observed in these houses.[31] Alypius' visit to Bethlehem, therefore, does not grant to the bishop of Thagaste such a preferred or exclusive status as the chief compiler of the *Regulations for a Monastery*. Nor is there any compelling reason from the standpoint of our present liturgical knowledge why north Africa must cede to Gaul or Italy as the *locus originis* of this monastic code.

A possible Italian origin for the *Regulations for a Monastery* is suggested by the fact that *Sermon* 95 of Maximus of Turin twice offers a paraphrase of the verse from Acts 4: 32: 'nemo suum aliquid uindicaret' and 'nemo proprium aliquid uindicaret'.[32] Does Maximus' use of *uindicare* echo that found in l. 32 of the *Regulations for a Monastery*, which reads: *Nemo sibi aliquid suum uindicet proprium?* Does such a coincidence thereby establish a possible link with the Old Latin Versions of the Bible which were circulating in Italy? Again, how can we explain satisfactorily the coincidence between the canonical hours observed at Vivarium[33] and the monastic office in § 2 of the *Regulations for a Monastery*?

We have come to the limits at present imposed on us by the available evidence. I shall hazard a conjecture. If the theory of dual authorship were critically examined with thoroughness and precision on the grounds of the existing evidence, it would, I believe, be weakened appreciably. I have in mind a detailed assessment of the *Ordo Monasterii* along the same lines as John K. Coyle's study, *Augustine's 'De Moribus Ecclesiae Catholicae'* (Fribourg, 1978). Such a comprehensive study would, in my opinion, strongly suggest that Augustine single-handedly composed the complete text. That is to say, he holds as strong a claim to this title as does Alypius. This at least is a reasonable hypothesis. Meanwhile, the author of the *Regulations for a Monastery* remains anonymous and its place of origin is by no means established with certainty.

---

[30] See Ch. IV n. 31.
[31] See Ch. IV n. 30.
[32] CCL 23. 63–4. Here *Sermo* 17, ed. Mutzenbecher.
[33] See n. 26 above.

Select Bibliography

The reader is also referred to the sections 'Monachisme' and 'Règle' of the 'Bulletin augustinien' in the *Revue des études augustiniennes* (Paris, 1955–   ).

1. General

ANDRESEN, C., *Bibliographia Augustiniana* (Darmstadt, 1973), 89–94.

BAVEL, T. VAN, *Répertoire bibliographique de saint Augustin 1950–1960* (Steenbrugge, 1963), 365–75, nos. 2288–339.

GINDELE, E., *Bibliographie zur Geschichte und Theologie des Augustiner-Eremitenordens bis zum Beginn der Reformation* (Berlin–New York, 1977), 25–33, nos. 230–315.

MEIJER, A., DE, 'Bibliographie historique de l'Ordre de Saint Augustin 1980–1984', *Augustiniana*, 35 (1985), 7–9, nos. 4220–34.

—— and SCHRAMA, M., 'Bibliographie historique de l'Ordre de Saint Augustin 1945–1975', *Augustiniana*, 26 (1976), 46–8, nos. 75–105.

————, 'Bibliographie historique de l'Ordre de Saint Augustin 1975–1980', *Augustiniana*, 31 (1981), 7–8, nos. 3241a–8.

VERHEIJEN, L., *Règle de Saint Augustin*, ii. *Recherches historiques* (Paris, 1967), 221–39.

2. Twentieth-Century Critical Editions
(The list is chronological.)

GOLDBACHER, A., *S. Augustini Epistolae*, 4, CSEL 57 (Vienna, 1911), 356–71.

SCHROEDER, P., 'Die Augustinerchorherrenregel: Entstehung, kritischer Text und Einführung der Regel', *Archiv für Urkundenforschung*, 9 (1926), 271–306.

DE BRUYNE, D., 'La première Règle de saint Benoît', *Revue bénédictine*, 42 (1930), 316–42.

VEGA, A. C., *La Regla de San Agustín: Edición crítica, precedida de un estudio sobre la misma y los códices de El Escorial* (El Escorial, 1933).

ARBESMANN, R. and HÜMPFNER, W., *Jordani de Saxonia liber vitasfratrum* (New York, 1943), 491–504.

VERHEIJEN, L., *La Règle de saint Augustin*, i. *Tradition manuscrite* (Paris, 1967), 'Obiurgatio', 105–7; 'Ordo Monasterii', 148–52; 'Praeceptum', 417–37.

3. *English Translations of Augustine's Rule*

BAVEL, T. J. VAN, *The Rule of Saint Augustine: Introduction and Commentary*, Eng. tr. R. Canning (London, 1984).

CLARK, M. T., *Augustine of Hippo: Selected Writings*. Preface by Goulven Madec (New York, 1984), 479–93.

HAND, T. A., *The Rule of Saint Augustine: Commentary by Alphonsus Orozco* (Dublin, 1956).

RUSSELL, R. P., *The Rule of Our Holy Father St. Augustine* (Villanova, 1976).

TOURSCHER, F. E., *The Rule of Our Holy Father St. Augustine*. Revised by Robert P. Russell (Villanova, 1946).

ZUMKELLER, A., *The Rule of St. Augustine*. Eng. tr., L. Meyer (Cleveland, 1960). Also tr. by J. C. Resch (De Pere, Wis., n.d.).

4. *Special Studies*

ARBESMANN, R., 'The Question of the *Regula Sancti Augustini*', *Augustinian Studies*, 1 (1970), 237–61.

——, 'The Attitude of Saint Augustine Towards Labor', in D. Neiman and M. Schatkin (eds.), *The Heritage of the Early Church* (Rome, 1973), 245–59.

ARMAS, G., 'Visión sinóptica de la vida religiosa según san Agustín', *Augustinus*, 24 (1979), 205–13.

BARDY, G., *Saint Augustin: L'homme et l'œuvre* (7th edn., Paris, 1948).

BAVEL, T. J. VAN, '"Ante omnia" et "in Deum" dans la "Regula Sancti Augustini"', *Vigiliae Christianae*, 12 (1958), 157–65.

——, 'Inferas—Inducas: A propos de Mtth. 6, 13 dans les œuvres de saint Augustin', *Revue bénédictine*, 69 (1959), 348–51.

——, 'Parallèles, vocabulaire et citations bibliques de la "Regula Sancti Augustini": Contribution au problème de son authenticité'. *Augustiniana*, 9 (1959), 12–77.

——, 'La espiritualidad de la Regla de san Agustín', *Augustinus*, 12 (1967) 433–48.

——, 'The Evangelical Inspiration of the Rule of Saint Augustine', *The Downside Review*, 93 (1975), 83–99.

——, *Christians in the World: An Introduction to the Spirituality of St. Augustine* (New York, 1980).

BENITO Y DURÁN, A., 'Los monacatos de san Basilio y san Agustín y su coincidencia en el pensamiento del trabajo corporal', *Augustinus*, 17 (1972), 357–95.

BISHKO, C. J., 'The Date and Nature of the Spanish "Consensoria monachorum"', *American Journal of Philology*, 69 (1948), 337–95.

BOLGIANI, F., *La conversione di s. Agostino e l'VIII libro delle 'Confessioni'* (Turin, 1956).

BONNER, G. I., '*Libido* and *Concupiscentia* in St. Augustine', *Studia Patristica*, 6 (Berlin, 1962), 303–14.

——, *St. Augustine: Life and Controversies* (London 1963; 2nd edn. Norwich, 1986).

——, 'The Extinction of Paganism and the Church Historian', *Journal of Ecclesiastical History*, 35 (1984), 339–57.

BRADSHAW, P. F., *Daily Prayer in the Early Church* (London, 1981).

BROCKWELL, C. W., 'Augustine's Ideal of Monastic Community: A Paradigm for his Doctrine of the Church', *Augustinian Studies*, 8 (1977), 91–109.

BROOKE, C., *The Monastic World 1000–1300* (New York, 1974).

BROWN, P., *Augustine of Hippo* (London, 1967).

——, 'The Philosopher and Society in Late Antiquity', *The Center for Hermeneutical Studies in Hellenistic and Modern Culture*, Colloquy 34 (Berkeley, 1980), 1–41.

——, 'Augustine and Sexuality', *The Center for Hermeneutical Studies in Hellenistic and Modern Culture*, Colloquy 46 (Berkeley, 1983), 1–41.

CHADWICK, H., 'The Role of the Christian Bishop in Ancient Society', *The Center for Hermeneutical Studies in Hellenistic and Modern Culture*, Colloquy 35 (Berkeley, 1980), 1–47.

——, 'The Ascetic Ideal in the History of the Church', *Studies in Church History*, 22 (1985), 1–23.

——, *Augustine*. Past Master Series (Oxford, 1986).

CILLERUELO, L., *El monacato de s. Agustín y su Regla* (Valladolid, 1947).

——, 'Nota sobre la fecha de composición de la *Regula Augustini*', *Archivo Agustiniano*, 55 (1961), 257–61.

——, *El monacato de san Agustín* (Valladolid, 1966).

——, 'Conclusiones sobre la *Regula Augustini*', *Revista agustiniana de espiritualidad*, 10 (1969), 49–86.

——, 'Evolución del monacato agustiniano', *Estudio agustiniano*, 15 (1980), 171–98.

CLÉMENT, J.-M., *Lexique des anciennes règles monastiques occidentales* (2 vols., Steenbrugge, 1978).

COX, P., *Biography in Late Antiquity: A Quest for the Holy Man* (Berkeley, 1983).

COYLE, J. K., *Augustine's 'De Moribus Ecclesiae Catholicae'* (Fribourg, 1978).

CROUZEL, H., 'Marriage and Virginity: Has Christianity Devalued Marriage?', *The Way*, Supplement 10 (1970), 3–23.

DESPREZ, V., *Règles monastiques d'occident, IVᵉ–Vᵉ siècle: d'Augustin à Ferréol*. Collection Vie monastique, 9 (Maine-et-Loire, 1980).

DICKINSON, J. C., *The Origins of the Austin Canons and their Introduction into England* (London, 1950).

SELECT BIBLIOGRAPHY   175

FERRARI, L. C., 'Paul at the Conversion of Augustine: *Conf.* VIII, 12, 29–
30', *Augustinian Studies*, 11 (1980), 5–20.
——, 'Ecce audio vocem de vicina domo: *Conf.* 8, 12, 29', *Augustiniana*,
33 (1983), 232–45.
——, *The Conversions of Saint Augustine* (Villanova, 1984).
FOLLIET, G., 'Aux origines de l'ascétisme et du cénobitisme africain',
Saint Martin et son temps. Studia Anselmiana, 46 (Rome, 1961), 25–44.
——, '"Deificari in otio": Augustin, *Ep* 10, 2', *Recherches augustiniennes*,
2 (1962), 225–36.
FREND, W. H. C., *The Rise of Christianity* (London, 1984).
FRY, T. (ed.), *RB 1980: The Rule of St. Benedict* (Collegeville, 1981).

GAVIGAN, J., *De uita monastica in Africa septentrionali inde a temporibus
sancti Augustini usque ad inuasiones Arabum* (Turin, 1962).
GRECH, P., 'The Augustinian Community and the Primitive Church',
Augustiniana, 5 (1955), 459–70.
GUARDINI, R., *The Conversion of Augustine* (Westminster, Md., 1960).

HACKETT, M. B., 'The Rule of St. Augustine and Recent Criticism', *The
Tagastan*, 20 (1958), 43–50.
HALLIBURTON, R. J., 'The Inclination to Retirement—the Retreat of
Cassiciacum and the "Monastery" of Tagaste', *Studia Patristica*, 5
(Berlin, 1962), 329–40.
——, 'The Concept of the *"Fuga saeculi"* in St. Augustine', *The
Downside Review*, 85 (1967), 249–61.
HANSLIK, R., *Benedicti Regula*, CSEL 75 (Vienna, 1960).
HENRY, P., *The Path to Transcendence: From Philosophy to Mysticism in
Saint Augustine*. Eng. tr., *La vision d'Ostie* (Pittsburgh, 1981).
HOARE, F. R., *The Western Fathers* (London, 1954).
HÜMPFNER, W., 'Die Mönchsregel des heiligen Augustinus', *Augustinus
Magister* (Paris, 1954), 241–54.

JOHNSON, L. T., *Sharing of Possessions* (Philadelphia, 1981).

KELLY, J. N. D., *Jerome: His Life, Writings, and Controversies* (London,
1975).
KIRSCHNER, R., 'The Vocation of Holiness in Late Antiquity', *Vigiliae
Christianae*, 38 (1984), 105–24.
KÖNIG, D., *Amt und Askese: Priesteramt und Mönchtum bei den
lateinischen Kirchenvätern in vorbenediktinischer Zeit*. Regulae Benedicti
Studia, Supplementa, 12 (Archabbey of St. Ottilia, 1985); on Augustine,
pp. 133–67.

LA BONNARDIÈRE, A.-M., *Biblia Augustiniana: Les Épîtres aux Thessaloniciens, à Tite et à Philémon* (Paris, 1964).
——, *Recherches de chronologie augustinienne* (Paris, 1965).

LADNER, G. B., *The Idea of Reform: Its Impact on Christian Thought and Action in the Age of the Fathers* (Cambridge, Mass., 1959).

LAMBOT, C., 'La Règle de saint Augustin et saint Césaire', *Revue bénédictine*, 41 (1929), 333–41.

——, 'Saint Augustin a-t-il rédigé la Règle pour moines qui porte son nom?' *Revue bénédictine*, 53 (1941), 41–58.

——, *Sancti Aurelii Augustini sermones selecti duodeviginti* (Utrecht, 1950).

LANDES, P. F., *Augustine on Romans*. Texts and Translations, 23 (Chico, 1982).

LAWLESS, G., 'The Rule of St. Augustine as a Mirror of Perfection', *Angelicum*, 58 (1981), 460–74.

——, 'Enduring Values of the Rule of Saint Augustine', *Angelicum*, 59 (1982), 59–78.

——, 'On Understanding Augustine of Hippo', *The Downside Review*, 100 (1982), 31–46.

——, 'Psalm 132 and Augustine's Monastic Ideal', *Angelicum*, 59 (1982), 526–39.

——, '*Ordo Monasterii*: A Double or Single Hand?', *Studia Patristica*, 17 (Oxford, 1982), 511–18.

——, '*Ordo Monasterii*: Structure, Style and Rhetoric', *Augustinianum*, 22 (1982), 469–91.

——, 'The Monastery as Model of the Church', *Angelicum*, 60 (1983), 258–74.

——, 'A Breach of Monastic Poverty in the Fifth Century: Augustine's *Sermon* 356', *Studia Abbati Carolo Egger a confratribus oblata* (Rome, 1984), 47–60.

——, 'Augustine's Burden of Ministry', *Angelicum*, 61 (1984), 295–315.

LECLERCQ, J., *Otia Monastica: Études sur le vocabulaire de la contemplation au Moyen Âge*. Studia Anselmiana, 51 (Rome, 1963).

LIENHARD, J. T., *Paulinus of Nola and Early Western Monasticism* (Cologne–Bonn, 1977).

——, 'Index of Reported Patristic and Classical Citations, Allusions, and Parallels in the *Regula Benedicti*', *Revue bénédictine*, 89 (1979), 230–70; on Augustine, pp. 236–9.

LODS, M., 'La personne du Christ dans la "conversion" de saint Augustin', *Recherches augustiniennes*, 11 (1976), 3–34.

LOF, L. J. VAN DER, 'The Threefold Meaning of *Serui Dei* in the Writings of Saint Augustine', *Augustinian Studies*, 12 (1981), 43–59.

LORENZ, R., 'Die Anfänge des abendländischen Mönchtums im 4. Jahrhundert', *Zeitschrift für Kirchengeschichte*, 77 (1966), 1–61.

LORIÉ, L. Th., *Spiritual Terminology in the Latin Translations of the* Vita Antonii *with Reference to Fourth and Fifth Century Monastic Literature* (Nijmegen, 1955).

LOUTH, A., *The Origins of the Christian Mystical Tradition* (Oxford, 1981).

LUDWIG, D. L., *Der sog. Indiculus des Possidius: Studien zur Entstehungs- und Wirkungsgeschichte einer spätantiken Augustin-Bibliographie* (Göttingen, 1984).

McCARTHY, M., *The Rule for Nuns of St. Caesarius of Arles: A Translation with a Critical Introduction* (Washington, DC, 1960).

MacMULLEN, R., *Paganism in the Roman Empire* (New Haven 1981).

MANDONNET, P., *Saint Dominique* (2 vols., Paris, 1937).

MANDOUZE, A., *Saint Augustin: L'aventure de la raison et la grâce* (Paris, 1968).

MANRIQUE, A., *La vida monástica en San Agustín* (El Escorial–Salamanca, 1959).

——, *Teología agustiniana de la vida religiosa* (Madrid, 1964).

——, 'Nuevas aportaciones al problema de la "Regula Sancti Augustini"', *La Ciudad de Dios*, 181 (1968), 707–46.

——, 'Autenticidad de la "Regla de S. Agustín"', *Estudio Agustiniano*, 12 (1977), 335–42.

MEALAND, D. L., 'Community of Goods and Utopian Allusions in Acts II–IV', *Journal of Theological Studies*, NS 28 (1977), 96–9.

MEER, F. VAN DER, *Augustine the Bishop* (New York, 1961; repr. 1983).

MEREDITH, A., 'Asceticism—Christian and Greek', *Journal of Theological Studies*, NS 27 (1976), 313–32.

MERLIN, N., *Saint Augustin et la vie monastique* (Albi, 1933).

MONCEAUX, P., 'Saint Augustin et Saint Antoine: Contribution à l'histoire du monachisme', *Miscellanea agostiniana* (Rome, 1931), ii. 61–89.

MORÁN, J., 'Notas sobre el monacato agustiniano', *La Ciudad de Dios*, 175 (1962), 535–47.

——, 'En torno a la primera experiencia monástica de san Agustín', *Augustinianum*, 7 (1967), 338–48.

MORIN, G., 'L'ordre des heures canoniales dans les monastères de Cassiodore', *Revue bénédictine*, 43 (1931), 145–52.

O'CONNELL, R., *Art and the Christian Intelligence in St. Augustine* (Cambridge, Mass., 1978).

O'DONNELL, J. J., 'The Demise of Paganism', *Traditio*, 35 (1979), 45–88.

——, *Augustine*. Twayne's World Author Series (Boston, Mass., 1985).

O'MEARA, D. (ed.), *Neoplatonism and Christian Thought* (Norfolk, Va., 1982).

O'MEARA, J., *The Young Augustine* (London, 1954; reprinted 1980).

ORBAN, A.-P, 'Augustinus und das Mönchtum', *Kairos*, 18 (1976), 100–18.

OROZ-RETA, J., 'Saint Augustin et saint Fructueux: parallèles doctrinaux de leur règles monastiques', *Studia Patristica*, 10 (Berlin, 1970), 407–12.

PELLEGRINO, M., *Possidio, Vita di Agostino*. Verba Seniorum, 4 (Alba, 1955).

PERLER, O., *Les Voyages de saint Augustin* (Paris, 1969).

QUACQUARELLI, A., *Lavoro e ascesi nel monachesimo prebenedettino del IV e V secolo*. Quaderni di *Vetera Christianorum*, 18 (Bari, 1982).

QUINOT, B., 'C. Litteras Petiliani III, XL, 48 et le monachisme en Afrique', *Revue des études augustiniennes*, 13 (1967), 15–24.

REA, P., 'A Pattern of Community and Apostolic Life', *The Clergy Review*, 68 (1983), 246–50.

RIST, J. M., *Plotinus: The Road to Reality* (Cambridge, 1967).

ROUSSEAU, P., 'The Spiritual Authority of the "Monk-Bishop": Eastern Elements in some Western Hagiography of the Fourth and Fifth Centuries', *Journal of Theological Studies*, NS 22 (1971), 380–419.

——, 'Augustine and Ambrose: The Loyalty and Singlemindedness of a Disciple', *Augustiniana*, 27 (1977), 151–65.

——, *Ascetics, Authority, and the Church in the Age of Jerome and Cassian* (Oxford, 1978).

RUBIO, L., 'La norma fundamental de la vida monástica según San Agustín y otras reflexiones en torno a la Regula Augustini', *La Ciudad de Dios*, 183 (1970), 189–235.

RUNIA, D. T. (ed.), *Plotinus amid Gnostics and Christians* (Amsterdam, 1984).

RUSSELL, R. P., 'Cicero's "Hortensius" and the Problem of Riches in Augustine', *Augustinian Studies*, 7 (1976), 59–68.

SAGE. A., *La Règle de saint Augustin commentée par ses écrits* (Paris, 1961).

——, *La vie religieuse selon saint Augustin* (Paris, 1972).

SALAS, A., 'La "koinônia" bíblica y la "communitas" agustiniana', *La Ciudad de Dios*, 182 (1969), 232–8.

SANCHIS, D., 'Pauvreté monastique et charité fraternelle chez saint Augustin: Le commentaire augustinien de Actes 4, 32–35 entre 393 et 403', *Studia Monastica*, 4 (1962), 7–33.

SEILHAC, L. DE, *L'Utilisation par s. Césaire d'Arles de la Règle de s. Augustin: Étude de terminologie et doctrine monastiques* (Rome, 1974).

STANCLIFFE, C., *St. Martin and his Hagiographer: History and Miracle in Sulpicius Severus* (Oxford, 1983).

TRAPÉ, A., *Sant'Agostino: La Regola* (2nd edn.; Rome, 1986).

VEGA, A. C., *El 'De Institutione Virginum' de San Leandro de Sevilla* (Escorial, 1948).

——, 'Notas histórico-críticas en torno a los orígenes de la Regla de San Agustín', *Boletín de la Real Academia de la Historia*, 152 (1963), 13–94.

——, 'Una posible fuente de la Regla de san Agustín', *Augustinus*, 12 (1967), 473–83.

——, 'La autenticidad y destinatarios de la "Regula Augustini" ante la crítica de hoy', *Revista agustiniana de espiritualidad*, 11 (1970), 167–76.

VERHEIJEN, L. 'La "Regula Sancti Augustini" ', *Vigiliae Christianae*, 7 (1953), 27–56.

——, 'La vie de saint Augustin par Possidius et la "Regula Sancti Augustini" ', *Mélanges offerts à mademoiselle Christine Mohrmann* (Utrecht, 1963), 270–9.

——, *La Règle de saint Augustin*, I, *Tradition manuscrite*; II, *Recherches historiques* (Paris, 1967).

——, 'The Straw, the Beam, the "Tusculan Disputations" and the "Rule" of Saint Augustine: On a Surprising Augustinian Exegesis', *Augustinian Studies*, 2 (1971), 17–36.

——, *Saint Augustine: Monk, Priest, Bishop* (Villanova, 1978).

——, 'Eléments d'un commentaire de la Règle de saint Augustin, XIII: Le très difficile chapitre quatrième, le célibat monastique et la sollicitude pour les pécheurs', *Augustiniana*, 29 (1979), 43–86.

——, *Saint Augustine's Monasticism in the Light of Acts 4, 32–35* (Villanova, 1979).

——, *Nouvelle Approche de la Règle de saint Augustin*, Coll. vie monastique, 8 (Abbaye de Bellefontaine, 1980).

——, 'La tradition manuscrite de l'Obiurgatio (Lettre CCXI, 1–4 d'Augustin) et de la Regularis Informatio', *Augustiniana*, 30 (1980), 5–9.

——, 'Eléments d'un commentaire de la Règle de saint Augustin.

——, XV: Comme des amants de la beauté spirituelle: Dans Augustin évêque', *Augustiniana*, 32 (1982), 88–136.

——, XVI: 'Non pas à moins de deux ou trois', *Augustiniana*, 32 (1982), 255–62. XVII: 'Les livres', 262–5.

——, XVIII: 'Le De Sancta Virginitate de saint Augustin et sa structure: Un complément à l'étude du chapitre quatrième', 266–81.

——, XIX: 'Comme des amants de la beauté spirituelle: Dans les œuvres du jeune Augustin', *Augustiniana*, 33 (1983), 86–111.

——, XX: 'La charité ne cherche pas ses propres intérêts', *Augustiniana*, 34 (1984), 75–144.

——, 'La Règle de saint Augustin: L'état actuel des questions (début 1975)', *Augustiniana*, 35 (1985), 193–263.

VILANOVA, J. E. M., *Regula Pauli et Stephani* (Montserrat, 1959).

VILLEGAS, F., 'La "Regula Monasterii Tarnantensis": texte, sources et datation', *Revue bénédictine*, 84 (1974), 7–65.

VOGÜÉ, A. DE, 'Saint Benoît et son temps: Règles italiennes et règles provençales au VIᵉ siècle', *Regulae Benedicti Studia*, 1 (1972), 169–93.

WARFIELD, B. B., *Studies in Tertullian and Augustine* (Oxford, 1930; repr. Westport, 1970).

WEISKOTTEN, H. T., *Sancti Augustini vita scripta a Possidio episcopo* (Princeton, NJ, 1919).

WILMART, A., 'Operum S. Augustini elenchus a Possidio eiusdem discipulo Calamensi episcopo digestus', *Miscellanea agostiniana* (Rome, 1931), ii. 149–233.

WUCHERER-HULDENFELD, A., 'Mönchtum und kirchlicher Dienst bei Augustinus nach dem Bilde des Neubekehrten und des Bischofs', *Zeitschrift für katholische Theologie*, 82 (1960), 182–211.

ZUMKELLER, A., *Das Mönchtum des heiligen Augustinus* (2nd edn. Würzburg, 1968; Eng. tr., *Augustine's Ideal of the Religious Life*, New York, 1986).

——, 'Ursprung und spirituelle Bedeutung der Augustinusregel: Eine notwendige Richtigstellung zu dem Werk Christopher Brooke's "Die grosse Zeit der Klöster 100–1300"' (deutsch: Freiburg, 1976). Ordens-Korrespondenz. *Zeitschrift für Fragen des Ordenslebens*, 19 (1978), 287–95.

——, 'War Augustins "monasterium clericorum" in Hippo wirklich ein Klöster? Antwort auf eine neue Hypothese A.-P. Orbans', *Augustinianum*, 21 (1981), 391–7.

Index

Biblical references below do not take account of Ch. VII. Parenthetical figures refer to divisions of Augustine's texts.

Divjak, J. 27 n. 41
Dorotheos of Gaza 136

Eighty-three Different Questions 48–9,
    61–2, 151, 156
Eleusinus 62
Epiphanius 137
ἐπιστροφή ix
    see also Plotinus
Erasmus 125–6, 136, 143
Eudoxius, abbot 49
Eugippius 124, 128, 131, 134, 135
Eusebius of Vercelli 42
Eutropius, bishop of Valencia 131
Evagrius of Antioch 41
Evodius 25, 38, 39, 43, 44, 52, 57, 59

fasting 85 (1), 111 (3.1)
Faul, D. 151 n. 96
Florentina 139
Folliet, G. 51 n. 41
forgiveness 99–101 (2–3), 103 (2), 116–
    17 (2–3), 118 (2)
fraternal correction 91–3 (7–11), 113–
    14 (7–11)
fratres 55–6; frequency in the *Rule* 159
Fructuosus of Braga 139
fuga mundi 35

Gaius 54
Gaultier, bishop 140, 141
Gavigan, J. 17 n. 22, 52 nn. 44, 46, 62 n.
    110, 149 n. 87, 168 n. 13
Gelasius II, Pope 165
Gift of Perseverance, The 150
gifts 93 (11), 114 (11), 137
Goldbacher, A. 138 n. 53, 146 n. 77
Good of Marriage, The 18 n. 24
Gregory the Great vii
Gregory Nazianzen 52
grumbling 75 (5), 95 (1), 97 (5, 9) 114
    (1), 115 (5), 116 (9)

Hackett, M. B. 168 n. 14
Hadrumetum 150, 151, 159
Halliburton 32 n. 25, 35 n. 42, 44 n. 39,
    129 n. 22
Hanslik, R. 131 n. 28
hatred 99 (1), 116 (1)
health 97 (5), 115 (5)
Héloïse 141–2, 143
Henry of Friemar 142
Hilary of Arles 161

Hipparchia 25
Hippo 58–62, 149, 151, 156, 158, 159
Holy Virginity 21, 59 nn. 90–1
Honoratus 52
Honoratus of Lérins 161
Hümpfner, W. 148 n. 79, 168 n. 9

Immortality of the Soul 39
Innocentius 47
interiority 35
Irungus of Saint-Emmeram 141
Isidore of Seville 131–2, 134, 139
Isocrates 155

Januarius 152
Jerome 11, 16, 26 n. 38, 33, 41–2 n. 26,
    156, 170
    Letter to Eustochium 42 n. 32
Jesus Christ 22, 23–7
    authority of Christ 33
    'fragrance of' 103 (1), 117 (8)
    interior teacher 53
    'in the name of' 79 (11)
Jordan of Saxony 125, 142

La Bonnardière, A. M. 132 n. 35, 151
    n. 96
Ladner, G. B. 168 n. 15
Lambot, C. 123 n. 5, 144 n. 70, 145 n.
    74, 146–7
lamp-lighting (*lucernarium*) 75 (2, 3)
Later Version of the *Rule* (*Regula
    recepta*) 165–6
laundry 95–7 (4), 115 (4), 136–7
Le Large, Alain 144
Le Proust, Ange 143
Leander of Seville 131, 139
lectio divina see Scriptures
Leontius, St 15
Leporius 62
Licentius 29, 30, 31
Lienhard, J. T. 16 n. 21, 126 n. 14, 131
    n. 28
life in community 3, 4 nn. 2–3, 25, 40,
    43–4, 57
    see also common life
Life of Happiness, A 29, 30–1
Liturgy of the Hours 75 (2), 167, 169 n.
    26, 170
Lorenz, R. 169 n. 22
Lorié, L. Th. 56 n. 73, 160 n. 6, 161 nn.
    7, 8
Louth, A. 38 n. 3